PRAISE FOR PETER CHARLES HOFFER'S
PAST IMPERFECT

"A thoughtful work. . . . Believe it or not, tracking teaching trends in American history is fascinating stuff. . . . [Hoffer's] tutorial on changes in historical standards is a good tool as we learn to sort out good scholarship from bad." —*Seattle Times*

"A tough-minded new book." —*Seattle Post-Intelligencer*

"[Hoffer] provides a brilliant analysis of changes in history writing in America, showing that there has long been a tension between those who want history to be celebratory, even if that requires whitewashing the past, and those who approach the past critically. He also explores the tension between popularizers of history, such as Ambrose, Goodwin, and Ellis, and those who believe that history should be conveyed primarily through maximum security monographs." —*St. Louis Post-Dispatch*

"A professor of history takes to the woodshed not only the recent high-profile plagiarizers and prevaricators (Bellesiles, Goodwin, Ambrose, Ellis) but also those whose acts of omission and commission made possible the whole dreary mess. The proof he assembles is devastating—particularly the side-by-side comparisons of texts. There is no question that Stephen Ambrose and Doris Kearns Goodwin played fast and loose with secondary sources, no question that Michael Bellesiles fabricated data for his *Arming America* (2000), no question that Joseph Ellis . . . lied about serving in Vietnam. What emerges in this well-researched assessment of a nasty problem are both the author's love for his discipline and his grief for the losses it has sustained." —*Kirkus Reviews*

"Hoffer argues with powerful restraint that the American Historical Association should speak out more clearly against unethical practices by historians. . . . Make[s] the case clearly and forcefully that historians' violations of common standards of ethics are not to be taken lightly, by their colleagues or by their readers." —*Los Angeles Times*

"Hoffer contends that his profession 'has fallen into disarray' and aims a polemical blast at his fellow historians for condoning sloppy scholarship and [an] anything-goes political climate. . . . Hoffer is a respected scholar whose previous work has generally earned the esteem of his peers. Now, setting himself up as judge, jury, and executioner, Hoffer puts historians in the dock—and throws the book at them." —*The Boston Globe*

"An adviser to the American Historical Association on plagiarism, Hoffer focuses on the four most notorious recent cases of professional historical misconduct in this useful and reasonably argued study. . . . Hoffer examines these cases in the broader context of the professionalization of history, the battle between academic and popular history, and professional standards. Those concerned with the integrity and future of the field will find this analysis illuminating." —*Publishers Weekly*

". . . *Past Imperfect* examines the plagiarism scandals of the discipline and bemoans the chasm between popular and academic historians." —*The Washington Post*

"Although recommended for all historians, *Past Imperfect* is one of the most important books history graduate students and newly hired historians will ever read. It is a fascinating history of our profession." —Peter Brush, Vanderbilt University Library

Past Imperfect

Facts, Fictions, Fraud—
American History from
Bancroft and Parkman
to Ambrose, Bellesiles,
Ellis, and Goodwin

PETER CHARLES HOFFER

 PUBLICAFFAIRS NEW YORK

For Natalie, A Get Well Gift.

BOOK DESIGN AND COMPOSITION BY JENNY DOSSIN. TEXT SET IN ITC NEW BASKERVILLE.

Library of Congress Cataloging-in-Publication data
   Hoffer, Peter Charles, 1944–
   Past imperfect : facts, fictions, fraud—American history from Bancroft and Parkman to Ambrose, Bellesiles, Ellis, and Goodwin / Peter Charles Hoffer.—1st ed.
     p. cm.
   Includes bibliographical references and index.
   ISBN–13: 978-1-58648-244-0; ISBN–10: 1-58648-244-0
   1. United States—Historiography. 2. United States—History—Philosophy. 3. Historiography—Social aspects—United States—History—20th century. 4. Historiography—Political aspects—United States—History—20th century. 5. Historians—United States—Biography. 6. Bellesiles, Michael A. 7. Goodwin, Doris Kearns. 8. Ambrose, Stephen E. 9. Ellis, Joseph J. 10. Professional ethics—United States—Case studies. I. Title.
E175.H54 2004
973'.072—dc22   2004048653

ISBN–13: 978-1-58648-445-3; ISBN–10: 1-58648-445-1

CONTENTS

PREFACE

T HE FIRST WEEKS OF JANUARY 2001 WERE BUSY
ones for our nation's top historians. Jan Lewis, professor of
early American history at Rutgers, and Pauline Maier, who taught
colonial history at MIT, faced the daunting task of ranking hundreds
of books submitted for the Bancroft Prizes and the Pulitzer Prize.
Their input as members of the prize committees would be very influential on two books on early America, their own specialty. One was
Arming America: The Origins of a National Gun Culture, Michael Bellesiles's thickly footnoted and highly controversial study of gun ownership in America; the other was *Founding Brothers: The Revolutionary
Generation,* Joseph Ellis's slickly written and imaginatively framed
account of the Founders of the republic. The two books had behind
them the oomph of a leading trade book publisher, Alfred A. Knopf.
Bellesiles, a history professor at Emory University, and Ellis, at Mount
Holyoke, were themselves busy teaching, giving interviews to the
media, and planning their next writing ventures.

Doris Kearns Goodwin, whose books on Lyndon Johnson (*Lyndon
Johnson and the American Dream*), the Kennedy women (*The Fitzgeralds
and the Kennedys*), and the Roosevelts (*No Ordinary Time: Eleanor and
Franklin — The Home Front in World War II*) had brought her a Pulitzer
Prize in 1995 and membership on the Pulitzer Prize Board, was writing her next book, a major biography of Abraham Lincoln, for
another leading trade publisher, Simon & Schuster. She was a regular

on PBS's *News Hour*, a veteran of the lecture circuit, and one of the most respected and recognizable of the "talking heads" on the educational cable TV channels. Stephen Ambrose, who had retired from university teaching but had busied himself giving lectures on history, had two books near the top of the all-time best-seller list: *Undaunted Courage: Meriwether Lewis, Thomas Jefferson, and Opening of the American West* and *Band of Brothers: E Company, 506th Regiment, 101st Airborne, from Normandy to Hitler's Eagle's Nest*. His gruff voice, kindly manner, and the enormous rapport he had with his readers had made him America's best-loved historian.

Unlike the ancient Romans, we Americans have not created the office of state historian, but if we had, all four of these historians might easily have had a claim to hold it. Ellis would win the Pulitzer Prize, Bellesiles one of the Bancrofts. Ambrose's *Band of Brothers* would become a much-viewed cable miniseries. *Wait Till Next Year*, Goodwin's memoir of her father and the Brooklyn Dodgers, just re-released in paperback, touched Americans' hearts. The rest of the historical profession might well have gloried in the success of all four of these scholars, for they had done something that many of us dreamed of doing—they had bridged the chasm between the professional practice of history and the popular exposition of it. Trained as academics, with doctorates from top-ranked universities and possessing classroom teaching experience, they had carried history to mass audiences and convinced those audiences that what all of us did was worth reading. They had earned the trust of general readers while winning the highest accolades that the profession could bestow on its own. They had their critics, but it seemed to many of us in the history-teaching profession that they had the right kind of enemies. It is not everyone who has Charlton Heston, then the president of the National Rifle Association, condemning their history books in public.

Then the sky fell in on all four of them. By the closing months of 2002 Ambrose and Goodwin had been accused of plagiarism; Bellesiles, of misrepresenting and perhaps even falsifying his research findings; and Ellis, of fabricating episodes in his own life. Ambrose, admitting no substantial misconduct, would die at the end of the 2002 with a cloud over his entire career. Goodwin conceded that mistakes had been made in the writing of her books, and stepped down from some of her distinguished posts. Ellis also confessed to error, was deprived of his chair in the history department at Mount Holyoke College, and went a year without teaching. Bellesiles resigned under fire from Emory University's history department.

A bewildered reading public was left with a series of sad, perplexing questions: What had the four actually done that set off the firestorm of criticism? Were the alleged offenses, if substantiated, really so terrible? And if guilty as charged, why had four highly honored individuals engaged in such misconduct? Then again, perhaps there was a sinister conspiracy behind the accusations, motivated as much by politics as by concern for scholarly standards or intellectual honesty.

Professional historians were just as shocked, for we knew these four as colleagues and coworkers, but our questions were different from the general public's. We needed to know whether we were somehow complicit in their fall from grace. Was the way we do history itself on trial in the alleged misconduct of the four? Did the cases tell us something we should know about the writing of history over the past decades, and what warning did they give us about the writing of history in the years to come?

I am not the first to address myself to these questions. Reporters and commentators, including a number of historians, have already tried to assess the meaning of the episodes and determine the motives of the principals in them. Indeed, in some quarters of the academic world, hand-wringing about these cases has become a minor industry.

This book goes beyond these convenient and sometimes self-serving displays of dismay. First, it places the four cases in the context of the often troubled and always contested evolution of historical writing in America—for in truth, what seemed to many at the time to be grave and almost inexplicable departures from the ethical canon of scholarship were in fact predictable, perhaps even inevitable.

Second, the book examines the four cases in far more detail than anyone has yet done. As the architect Mies van der Rohe once said, God is in the details. By assembling the evidence on both sides and assessing it from the perspective of a working historian, I am able to offer informed, contextualized judgments. In this, my aim is not to expose, indict, or titillate, but to explain to people who love to read history how the history profession has fallen into disarray and controversy.

Although I am a professional historian—I teach history at the University of Georgia, in Athens, and oversee the work of doctoral candidates—I have not written this book for my colleagues. They know most of it already. It is a book about history for nonhistorians. Thus I hope that my colleagues will forgive me if I do not cite many estimable scholars; I know full well that the vast majority of today's college and university history instructors belong on an honor roll of hard-working, decent, and honorable men and women. I have not forgotten them. But the purpose of this book is to traverse a broad landscape and map its contours; I have not time to stop and admire each striking bit of scenery.

My perspective on these cases is quite specific and may differ from that of some of my colleagues in the historical profession because of my service on the American Historical Association's Professional Division. At the end of the nineteenth century, the United States Congress gave to the newly formed American Historical Association a charter and told its founders to take good care of the writing of American history. Thirty years ago, to further that goal, the AHA created a Professional Division. To this division the AHA gave the authority to inquire into suspected wrongdoing by all historians, popular and academic. I sat on this body from 2002 to 2004. Among our duties was to hear and decide complaints about a wide variety of alleged misconduct, including plagiarism, misrepresentation of credentials, and falsification of research findings. None of the four cases above were referred to our committee—if they had been I would have been barred from writing about them by our confidentiality rules—but in this book I have applied to them the standards that we used when we heard complaints.

I have constructed from published and unpublished materials a record for the four cases similar to that the Professional Division would have received had the cases come to us. To this record I have added the results of interviews, but only for background purposes—that is, to make the case easier for readers to understand. It is true that I have played all of the roles in the drama—complainant, defender, trier of fact, judge of law—it's a one-man show. But that is what historians routinely do when they are researching and writing history. They examine documents and listen to oral testimony. They alternately attack and defend in their minds the veracity and validity of their sources, and then decide how much weight to put on them in the final analysis.

ACKNOWLEDGMENTS

T HIS BOOK IS SOMETHING OF A VALEDICTORY FOR me—not because I played a central role in any of its fascinating tales, but because I have taught the history of historical writing for many years. I know many of the players in the drama (and many more, when they learned I was writing this book, brought me their tales), for this is the story of my generation of historians. We made this academic world, with its pressures to publish or perish, its fascination with ideology, and its readiness to stand in judgment of others. We have to take responsibility for it.

I am indebted to a number of individuals who aided me—they of course bear no responsibility for my errors. To those colleagues and friends who provided background factual information or let me use unpublished materials, including Richard B. Bernstein, Paul Finkelman, Michael Gagnon, John T. Juricek, Stanley N. Katz, Allan Kulikoff, Jesse Lemisch, Sanford Levinson, J. Morgan Kousser, Peter Onuf, Robert B. Townsend, and Jeff Young, I offer heartfelt thanks. Members of the Professional Division of the American Historical Association with whom I have served—Vice President William Cronon, James Grossman, Maureen Nutting, Susan Stuard, and Denise Youngblood—helped shape my ideas of the ethics of our profession. Arnita Jones, executive director of the AHA, and Sharon Tune, her assistant, helped me understand their organization, which is the senior association in our profession. Bernstein, Cronon, Katz, Kulikoff, Onuf, and

Gary B. Nash have offered comments on parts of the manuscript, for which I am grateful. Katherine Scott copyedited the manuscript with verve and skill. To my editor, Clive Priddle, and my agent, Scott Waxman, I can say with absolute truth and candor: this book would not have been written without them.

Past Imperfect

Two-Faced History

AMERICAN HISTORY IS TWO-FACED, LIKE THE ANCIENT Roman god Janus. One face proudly bears the accomplishments of heroes and heroines and reflects the rise of a handful of isolated European enclaves in a vast wilderness to the greatest democratic and industrial power in the world. On this face of our history are chiseled the essential facts that everyone is expected to know about our past, along with a series of useful fictions that celebrate our achievements. This celebratory version of our history has a very old pedigree, going back to the first Fourth of July orations at the end of the eighteenth century. The other face bears a different, less appealing, aspect. On its facets one sees the sad tales of the displacement of native peoples, the wickedness of slavery, the exploitation of workers and nature, and the many failed promises of equality and justice that have marked American history from its inception. I have called this the "new history," following a usage made popular in the turbulent 1960s.

These are the two countenances of American history, both exhibiting substantial truths, but neither, like the faces of Janus, able to regard the other. Because American history is two-faced, everyone who undertakes to write about or teach American history in a thorough manner has an almost intolerable burden: to balance a critical approach and a rightful pride. The effort to carry that burden began with the creation of the American nation, continued through two centuries of historical scholarship, and provides the context for the achievements and the failings of Ambrose, Bellesiles, Ellis, and Goodwin. For in different ways they tried to shoulder that burden, and in different ways it proved too heavy for them.

All of the four knew that Americans want and need a history that reassures us that we can manage our democracy, find a way to work through our cultural conflicts, make use of our diversity, and give every American the opportunity to fulfill his or her dreams. Americans certainly want and perhaps need heroes, and this presses us to see the strengths and achievements of past generations. Thus, perhaps too often we ask for simple, straightforward historical answers to highly complex questions. Historians should not be insensitive to the needs and wants of their countrymen, but neither can we ignore the way that they may lead historians to bend facts and dictate interpretations—demanding fabrications, rewarding falsehoods, and promoting repetition of soothing phrases and inspirational slogans. For we also need a history that is critical of the past and critical of itself, a history that is always trying to instruct us by bitter example and by self-examination.

On July, 5, 2003, my nineteen-year-old son and I visited the newly opened National Constitution Center in Philadelphia, two blocks from Independence Hall. We joined eager crowds surging through the exhibits. I asked a few people what they were looking for, and they answered that they had come to celebrate the founding of the greatest nation the world had ever seen. They were proud to be Americans, and assumed that the objects and the demonstrations in the center would foster that pride. None told me that they had come to find evidence of oppression, even though the newspapers that week had been full of the efforts of civil rights groups to create some kind of memorial to the slaves brought to the city by the very men who framed the new Constitution. The sites of the slave quarters, unmarked, were no more than a block away from the new center.[1]

My favorite room was the hall of signers, containing a tableau-vivant of life-size posed bronze statues of the delegates to the Constitutional Convention of 1787. As I stood next to the figure of James Madison, I imagined conversing with him about his views. I knew that we did not have much in common other than our love of history. He was a Virginia planter, a member of a land-owning, ruling elite, and a slaveholder highly suspicious of democracy, equality, and the masses. I do not share any of these characteristics with him, but have written many pages about him. The intellectual assumption that we historians, so different from the people we write about, can leap over the years and enter into their minds and hearts, the fragile but enduring faith in a scholar's imagination and learning, is the foundation on which all historical scholarship is built.

My son interrupted my reverie and asked me to join him at the multimedia presentation on the history of the Constitution. Averse to what I anticipated would be a mindless celebration of 216 years of unalloyed liberty and progress, I reluctantly consented. We found seats in a steeply banked theater in the round, enjoyed an introduction of stirring images and sound effects, then for 15 minutes listened to an actor reciting the lines in a script. As he began to speak, I recalled another occasion, nearly a quarter century before, when I heard a National Park Service guide's recitation during a tour of Independence Hall. His account did not mention people of color, slaves, or women at all. Indeed, it sounded as though there was nothing particularly revolutionary about the Revolution. How different was the actor's narrative; it was not uncritically patriotic and self-congratulatory. His script conceded how the Constitution bowed to slave owners and how it left out the rights of women, minorities, and Indians.

It seemed that our story—the story we tell ourselves about ourselves, in a word, our history—had mutated. Instead of one people, with one great dream that we fulfilled, we had become many people, with many dreams, some not yet fulfilled. Instead of unalloyed progress, we had a mixture of achievement and turmoil. Those who were marginal in earlier accounts had become central; once powerless victims now exercised agency; and the dispossessed and enslaved gained a history worth knowing. The exhibits and the multimedia show at the National Constitution Center certainly celebrated the achievement of the Founders, but also they raised questions about inclusiveness, diversity, and contested values. The distinguished professional historians on the advisory board of the council of the center—the University of Pennsylvania's Richard Beeman, among others—insisted on going beyond mere celebration, but stopped short of depicting "the American experience in liberty and constitutional justice as a fraud and a sham."[2]

But how could our past itself change? Surely the events of 1776 and 1787 happened as they happened. How could the history we teach and write change so much when the past could not change at all? Were we simply inventing a new past to suit current needs and ideals—a past more welcoming to diversity, dissent, and minority rights? Was everything in history a matter of interpretation and perspective, or were there basic facts and great truths that should not be made the subject of contemporary fads?

One of the foremost academic historians of the 1950s and 1960s, Harvard University's Oscar Handlin, titled his personal memoir *Truth in History* because that is what he thought historians should be seeking. He was upset by the rise of what others had called "politically correct history," warned against faddish reinterpretations, and decried "theoretical political considerations." As if in reply, Eric Foner, one of the most respected historians of the 1980s and 1990s, insisted that truth itself was culturally constructed in the past as it is in the present. History did not reveal truths; it revealed the struggle among people to define their beliefs as truth and their opponents' ideas as falsehoods. Thus "history always has been and always will be regularly rewritten." In other words, historians were always rewriting the past.[3]

But many Americans are uncomfortable with that process of continual renewal. They demand that certain themes not vanish from our history. The most important of these is our desire to celebrate our past. As the literary critic Norman Podhoretz insists in *My Love Affair with America*, the "institutional structure of American democracy . . . must be defended against the people both at home and abroad who thought that it was bad. . . . More than merely being defended, it deserved . . . to be 'celebrated.'" The political theorist Thomas G. West put the need for finding and celebrating heroes more plaintively in his *Vindicating the Founders*: "Although America has not always lived up to her own best principles, she has a great and noble heritage. It would be a shame if that heritage were to be squandered because of misunderstandings and distortions of the Founders' principles by today's intellectuals." Historians who would undermine this view of history with their critical ideology become the enemy in this "culture war." As the historian Joseph Ellis explained

> A kind of electromagnetic field, therefore, surrounds this entire subject [of our founding], manifesting itself as a golden haze or halo for the vast majority of contemporary Americans, or as a contaminated radioactive cloud for a smaller but quite vocal group of critics unhappy with what America has become or how we have gotten here.[4]

The value of celebratory history, in theory at least, is that it brings Americans together in harmony. The other side of the story is that celebratory history hides the blemishes, the injustice, oppression, and divisiveness that marred our past. The most tangible manifestation of the celebratory ideal is the historical theme park. In the 1970s, there was a boom in what Michael Kammen, a historian of American culture, called, "the heritage phenomenon." Historical parks, exhibitions, preservation societies, and living history museums blossomed all over America. Some were public, others commercial. All valuable and praiseworthy on their face, they were vehicles for promoting consensus, even when, like Gettysburg National Park, the historical event they commemorated was one of violent divisiveness. Thus when I visited Gettysburg, my historical guide stressed the common values, heroism, and sacrifice of the Union and Confederate troops and never mentioned the issues of slavery and sectional animosity that led to the Civil War and the carnage at battles such as Gettysburg. Kammen was concerned that many of the historical theme parks masked "an ideologically useful" task, a "self-indulgent" defense of traditional ideas that celebrated a nonexistent past.[5]

Over the past decade I have visited many memorial parks, historical reenactments, living museums, and historical sites relating to early
American history and seen evidence of their inspirational power and
their ideological bias. I have enjoyed the efforts of the reenactors and
conservators, and have learned much from them. I believe that the
experiences they recounted provide a deeply moving sense of the
accomplishments of our forebears. I also encountered a sanitized
past. Colonial Williamsburg, for example, did not present an accurate
picture of the importance, or the horrors, of slave life in Virginia's
colonial capital, though the reenactors included people of color discussing slavery. None of Jamestown Festival Park's many exhibits
revealed the mortal enmity between colonists and Indians. Instead,
the captions in the display cases and the talks of the reenactors suggested a harmonious, if harsher, time.[6]

In recent years, the conceptual gap between a comforting celebration of our past on one side and a demanding critique of our past
shortcomings on the other has become a yawning political rift, conservatives standing on one side of it, ignoring the need for self-criticism,
and liberals on the other, demanding reparations for the victims of
past misdeeds. On September 17, 2002, President George W. Bush
made clear where he stood. He announced a National Endowment for
the Humanities initiative called "We the People" that would sponsor
"projects designed to explore significant events and themes in our
nation's history" and an annual "Heroes in History" lecture by a
scholar "on an individual whose heroism has helped to protect America." He had as little use for criticism of his policies from historians as
he did for critical historical writing. When some historical experts
questioned his rationale for the Second Iraq War, President Bush furi-
ously assailed "revisionist historians" for undermining the consensus
necessary to prosecute the war. Liberal historians, led by James M.
McPherson, president of the AHA, replied that "there is no single
immutable 'truth' about past events and their meaning. . . . Revision is
the lifeblood of historical scholarship. . . . Without revisions we might
be stuck with the images of Reconstruction that were conferred by D.
W. Griffith's *Birth of a Nation*," a film of such transparent racism that it
has become the epitome of malignly distorted consensus history.[7]

But the contest for control of our history is much more complex than a simple conservative celebrant versus liberal critic lineup. Early in 2003, Republican Representative Joe Wilson of South Carolina proposed a national park site to commemorate the history of Reconstruction. It would have brought federal dollars and thousands of visitors to depressed Beaufort County. Who could oppose a public history project that would also benefit the economic welfare of a local area? The Sons of Confederate Veterans is who. They wanted a veto on potentially offensive exhibits, claiming that Reconstruction was a "blight" imposed on the South by carpetbaggers and federal troops. Jefferson Mansell, director of the Historic Beaufort Foundation, replied that "history is not always pretty. It is often controversial and open to interpretation." He continued that all South Carolinians who suffered after the war would be included in the exhibits, but the Sons of Confederate Veterans were not mollified. The split was there, all right, and where one stood depended on what one wanted from history.[8]

It would be reassuring to think that professional historians could find a way to bridge this gap. We are a nation that honors the professionally trained person and turns to professionals when something has gone wrong. Lawyers, doctors, and psychological counselors are all professionals. Modern professional historical study, in the hands of well-trained, supposedly objective practitioners, should save us from short-sighted, partisan, adversarial contests over the uses of our history. In the hands of the professionals, no one supposedly need fear "revisionism," for all revision would be improvement and refinement of knowledge. As one of the most honored members of our profession, the late Daniel Boorstin, told an audience at the Library of Congress in December, 2000, "For me the task of the historian is not to chisel a personal or definitive view of the past on granite. Rather, it is to see the iridescence of the past, fully aware that it will have a new and unsuspected iridescence in the future."[9]

But professionalization of its members has not brought harmony to the historical academy. Although the American Historical Association's *Statement on Standards of Professional Historians* urges all historians to show "an awareness of [our] own bias and a readiness to follow sound method and analysis wherever they may lead," in fact, as the historian Lawrence Levine recently wrote, "Academic history in the United States . . . has not been a long happy voyage in a stable vessel characterized by blissful consensus about which subject should form the indisputable curriculum; it has been marked by prolonged and often acrimonious struggle and debate." Professional historians valued the mastery of facts but vigorously challenged one another's interpretations of those facts.[10]

Until our own day, professional historians' quarrels with one another have not had the same visibility as their publications. Disputes within the profession generally stayed there. Indeed, relative invisibility had brought a kind of oracular authority to the historical profession, especially for historians at elite universities. Such scholars were held in a special esteem, occupying a pedestal they had built for themselves with all their talk of special training, long apprenticeships, peer (collegial) review, and blind refereeing of book and article manuscripts (the reviewer not knowing the author) prior to their acceptance for publication.

In our age of talking historians' heads—on the History Channel, in documentaries like Ken Burns's *Civil War,* and on C-Span's *Booknotes*— for the first time many Americans have the opportunity to see and hear elite professional historians. Professional historians who also or primarily write for general audiences now "do the circuit" at the huge bookstore chains like Barnes & Noble and Borders, giving spiels and signing copies of their latest books. Leading trade publishers schedule their historians' appearances on television and radio as part of advertising campaigns for books. The impact of the marketing of popular history has been immense. Near-celebrity status for these historians has meant a magnification of both their importance and their flaws.

There is a lot more institutional support for history now than ever before, too. It is big business. The only historians who got rich in the 1940s and 1950s were the ones with successful textbooks. Today, the salaries of the star professors, the royalties from best-selling books, and the honoraria of doing the lecture circuit have moved the top tier of the profession out of genteel poverty into the upper middle class. One colleague much in demand on the military and diplomatic history lecture circuit explained to me that he would not give any more invited talks unless he was paid a minimum of $1,500. And that is chicken feed compared to the fees commanded by some of the best paid historians, including two of the individuals discussed at length in this book.

Leading professional historians can also rely for support on well-endowed universities and private foundations. In one recent biography of the architect Frank Lloyd Wright, the author Meryle Secrest thanked "four main foundations and research centers" and then listed another 91 institutions and organizations. In the opening pages of his recent exploration of the idea behind the new history, *The Opening of the American Mind: Canons, Culture, and History,* Lawrence Levine revealed that the book began life as his presidential address to the Organization of American Historians in 1993. Before and after, he had "tried out the ideas" on "a wide variety of academic audiences from Colby College in Maine on one side of the country to the Stanford Humanities Center on the other." The individual chapters began to take form as lectures at George Mason University, to which Levine had migrated after long service at the University of California at Berkeley. Before another year had passed revised versions of the chapters became the Carl Becker Lectures at Cornell. A John Simon Guggenheim Foundation fellowship and a short stay at the Rockefeller Foundation Study and Conference Center in Bellagio, Italy, permitted Levine to put the finishing touches on the work. He did not work alone: "Once again I have been privileged to work with research assistants who aided me with consummate skill and unfailing thoughtfulness."[11]

Wherever one stood in this quarrel over the value and use of history, whatever one's politics, it was clear that the divide between celebratory history and critical history had grown wider. But those on both sides did not recognize that the contest for control of America's past started in the first years of the nation. Historical writing then was just as politically potent, just as partisan, as it was at the end of the twentieth century. Moreover, the framing of historical writing in the formative years of our republic set the stage for the current controversy—and the crisis in historical confidence that it has spawned.

———————

This book is in two parts. Part I offers a brisk and pointed background description of the first 200 years of historical writing in America. Part II presents a thorough examination of the cases of Bellesiles, Ambrose, Goodwin, and Ellis, in that order. The two parts are linked, for these cases, and the profession's response to them, could not have happened at a time other than when they did. History—the history of our profession—gave the four controversies their shape just as it dictated their outcome.

PART I

Facts and Fictions

T HE FOUNDERS OF OUR NATION BELIEVED THAT HIS-
tory was not just a subject of study, it was a treasure trove of
political lessons and a means of social and intellectual self-justifica-
tion. One could, and the founders did, use history to debate present
goals. Unlike some other new nations, where the state imposes an
official history, Americans in the first century of the republic disputed
the meaning of the country's past. Some argued that the American
Revolution reflected our deep distrust of traditional authority and
our yearning for equality, and was truly revolutionary in that it
changed politics and the law profoundly. Others found in the same
events proof of continuity: our rights were inseparable from and grew
out of traditional religious and social usages.

By end of the nineteenth century, however, one view of our history
had gained a dominant place. According to this view, we were one
people, forming one nation, with one history. Those whose stories did
not fit this master narrative were shunted to the side. It was a self-congratulatory tale, told by a white, Protestant elite, and it proved that
members of this elite were entitled to their paramount political and
economic position in the United States. It also concerned itself little
with the dangers of fabrication, falsification, and plagiarism. Indeed,
insofar as it labored to exclude people of color, women, servants, and
slaves, it embraced profound fictions. In 1959, the historian John
Higham gave this view of history a name: "consensus history."[1]

The nineteenth-century historians were amateurs—gifted amateurs, to be sure, but still amateurs, not because they were inept or
inattentive to their research or writing but because they did not earn
a living teaching or writing history. (They had family money or they
had other paying jobs.) By the beginning of the twentieth century,
university-trained "professional" historians had arrived on the scene.
Dismissing and sometimes condemning the work of their amateur

predecessors, they promised a new, scientifically verifiable account of our past. Fact would replace fiction. Though they touted their professional canon (as much to separate themselves from and elevate themselves above their amateur rivals as to improve the accuracy of historical scholarship), the new professionals did not abandon the essentials of consensus history. Instead, in profound and disturbing fashion, they clove to it with as much passion as the amateurs. The professionals simply changed consensus history from a branch of nationalistic literature to an academic science.

And this move further insulated consensus history from charges of falsification, plagiarism, and fabrication—for that is exactly what consensus history permitted. Although the new professionals condemned unethical scholarship, the history they produced was still built on a series of comforting falsehoods: that certain people were more equal than others when it came to inclusion in the story; that oppression or exploitation was never central to any part of that story; that Americans had little to be ashamed of and no reparations were owed because of our past. It relied on plagiarism—repeating, without citation and without criticism, the old self-sustaining truisms, as though they were not the precise language of past writers but a kind of secular Scripture. And fabrication, the passing on of unsupportably racist opinions as historical facts, was not just common, it was necessary to maintain the whole. In this polluted climate of opinion, no one could charge consensus historians with unethical behavior or unprofessionalism for doing what their predecessors had done, even when history writing and some leading historians came to serve repressive political forces in the Gilded Age (1880–1900), during the first Red Scare (1919–22), and in the height of the Cold War era (1946–76).

But by the 1960s, a time of turmoil for all Americans and particularly for younger scholars, the themes of consensus history not only appeared intellectually unsupportable, they came to seem morally censurable. The gates of the academy had opened to different kinds of professional historians—Jews, women, blacks, ethnic minorities— with much less of a personal stake in the great success story that propelled the old consensus narratives. These younger professional historians fashioned a new concept for the way that history should be presented. They called it "new history," and within two decades it had established itself as orthodoxy in the major universities and had largely supplanted consensus history as the approach used in the training of the next generation of scholars. It also transformed the way history was taught to undergraduates, and the way that the profession presented itself to the public.

The new history did not celebrate uniformity, progress, and conquest. Instead, it argued for critical thinking, diversity, and moral self-assessment. It brought new figures into the master narrative, people who had been marginal or invisible in the consensus account. Those who adhered to the new doctrine admitted history would change as historians' interests and backgrounds changed, but insisted that the multiple and multiplying perspectives did not so much undermine the goal of objective historical knowledge as broaden it.

The new history was not armored against charges of falsification, fabrication, and plagiarism, however, and the members of the increasingly ethnically and racially diverse profession did not have the same motivation as their predecessors for shielding established historical writers or conventional historical writing from criticism. Quite the reverse was true: the new history and its promoters took a perverse delight in bashing one another, sometimes in public. In fact, when highly controversial works like *Time on the Cross*, a study of antebellum southern slavery by the economists Robert Fogel and Stanley Engerman, appeared in 1974, the authors and their critics appeared on panels at national conventions to debate the book, then wrote more books to continue the debate in print.[2]

In its candor, and its apparent delight in disputation, the new history opened itself to a kind of external criticism that the consensus historians never faced. Indeed, unintentionally, the new history controversialists undermined the authority of the profession in the eyes of the public. And when the promoters of the new history became combatants in the culture wars of the 1980s and 1990s, they found a conservative backlash of frightening proportions lying in wait. In a series of highly publicized encounters, advocates of the new history found themselves fighting not only for it, but for the authority of the entire history profession against an army of conservative educators, pundits, and politicians. The result of these combats was a profession that had become politicized and highly sensitive to threats to its own authority.

The new history had also distanced itself from popular history written for general readers in a way that even the first consensus professionals could not have anticipated. The new history embraced methodological sophistication, borrowing from European literary criticism, social science statistical measures, and all manner of other academic novelties that general readers could not understand. The best and brightest of the new historians were soon writing only for one another. The result was that the general public could easily be persuaded that the academic historians did not see history as it should be seen—something to be shared with all Americans, and something that would make all Americans proud.

At the same time, the market for popular history was growing and there were millions of dollars to be made if one could tap that market. The politicization of history, the growing gap between the professors and the popularizers, and the temptations of the marketplace would set the stage for the Bellesiles, Ambrose, Goodwin, and Ellis dramas.

CHAPTER 1

The Rise of
Consensus History

ONCE UPON A TIME, HISTORY MEANT EVERYTHING
to Americans and historians were revered and trusted. For
everyone knew that history's lessons were immutable and inescapable. Those who did not know history were fated to suffer its judgment for their ignorance.

From the first days of our nation's existence, American thinkers
and political leaders were exceptionally sensitive to the lessons of history. Although our version of republicanism was without precedent or
parallel, Americans scanned the historical record for clues and
omens to the prospects of their revolutionary experiment. The new
United States of America was vast in space and potential but weak mil-
itarily and surrounded by old enemies. Its state and federal constitutions were marvels of ingenuity, but untested, and many feared that
the geographical distances that separated North from South and East
from West would foster anarchy. The founders worried about disorder at the bottom of society and corruption at the top—causes of the

decline and fall of prior republics. Thus there was both anxiety and
exaggeration in the historical claims of men like Noah Webster when
he wrote of the federal Constitution, in 1788: "This Western world
now beholds an era important beyond conception. . . . The names of
those men who have digested a system of constitutions for the American empire, will be enrolled with those . . . collected by posterity."[1]

To the foremost men of the Revolutionary generation the verdict
of history was especially prized and poignant, for the creation of the
new nation was their life's work. They feared as much posterity's judgment of them as of their creation. Shortly before he died, Jefferson
wrote to his longtime friend James Madison, "It has also been a great
solace to me to believe that you are engaged in vindicating to posterity the course we have pursued. . . . Take care of me when [I am]
dead." There was danger in too critical a reading of American history,
as Madison himself, some years later, wrote to a correspondent, "Our
history, short as it is, has already disclosed great errors sanctioned by
great names." He was alluding to the division of the country along
sectional lines, into pro- and antislavery factions. Madison was a real-
ist in politics but he knew that such realism in history could be fatal to
national unity. Only the right kind of history could save the new
republic from itself.[2]

Useful Facts

Here, at the dawn of what Jefferson called the "great experiment"
in republican self-government, was the same dilemma that the
council of the National Constitution Center would later face in planning its exhibits. How should history best be used? For the generation
that succeeded Jefferson and Madison, the problems of national unity
seemed dire. Bitterly divisive political parties, unanticipated by the
Founders, had arisen to contest state and national elections. Behind
these parties lay a festering controversy over the spread of slavery into
the western lands.

In this moment of incipient crisis, state historical societies, Fourth
of July orators, and popular writers agreed that by celebrating our his-

tory we might heal our political differences. Look to the Founders, these historical boosters argued; praise, exalt, and honor them. Ignore their faults and failings, for the message must be an uplifting one to which everyone can subscribe. The greatest of the Founders, George Washington, became at the hands of the itinerant bookseller and preacher Mason Weems an unblemished paragon of virtue, whose "great talents, constantly guided and guarded by religion he put at the service of his country." In his 1823 biography of the Revolutionary lawyer James Otis, Jr., the Boston author, merchant, and diplomat William Tudor praised the "real equality of political ideas" on the eve of independence. Timothy Flint, like Weems a missionary and author, waxed even more eloquent on "the first settlement of the country . . . the singular character of the first adventurers, who seem to have been a compound of the hero, the philosopher, and the farmer, and the savage."[3]

Scholars and men of letters in the new nation proposed that history had a vital purpose. A contemporary review of an 1835 edition of Washington's letters, edited by Reverend Jared Sparks, pronounced: "Nothing can be of more profit to Americans, and especially to the youth of our land, than to recur, and that frequently, to the labours and sentiments of our revolutionary leaders." Nothing was better suited to reduce the "heats of modern party warfare" than the cool patriotism and dedication of Washington and his cohorts.

Against the vast profit perceived in this approach, what reader could object to the historians' rearrangement of their subjects' language, or to their selective use of facts? It did not seem to matter to readers that Sparks regularly altered Washington's words, or sometimes pasted one piece of a document into another document entirely. After all, the entire purpose of editing the letters was moral instruction, and ministers like Sparks long had the tradition of cutting and pasting Scripture in their sermons.[4]

Permission to fabricate (as in manufacture) was not a license to lie, but it did give carte blanche when it came to deciding what was important, worth inclusion in the narrative, and what could be ignored or dismissed. One of the major historical projects of the 1830s was Peter Force's collection of documents on the American Revolution. Force, a

New Yorker by birth and a Washington, D.C., politician, printer, and newspaper editor later in life, lobbied hard for and gained a subvention from Congress to compile the papers, and historians all over the country waited eagerly as he performed the work. Robert Walsh, the editor of the Philadelphia-based *American Quarterly Review*, kept a special watch on Force's progress, for it subscribed to his aim, "to place history upon an immovable basis, and to make it, what all history ought to be, a record of facts, beyond cavil or doubt—a simple relation of what actually occurred, clothed in the plain and noble garb of truth." For Force and those who reviewed his work assumed that there was a core of indisputable facts that could be uncovered by hard work and honest reporting. These facts would prove what the American historians and their readers needed the facts to prove: that the republic was safe. It would not repeat the errors that had doomed all republics before it, not if it learned the lessons of its past. Because history was based on such immutable facts, historians could never be guilty of plagiarizing. One could never steal a fact from another author, even if one used the same language, word for word. Facts could not be the property of anyone.[5]

Today, most professional historians would agree that historical facts are not stones one finds lying about. They are instead little arguments constructed from evidence. In insisting on the existence of a core of irreducible and essential facts, thus, the historians of the new republic arrogated to themselves the authority to decide what belonged in the corpus of our history and what did not. White, Protestant, Anglo-Saxon New Englanders were thus freed to identify themselves and their coterie as the makers of the American success story. Their forebears needed space for their farms and herds, and they took it from the native inhabitants. They needed cheap and plentiful labor, and found it in a system of chattel slavery. They needed to spawn new generations of their own superior kind, for which purpose the mothers of the race were divinely appointed and naturally suited, the historians believed. The necessary and logical consequence of their assumptions about history was that Indians, African Americans, and women could not be the center of the tale. Indeed, they must be pushed to its edges—or American history would become a story of oppression, the very opposite of what its chroniclers wanted and needed it to be.

The Giants:
George Bancroft
and Francis Parkman

George Bancroft and Francis Parkman, the two giants of nineteenth-century American historical writing, understood implicitly that a serviceable American history—serviceable for their ends—must be narrowly tailored. It must convince readers of the heroism and achievement of the hardy breed of New England men; prove that those men deserved, indeed were ordained, to rule; and excuse, rationalize, or reformat the whole of the tale so that oppressed groups vanished from it. In this they were spectacularly successful, insofar as that success could be measured by their reputation and sales.

In 1834, the same year that the conservative, Whig Party–supporting *American Quarterly Review* was laying out the ethical canons for American historians, George Bancroft published the first volume of his monumental ten-volume *History of the United States,* the last volume of which appeared in 1874. Bancroft's *History* was to become the standard work on American history for generations. Bancroft was the son of a minister, and he entered Harvard at age 13, in 1813. After he graduated, he went to Europe and earned degrees in German universities, then returned to found a school in Northampton, Massachusetts. Later he would engage in Democratic politics (holding, before he was done, at various times an ambassadorship and the post of Secretary of War). He did most of the research for his volumes between 1831 and 1834, though he continued to write and revise until his mental powers failed late in life. When he died in 1891, he was the most honored of our historians, and his works were widely read.[6]

Bancroft saw himself as a scholar and regarded his work as a major contribution to knowledge. As he wrote in his preface,

I have endeavored to impart originality to my narrative, by deriving it from writings and sources which were the contemporaries of the events that are described. . . . Much error had become incorporated within American history. . . . The early history was often written with a carelessness which seized on rumor and vague recollection as sufficient authority for an assertion which satisfied prejudice by wanton perversions.

This was both strong and critical language. Bancroft was careful to alert his readers in his footnotes when he disagreed with another historian's reading of the primary (original or documentary) sources. He was careful to provide the source of every quotation and to name the secondary sources (other scholars' works) that he consulted to hold the narrative together, and was effusive in his gratitude to others. "I have been most liberally aided by the directors of our chief public libraries, especially the library at Cambridge, on American history."

But Bancroft made no real distinction between primary sources and secondary sources. When a secondary source cited a passage from a primary source, Bancroft felt perfectly free to reuse the language of the secondary source in his own account without identifying it as such. He cited the secondary-source pages, but copied or closely paraphrased rather than quoted. Facts were facts, in whatever language they were reported. In effect, he turned all his sources, whether written by the actual actors or by later scholars, into primary sources. And when it suited his didactic purposes, he fabricated. He "felt free to change tenses or moods, to transpose parts of quotations, to simplify language, and to give free renditions." If the purpose of history was to tell stories that taught lessons, such "blending" could hardly be objectionable, and for contemporary reviewers, it was not.[7]

Bancroft believed that his job was to write a chronicle that would make his readers proud of their country's history. The first volume of his *History of the United States* was published at the height of the national battle over antislavery petitions in Congress, the beginning of the dispossession of the "civilized tribes" of Indians from their homelands in the Southeast (eventually they would be relocated to the Indian Territory in what is now Oklahoma), anti-Catholic rioting in northeastern cities, and the rise of workingmen's political parties.

But one would never imagine any of this was going on around Bancroft when he sounded the trumpet for our "precedence in the practice and the defense of the equal rights of man. . . . Prosperity follows the execution of even justice; invention is quickened by the freedom of competition; and labor rewarded with sure and unexampled returns." Although slavery was entrenched in half the nation and fully 20 percent of Americans could not claim the fruits of their labor, much less the freedom to walk away from their masters, Bancroft (who did not defend slavery personally) insisted that in the United States, "Domestic peace is maintained without the aid of a military establishment" and "Every man may enjoy the fruits of his industry." Although abolitionists were not welcome in the South and their writings were routinely opened at post offices and burned, Bancroft asserted that "Every mind is free to publish its convictions." Although law in almost all of the slaveholding states forbade slaves from learning to read the Bible and in the northern states Catholic churches were burned and convents looted by mobs, Bancroft boasted, "Religion, neither persecuted nor paid by the state, is sustained by the regard for public morals and the earnestness of an enlightened faith."

In order that the greater "truths" he beheld in American history not be obscured, in order that history uplift and inspire Americans, Bancroft decided that some Americans' part in that history must be elided or diminished. If they were moved to the center of the tale, American history would bear a sanguinary aspect. So Bancroft selected certain facts and ignored others in order that it appear that "the principles of liberty unite all interests by the operation of equal laws, blend the discordant elements into harmonious union." This was consensus history in the service of celebration and it was inherently fallacious. It falsified our history because it left out or dismissed the experience of more than half of America's population: Indians, women, servants, slaves, and immigrants.

Fifty years after writing his first encomium on American liberty, thirty years after the immensely destructive Civil War, ten years after the postwar Reconstruction failed and former slaves, now freedmen and -women, found themselves mired in sharecroppers' poverty and held captive behind the razor wire of Jim Crow segregation, in the midst of a great war between labor and capital that brought strikes and scab labor to American industrial sites—in the midst of all this, Bancroft looked back on the judgments he had made in his first volume, and persisted in his view that

> . . . the foregoing words, written nearly a half-century ago, are suffered to remain, because the intervening years have justified their expression of confidence in the progress of our republic. The seed of disunion has perished, and universal freedom, reciprocal benefits, and cherished traditions bind its many states in the closest union.[8]

The issue that agitated Americans above all others in both 1834 and in 1885 was the treatment of people of color. Bancroft knew that "the Negro race, from its introduction [into the colonies], was regarded with distrust," but who knew that "human bondage would become so strongly riveted" in some parts of the new land? The plight of the slaves was real, but it was not important to Bancroft's purpose, for it denied the fundamental thesis of consensus history. Slaves did not enjoy the bounties of liberty. So, too, Bancroft's handling of Native Americans reflected his commitment to a narrow and self-serving consensus history. When the colonists came from Europe to North America, he wrote, they found "an unproductive waste . . . its only inhabitants . . . a few scattered tribes of feeble barbarians, destitute of commerce and of political connection." Bancroft was wrong on all three counts, as any of the first settlers could have told him. Indians produced an abundance of crops in season—an abundance that the first Europeans noted with delight. Indians traded with one another and they formed political connections that endured for hundreds of years (longer than most European peace treaties).

Bancroft was not unsympathetic to the plight of what he saw as a few feeble redmen, but "Manifest Destiny" was his credo. He wrote in an age of ebullient imperialism, when the American eagle screeched triumphantly over the expansion of the United States. Thus, however much Bancroft might feel the pain of the mistreatment of the Indians, that pain merited no more than a few sympathetic asides. He lamented how the Spanish conquistadors in the sixteenth century "enslaved such as offended" them among the natives, and "on slight suspicion . . . cut off the hands of numbers of the natives for punishment or intimidation." He moralized that "the happiness, the life, and the rights of the Indians were held of no account." But he concluded that if the Indians were benighted victims, they were also too different, dispersed, and ultimately unimportant to require more than passing mention in his history.[9]

Bancroft's great rival as the foremost American historian of the nineteenth century was Boston-bred and Harvard-educated Francis Parkman. Like Bancroft, Parkman's labors spanned the better part of the century and his books assayed a broad swath of our history. Parkman's much admired multivolume narrative of the French and English struggle for the North American colonies was a classic, plain and simple. As John Fiske, the turn-of-the-century historian who edited the 1902 reissue of the volumes, wrote admiringly, the volumes "take their place in literature as permanent and secure" among the finest studies of human warfare.[10]

Parkman was as determined to be accurate and as meticulous in his use of the primary sources as Bancroft, and he was just as indifferent to issues of scholarly citation of secondary sources. As he prefaced his narrative of the French and Indian war, *Montcalm and Wolfe* (1884), "Besides manuscripts, the printed matter in the form of books, pamphlets, contemporary newspapers, and other published histories relating to the Americans' part of the Seven Years War, is varied and abundant, and I believe I may safely say that nothing in it of much consequence has escaped me. . . . The whole of this published and unpublished mass of evidence has been read and collated with extreme care." In other words, the secondary sources were mixed in with the mass of primary sources and no special effort was made to avoid plagiarism. Indeed, for all his care with the primary sources, including sending emissaries to copy documents in foreign archives,

Parkman was indifferent to any requirement of putting quotation marks around language directly copied from other historians. He read them, to be sure. Large portions of *Montcalm and Wolfe*, for example, those describing England, France, and the colonies on the eve of the war, have no reference notes at all, though they are meticulously detailed. He got that material somewhere, but the only citations in the book are to primary sources, which is the case for all the volumes. As Fiske recalled (having known Parkman from 1872 to the day of his death), Parkman read everything but "had not the tastes of a bibliophile."[11]

The excuse Fiske provided for Parkman's way of doing history was one that appeared often in all contemporary reviews of nineteenth-century American history. Parkman, said Fiske, was a man of letters, "with his naturalist's keen and accurate eye and his quick poetic apprehension. . . . Such realism is usually the prerogative of the novelist rather than the historian." Mastery of detail was not enough; it was Parkman's poetic gift that lifted his works to the pantheon of great history. Such borrowing as Parkman (and Bancroft) assayed from other authors was something that men of letters did all the time, without qualms—if not without controversy, as Edgar Allen Poe, Nathaniel Hawthorne, Samuel L. Clements (Mark Twain), and other authors discovered. Certainly plagiarism was an offense against good taste, but was not seen as a matter of professional ethics.[12]

Parkman's aim was an accurate account, but it was filled with what can only be regarded as misrepresentation at best and prejudice at worst. These derived not from intention to deceive, but from deep-seated opinions of his own that he never bothered to explore. Nearly blind and often lame, Parkman walked the warpaths that the Indians once traveled, but he saw only the dissolute ghosts of his own imagination—as he wrote in *The Jesuits in North America*—the "extremes of misery and degradation" he believed to be the Indians' assigned lot. For the Indians' role in his history was to people "the savage prologue of the American drama . . . coming to a close, [as] the civilization of Europe was advancing on the scene."

In fact, Parkman's near mania for accuracy in the historical details he provided served to prove what Bancroft assumed at the outset: the

Protestant, New England vision of American history was destined to prevail over all others. Parkman's immersion in historical materials permitted him to depict Indian life with great energy, but his prejudices never enabled him to see the Indians' world through their eyes or to give them any kind of credit for creativity or achievement. Though some Indians were of a higher "type" (a word Parkman used to mean racial characteristics), even those who cultivated the land instead of wandering over it and lived in extensive towns instead of isolated woven-reed wigwams were, in his view, inferior specimens to the European newcomers.

His account of the Canadian Huron Indians, in *The Jesuits in North America,* is an example of his perspective: "He who entered [a Huron Indian longhouse] on a winter night beheld a strange spectacle." (Of course, the Hurons would not have found it strange at all—for them it was home. A more sensitive historian would have realized this.)

The bronzed groups . . . eating, gambling, or amusing themselves with badinage: shriveled squaws, hideous with threescore years of hardship; grisly old warriors, scarred with Iroquois war-clubs . . . damsels gay with ochre and wampum; restless children pell-mell with restless dogs. Now a tongue of resinous flame painted each wild figure in vivid light; now the fitful gleam expired, and the group vanished from sight, as their nation has vanished from history.

He thought that the Hurons were superior to other Algonquians because of "the size . . . of their brains." Parkman subscribed to the emerging pseudo-science of phrenology. But he thought they were incapable of intellectual abstraction. To him, Indian religion was "a chaos of degrading, ridiculous and incoherent superstitions." Above all, Indian character was morally deficient: "That well known self control, which, originating in a form of pride, covered the savage nature of the man with a veil, opaque, though thin. . . . Though vain, arrogant, boastful, and vindictive, the Indian bore abuse and sarcasm with an astonishing patience."[13]

Parkman was a Victorian moralist, which explains at least in part his fascination with the outlandish along with his unreflecting arrogance in condemning it. But his biased moralism ensured that Parkman's brilliant pointillist depiction of Indian life ended up as little more than an artistic exercise in falsification and fabrication. The Hurons did not vanish from history. In 1867, when Parkman wrote these passages, there were still Hurons in Canada, as there are to this day. But for him "vanished from history" meant something larger and more important than a demographic fact. The Hurons had played a horrific but subsidiary role in the great competition between England and France for empire, and now they were no longer needed in the tale.

Consensus and the
History of the Ruling Race

As Bancroft selected the facts that described and established the trumph of American liberty, so Parkman favored the facts that proved the racial superiority of the Anglo-Saxon peoples. Behind the conquest of the Indian by the Anglo-American lay the latter's supposedly superior racial traits: "The Germanic race, and especially the Anglo-Saxon branch of it, is peculiarly masculine, and, therefore, peculiarly fitted for self-government. It submits its action habitually to the guidance of reason, and has the judicial faculty of seeing both sides of a question."[14]

The immense popularity of accounts like Bancroft's and Parkman's well into the 1880s and 1890s was not diminished by their prejudices. Indeed, Parkman's and Bancroft's readers, men and women of a supposedly superior type, held the historians in such high esteem precisely because they shared the historians' view of the world. Their history proved that the world was ripe for conquest by their readers and their kind. As Henry Adams, a representative of the next generation of their set, wrote in conclusion to his magisterial history of the administrations of Thomas Jefferson and James Madison:

> The continent lay before them, like an uncovered ore bed. They
> could see, and they could even calculate with reasonable accuracy,

the wealth it could be made to yield. With almost the certainty of a mathematical formula, knowing the rate of increase of wealth, they could read in advance their economic history.

At the end of the 1880s, young Theodore Roosevelt, another of the new generation of amateur historians, agreed that "much yet remained to be done before the West would reach its natural limits and would fill from frontier to frontier with populous common-wealths of its own citizens." Indians, by their very nature, in the 1880s as in 1816, could not be citizens, and thus, by definition (a perfect circularity), they did not belong in the story.[15]

The Founders of the nation had asked for a history that would showcase their achievements in the best light and provide a glue to hold the nation together. They were children of the Enlightenment who believed that universal laws governed politics and history just as they governed physics and chemistry, and the right kind of history would prove that the new nation would surpass the great republics of the past.

The next generation's historians were children of a romantic age, to whom differences meant more than similarities and the ideal of universal liberty had different implications than it did for Jefferson and his fellow Founders. It was a thoroughly racist age, and it saw in American history the rise of a ruling race. One Boston aristocrat, Henry Cabot Lodge, put it: "The men of each race possess an inde-structible stock of ideas, traditions, sentiments, modes of thought, an unconscious inheritance from their ancestors, upon which argument has no effect." The seeds or germs of superior cultures passed through the blood from generation to generation. History was the story of that inheritance, and American history was the tale of the rise of the Anglo-Saxon peoples. Historians drawn from this social and ethnic cadre agreed that in Anglo-Saxon or Teutonic blood lay the origins of freedom, democracy, and progress, and the narrative they crafted reflected this credo.[16]

At best, other races could learn how to adopt these institutions from the master races. At worst, hordes of inferior peoples would overwhelm their superiors and destroy civilization. Thus, Roosevelt, a student of these racial theories, insisted that the Indians had to make way for the Europeans, for if Indians

> . . . have often suffered terrible injustice at our hands . . . it was wholly impossible to avoid conflicts with the weaker race, unless we were willing to see the American continent fall into the hands of some other strong power, and even had we adopted such a ludicrous policy, the Indians themselves would have made war upon us.

The Indians had to move aside; history commanded it. Not by accident, Roosevelt was also an early and eager exponent of "eugenics," the science of reproductive engineering. He demanded that Anglo-Saxon mothers produce more babies of good stock, lest the ruling race be outnumbered by dark-skinned hordes.[17]

Was this vision false, fabricated, built only upon self-interested and repetitious assertions by a few that they were predestined to rule the rapidly expanding American empire? Not to the minds of the historians who expressed the vision and not to the many readers who shared their prejudices and their fears. For them, it was the essence of American history, explaining why the nation was destined to spread across the continent, conquering and assimilating everything in its path. Such scholarship fulfilled the narrowest of all the purposes assigned to history by the Founders. It reassured, justified, and made whole the experience of a people rent by a Civil War and challenged by rapid geographic expansion and torrents of immigration, but it did not truly reflect the struggles and the sacrifices of all Americans. It was winners' history written and read by the winners. For this reason, consensus history's fabrications, falsehoods, and plagiarism actually immunized it from criticism in elite and learned circles.

In retrospect one must recognize that consensus histories fit a self-serving pattern, but at the same time, one ought to see that pattern in the context of elite nineteenth-century American values and biases. This is what today's historians mean by "historical-mindedness," the ability that scholars must have to recognize the impact of past time and place on the ideas of people long ago. But is that "brooding omnipresence" of personal experience (to modify one of Oliver Wendell Holmes, Jr.'s most telling phrases), a bar to any historian's surmounting the values and desires of his own time and place? If the Bancrofts and Parkmans were merely prisoners of a racist and imperialist age, so much so that the facts they saw as immutable and compelling left out or ignored the suffering of most early Americans, how can we claim to be exempt from the same intellectual limitations? Is there any way to step outside our time and place, outside the formative influences that shape our opinions, and strive for a more objective history than one that simply bows to current prejudices?

In the 1880s and 1890s, as the last of the great nineteenth-century amateur historians like Bancroft and Parkman finally laid down their pens, a new generation of historians was appearing on the scene. They were the first American professional historians and they claimed to be free of the romantic prejudices of their immediate predecessors. Their work, they assured readers, would truly make history a science, free of the constraints of time and place, local bias, and regional interest.

CHAPTER 2

Professions
of History

A T THE END OF THE 1870S, HERBERT BAXTER ADAMS, recently returned from studying history at a German university and newly appointed to a teaching post at Johns Hopkins University, introduced the German *Seminarium* method of graduate study. The idea was that history could be made a science if the study of history was modeled upon the training of scientists. Thus, history would become a profession and have professional standards. The university would accept a few students each year to work toward a new degree (also imported from Germany), a doctorate in history, which would qualify them to teach history at the college level. Graduate students would gain their doctorates by writing a long research paper, called a dissertation, based on their study of primary sources of history. It had to be an original contribution to knowledge. Students would give progress reports on their research at the seminar, where they would be criticized by faculty and other students.

At the urging of Albert Bushnell Hart of Harvard's History Department, Harvard began offering its own history seminar for graduate students in 1885. Columbia University quickly followed suit, and soon Cambridge, Massachusetts, and New York City rivaled Baltimore as Meccas for young men seeking advanced degrees in history and planning on college teaching careers. They, like their mentors, wholly dissociated themselves from the romantic men of letters. In fact, the first professionals were quick to discern and decry evidence of fabrication and plagiarism in the work of the nineteenth-century amateur historians.[1]

In 1878, the Johns Hopkins University created the first academic press, the Johns Hopkins Publication Agency, to ensure publication of dissertations. Its first publications were dissertations on mathematics and chemistry; then, in 1882, the Studies in History and Political Science series was launched. The press's origin was inseparable from the new professionalism. Its purpose was not to sell books to a wide audience but to make available the latest, best research in history and other academic fields to professionals in the field and to give publication credentials to newly minted Ph.D.s.

In their effort to separate their own endeavor from that of the amateur historians, the professionals inadvertently created an entirely new genre of history, today termed popular history. Until the university presses appeared, all history was popular history or it did not get published. But the popular was frowned upon by the professionals; it demeaned their discipline and training. It was unscientific and unworthy of serious notice. University presses stuck to "monographs," works that were heavily researched and often tediously written.

To ensure what they saw as high standards in professional history, and to maintain the value of the Ph.D. by limiting access to it, Adams, Hart, and their ilk founded the American Historical Association in 1884 and began publication of the *American Historical Review* in 1895. Like the amateurs, the officers of the new national organization and the board of editors of the new journal were an elite; indeed, they came from the very same social stratum: Protestant, largely British in family origin, from the Northeast, well educated (often partly in Europe), and wholly committed, as Hart told the AHA in 1910, to a "genuinely scientific school of history, which shall remorselessly

examine the sources and separate the wheat from the chaff; which
shall critically balance evidence; which shall dispassionately and mod-
erately set forth results." But Hart had not abandoned the ideal of a
consensus history, and in this he departed little from the great and
noble dream of Bancroft and Parkman: "In history, too, scattered and
apparently unrelated data fall together in harmonious wholes." The
ideal of scientific history was simply a scientific-sounding version of
consensus history.[2]

The Professionals'
Consensus

If the new professionalism was not necessarily antagonistic to the
project of consensus history, one would expect that its ethical
canons, elucidated by men like Adams and Hart, would end the fabrication, plagiarism, and self-serving narrowness of the romantic school
of history. In fact, the reverse was true. Professionalism merely camou-
flaged the prejudices of its credentialed authors. One of the first
graduates of the Johns Hopkins Ph.D. program was a stern-faced and
sober-thinking Southerner named Woodrow Wilson. He would go on
to a career as a scholar and professor at Princeton University, and
become its president, then governor of the state of New Jersey, and
finally president of the United States, in 1912. So one might expect
that he would bring to his historical writing the scientific, impartial,
objective canon of professionalism.

Not so. In 1901, he edited a ten-volume collection of documents
on American history, and the introduction he wrote bears a remarkable resemblance to the thinking of the nineteenth-century consensus historians. It began with a set of factual assertions that were little
more than prejudices. When the English came to North America,
according to Wilson, they found "that the interior was one vast wilderness, grown thick with tangled forests." This was a factual error, as any
unbiased reading of the primary sources would immediately reveal.
The English found Indian gardens and palisaded towns. Wilson con-

tinued that North America exhibited a wildness that baffled some of the Europeans, but not for long those of Anglo-Saxon stock, a "whole race of venturesome and hardy" men, whose "sober mind" and "steady business sagacity" combined with "high imaginative hope" had led them to sea, and then "towards new ports and new homes in America." The "wild savagery" of the tribesmen did not deter the English, for the Indian "feared the white man with an overmastering dread." Actually, the first English accounts found the Indians admirable in many ways, and gave no evidence that the Indians dreaded the English. Wilson was not letting facts speak for themselves—he was choosing bits and pieces of evidence to support his own opinions. "Steadily, relentlessly, and by a masterful advance from settlement to settlement which they [the Indians] could in no wise withstand, they were pushed back into the forests." The outcome of the encounter of "savage" and "civilized" was never in doubt, and it was wholly consonant with the idea that the continent of North America belonged to the Anglo-Saxons, Wilson's own forbears.[3]

The condescending and biased tenor of Wilson's supposedly scientific account reappeared in his treatment of blacks. History was supposed to teach everyone to know their place. According to Wilson, during the Civil War, the South's slaves had remained "faithful and steady at their accustomed tasks . . . devoted in the service of the masters." Never independent, never fully capable of independent thought or moral action, blacks contributed little to the national saga. At best they were docile toilers, at worst dangerous vagabonds. When the crutch of slavery was removed, they "ignorantly" expected

> not freedom only, but largess of fortune. . . . The government would find land for them, would feed them and give them clothes. . . . They had the easy faith, the simplicity, the idle hopes, the inexperience of children. Their masterless, homeless freedom had made them the more pitiable, the more dependent, because under slavery they had been shielded, the weak and the incompetent with the strong and capable.

The notion that slaves were shielded by slavery is a remarkable one,

leading a dispassionate reader to ask, "shielded from whom," for the
casual cruelty of slavery was evident in the primary sources that Wilson was editing. Freed by the Thirteenth Amendment after the Civil
War, Wilson's freedmen were "helpless creatures . . . a dusky host of
pitiful refugees." In fact, many former slaves were refugees, but they
were actually looking for loved ones sold or carried away to distant
places. And some on the roads were not refugees at all, but migrants,
going north or west in search of better lives.[4]

It was not a professional dedication to thorough and unbiased
research and analysis that motivated Wilson, but his adherence
(indeed, his abiding commitment) to the prejudices of his time and
place. A son of the Confederacy, he shared its views on history. These
crossed the Mason-Dixon Line. Northerners like New Jersey's William
A. Dunning, a Columbia University history professor specializing in
the Reconstruction era, taught that "the freedmen were not, and in
the nature of the case could not for generations be, on the same
social, moral, and intellectual plane with the whites," and thus, with
freedom in hand after the Civil War they "wandered aimless but
happy through the country." Reconstruction failed not because of
white Southerners' violence against their black neighbors, but because
"it became increasingly apparent to reflecting men that . . . intelligence and political capacity were, indeed, almost exclusively in the
one race."

Dunning, like Bancroft and Parkman, believed in the immutability
of facts. Facts "must be taken squarely into account by historians"
when they wrote the nation's history. Dunning was so influential in
Reconstruction studies as to have his and his students' work commonly called "the Dunning school" and to gain him the presidency of
the AHA. Thus it was with unconscious irony that Dunning, in his
presidential address to the AHA, in 1913, admitted, "We must recognize frankly that whatever a given age or people believes to be true is
true for that age and people." I say ironically because he did not see
fit to apply that truism to his own work or his own age's historical
assumptions about race.[5]

Indeed, because they came from the same backgrounds and
shared many of the preconceptions of their amateur nineteenth-cen-

tury predecessors, turn-of-the-century professional historians adopted the fundamental assumptions of the old consensus history. Hart, in whose multivolume American Nation series Dunning's book, *Reconstruction, Political and Economic, 1865–1877*, appeared in 1907, is a perfect example. Hart was a descendant of abolitionists. He had no doubt that slavery had burdened the nation with a "terrible race and labor problem." But he was equally certain that the slaves' "shiftlessness, waste of their master's property, neglect of his animals, were almost proverbial, the looseness of the marriage-tie and immorality of even the best of the Negroes were subject of sorrow to those who felt the responsibility of them." Thus, for Hart, the political agitation that led to a Civil War was an unpleasant anomaly in our history, just as slavery itself was an anomaly and the presence of blacks was an anomaly in the larger story of one people's and one nation's progress toward greatness.[6]

By selecting and arraying facts in highly slanted ways, men like Hart and Wilson could bring consensus history up to date. It became a form of apology, excusing past harms the weak suffered and rationalizing the economic and political advantages the strong enjoyed. No better example of this exists than the way in which leading Southern historians made the slaves and the freedmen into the scapegoats for Southern problems. Thus Claude Bowers, in 1929, regarded Reconstruction as a "tragic era" and believed that blacks participating in public life presented an "astonishing" and hideous spectacle. Bowers's book was hugely popular, but as biased scholarship it paled in comparison to Paul Buck's deeply sentimental *The Road to Reunion 1865–1900* (1937), a Pulitzer Prize winner. Buck lamented that the end of the Civil War and the advent of "Negro rule" by an "inferior race" had brought to the South a "disorder worse than war, and oppression unequaled in American annals." In the meantime, the "nobility of sacrifices" of the Confederacy's bold warriors had been overwhelmed by force of numbers alone. He opined that only when the Negro and his Republican puppeteers were driven from their roosts could "peace and brotherhood" among the whites of North and South be achieved. Then, over time, with the eventual consent of the whites of the North, "the South" (by which Buck invariably meant the white South) would be allowed to deal with its "Negro problem" on its own. Then would the "stability of race relations" give "the Negro a chance . . . to take the first steps of progress." The same themes echoed in E. Merton Coulter's influential *The South During Reconstruction, 1865–1877* (1947), the first volume in the prestigious History of the South series at the Louisiana State University Press, for which Coulter was the series editor.[7]

Wilson, Dunning, Hart, and Buck all stood at the pinnacle of the historical profession in their time, and yet their writings demonstrated all the biased and questionable qualities of the old consensus history. They borrowed freely from their predecessors a body of supposedly incontrovertible "facts" that were in fact nothing but self-satisfied prejudices. They falsified and fabricated by omission and commission, and substituted opinion for scholarship.

One could try to excuse them by saying that they were merely prisoners of their time and place—they could see no other interpretation than the one they did. For at the same time these professionals were promoting the idea of a scientific history free of personal bias, a few of their number had reached an opposite conclusion—that all historical writing was "relative" to its time and place. There could be no pure science of history: at best it was just an elegant form of literary conjuring in which historians guessed at what could never be known; at worst, it came down to the sort of myth making that totalitarian regimes imposed on the masses.

Forms of historical skepticism had made their appearance among European intellectuals in the middle of the nineteenth century, and announced their arrival here in the work of Carl Becker, a professor of European history at Cornell University. In a 1908 essay he wrote of the scholarly process, "My own experience enters in. . . . New sources enable me to combine the elements of experience more correctly, but experience must furnish the elements to select from" in writing any account of the past. The past only lived "in present reality," and that reality was the historians', not the past's.[8]

But relativism never caught on among these first professionals— indeed, Becker was a historian of European ideas, not an Americanist at all. However, relativism's central point—that facts were not irreducible bricks that the historian piled up but little arguments that he fabricated from the pieces of evidence he selected—implied that the consensus view might not be the only one historians could adopt. If there were no central core of essential facts automatically more important than other facts, then historians could propose accounts of American history contrary to the consensus narrative. It did not matter whether these opposing views were dictated by the historian's time and place, as Becker seemed to imply, for relativism could be used in a far less profound manner to undercut consensus historians' claim to orthodoxy. And that is just what the so-called progressive historians attempted to do.

Progressive Historians

This new grouping within the ranks of professional historians, largely men trained after 1900, read the evidence differently from the consensus historians, and placed at the fore a different set of facts and stories, including sectional antagonism, class struggle, and the subjugation of minorities. In the work of Charles Beard and other progressive historians, American history bore a contentious and sometimes oppressive face. Had their ideas been pushed to their natural limits and spread through the profession, they might have revolutionized the way that historians, and their readers, saw our past.

Perhaps the advent of a progressive critique of older views of American history was inevitable, given the political developments in the country. Certainly the progressive historians were influenced in part by the Progressive political reformers' critique of corrupt politics and corrupting "robber barons" of big business. However they came to their views, the progressive historians proposed that American history was riven with conflict and competition. But such a critique could not have shaken the foundations of consensus history had not the progressives wielded the sword of relativism. And Charles Beard, the greatest of the progressive historians, thrust it home in a remarkable address to the AHA. Elected its president in 1935, in his presidential address he argued that scientific history was nothing more than a conceit. His targets were those who believed that "sound and credible" objective works on American history were a "noble dream" and should be pursued by all true scholars. For that, read "consensus historians." Beard knew that he and other progressive historians were being accused by those same conservative consensus historians of being "ignoble, unsound, discreditable, and weak," and that their supposedly "partial and doctrinaire" works were dismissed by the same scholarly apologists for the status quo. One can almost taste his venom as he parodied the traditionalists. They were not even good reporters of the AHA's own past, for had not his predecessors at the head of the AHA (he meant, I think, Dunning) written history with concerns "true to their age"? Historians invariably selected problems to tackle and arrayed evidence not "as the chemist sees his test tubes and compounds," but as "me," as interested parties.[9]

But if Beard was right that his opponents' claim to scientific accuracy was nothing more than an unsupported and (according to relativist theory) unsupportable claim, why should anyone place more faith in his own views? And in fact, progressive historians, faced with this dilemma, did not abandon all of the comforting tenets of consensus thought. Take, for example, Beard's slightly older contemporary, Frederick Jackson Turner. Turner, a professor of history at the University of Wisconsin, was the first of the progressive historians to propose that divisions within American history were as important as unities. Born and reared in Portage, Wisconsin, he argued that the frontier experience and the open spaces of the West, rather than the town meetings and the Anglo-Saxon heritage of New England, gave Americans their appreciation of individualism and democracy. As a result, Jackson postulated, sectional tensions—West vs. East, North vs. South —shaped the history of the country. "Each of these areas has had an influence in our economic and political history, the evolution of each into a higher stage has worked political transformations. But what constitutional historian has made any adequate attempt to interpret political facts by the light of these social areas and changes?" he asked. But—a very important but—Turner did not deny the core consensus thesis of one people, one nation, one history. He merely refocused its lens on the West. As he wrote in 1908,

The development of national self-consciousness and national unity went on with the development of sectionalism. Indeed, in one respect sectionalism may be regarded as a stage in the process of the increasing consolidation of American society. . . . As the result of sectional conflict itself, national self-consciousness became ascendant.[10]

Beard's own early work showed the same ambivalence about consensus as Turner's. Born in Indiana, his formative experience among socialist reformers in London appeared in his seminal work on the framing and ratification of the federal Constitution, *The Economic Interpretation of the Constitution of the United States* (1913). Here he argued that the Federalist framers of the Constitution were creditors in a nation wallowing in a sea of debt. Astutely they reasoned that a powerful national government with control of its own purse strings would defend private property against the demands of indebted farmers and urban poor. "A small and active group of men immediately interested through their personal possessions in the outcome of their labors . . . [the Federalists] were able to build the new government upon the only foundations which could be stable: fundamental economic interests." There was nothing in Beard's study that directly confuted the one people–one nation–one history approach. Like Turner, Beard merely offered a different historical interpretation—in his case, a different characterization of the motives of the Founders. Instead of all of them being disinterested patriots, all of them were self-interested lobbyists.[11]

Beard, with the assistance of his wife, Mary Beard, a women's and labor historian, expanded this class-and-conflict theme to all of American history. In the very first colonies they uncovered a skein of selfishness that Bancroft, Parkman, and their ilk had not mentioned. English colonizers were "merchant capitalists" who sought to exploit an underdeveloped region. The English sea-going heroes of Parkman and Wilson were banditti shooting and looting Spanish galleons on their way home from the colonies. In addition, the Beards stressed the importance of class differences in our past. The Beards categorized the majority of the colonists as "labor," among whom the Beards included "Negroes dragged out of Africa" to be slaves on American plantations.

The Beards attempted to rehabilitate the reputations of groups previously demeaned or neglected in traditional consensus histories. The native inhabitants (no longer savages marauding or skulking about) in their account exhibited a wide variety of ways of life, including "settled communities engaged in practicing the economic arts of forest, stream, field, and domesticity. With the Indians the pioneers entered into varied relations: from peace and friendship to treachery and massacre on both sides." There was trade, and sometimes only the Indians' willingness to trade, or simply to share food, enabled the colonists to survive. For the first time in a general text, the authors treated slavery as a major topic. The Beards recognized that one could not discuss tobacco production in the South without mentioning slave labor. They also noted that, in Reconstruction, "hundreds of Negroes, intelligent and educated, furnished some leadership for their bewildered people."

Finally, and perhaps most notably, their view of American history recognized the essential role of women. Seventy-five of the 489 pages in their textbook, *A Basic History of the United States,* were devoted in some way to women's experiences. The tenor of these is clear from one sample reference: "During this democratic development [of the antebellum era] women asserted claims to rights and privileges denied them in law and custom."[12]

The Beards did not totally reject the notion that American history had a central unity, or that it progressed toward greater liberty. Instead, they expanded the core story to include Indians, blacks, workers, and women among the people who belonged in the nation's chronicle. They enlarged the scope and cast of the drama, rather than rewriting the plot line. Had they so desired, they might have entirely discarded consensus history, but they elected instead to reinforce its grip. Who could blame them? Writing in the midst of the great war for democracy, after the greatest depression in our history, Americans wanted and perhaps even needed reassurance that they could work, live, and prosper together within the system of democratic capitalism.

No longer an academic (after teaching history at Columbia University for almost ten years, he had been driven from his post in 1917 by its conservative president Nicholas Murray Butler), Beard, publishing with trade presses, had become a popular historian himself, the most respected practitioner of the craft to make that transition in his day. He had no love for academicians or their supposedly scientific studies, and forfeited the leadership he might have exerted over the entire profession. What was more, angered at the slide toward American participation in World War II (Beard had come to detest our participation in the First World War, and felt guilt over his own efforts to support that war), Beard wasted much of his energy attacking President Franklin D. Roosevelt. When the war came, Beard supported it, but he had lost the moral edge that progressive history had always maintained. In his fall, sadly, the entire project of rewriting American history in terms of class struggle foundered.

Now, the very relativism that had given philosophical energy to the progressive critique of consensus history undermined the appeal of progressive history itself. If everything was relative, how was one to choose between rival interpretations of the past? How in particular could Allied leaders find inspiration in American history for the enormous task of defeating the Axis powers? Worse still, on what basis could one condemn totalitarian uses of history, like the Nazis' and the Fascists'—surely the most cynical of all uses of relativism?

In the World War II years, the influence of the progressive critique and of relativism itself waned. However sophisticated the progressives might have seemed in the 1920s and 1930s, their dismantling of consensus certainties and unities lent no aid to the crusade to save democracy and human dignity from the Nazis and the Fascists. In the wake of the war, a new totalitarian enemy loomed on the horizon, wielding a formidable theory of history of its own, and consensus history assumed a new task: saving American democracy from Communism and American history from Marxist dialectical materialism.

The Cold Warriors'
Consensus

A particular version of Marxist historical theory was one of the propaganda tools of international Communism. In the Soviets' twisted and self-serving version of Karl Marx's ideas, all history reflected the struggle for control of the means of production; capitalism was only one, passing, stage in that struggle; and the exploitation of the workers would end with a Communist state. The end of history was predetermined. Premier Nikolai Khrushchev put it in a somewhat unscholarly fashion when he said, "We will bury you." In the meantime, the Soviet Union's rendering of Marx's dialectical materialism justified political repression and collectivization of the economy of the Soviet Union.

For many American historians, the only answer to the challenge of historical Marxism was to reformat consensus history to fit the new role of the United States as the leader of the free world. As Columbia University's Allan Nevins and Amherst College's Henry Steele Commager explained the tide of American history in the 1963 edition of their *Pocket History of the United States,* "It was inevitable from the beginning" that settlement would sweep over the [North American] continent from east to west; that the savages would be overcome; that the progress of civilization would pass "through several marked stages" in which toleration of religion would gain ground and the power of European institutions like state churches would recede; that the "common heritage" of English language and political ideas would direct the nation on its upward course; that Negroes who knew their place would find freedom; and that a sturdy class of enterprising Southerners would emerge from the devastation of the Civil War to rebuild the South. It was the old consensus history, refitted and pressed into service in the global struggle against Communism.[13]

Commager and Nevins were supremely successful professional historians. Between them they crafted over a hundred books (Nevins had 79 and Commager 76), including their widely adopted textbook *America, the History of a Free People,* published in various editions throughout the 1940s and '50s. Commager was coauthor, with Samuel Eliot Morison and later William Leuchtenberg, of the leading American history college textbook of the 1960s, *The Growth of the American Republic.*

The U.S. history textbook of the 1950s was the most popular kind of American history book. It certainly outsold all other history books. Indeed, it represented a reunification of the professional and the popular in history, for although the authors were often leading professional historians, the volumes themselves had no reference notes —indeed none of the quasi-scientific apparatus that the first professionals had insisted would make amateur history obsolete. By the 1950s, college history textbooks and review books were big business. These books, periodically updated and reissued (the used textbook makes no money for the publisher or the author, hence the need to issue a new and improved version every so often), like those by Commager, Nevins, and Samuel Eliot Morison, all shared the celebratory, consensus view, and all were written to confute the claims of Marxism. The books freely borrowed and often copied from academic monographs with no attribution. Writing a textbook was tantamount to a license to steal.[14]

The only limitation on the use that textbook authors of this era could make of other, earlier accounts of the same events lay in the copyright laws protecting the specific language in prior publications. To get around the need for copyright permission from the authors or publishers of secondary sources, textbook publishers promoted the idea of an educational "fair-use" exception to copyright. In theory, the fair-use exception did not excuse the absence of citations, but in practice, textbook writers simply borrowed with both hands and never said thank you. After all, all the textbooks supposedly did was inform readers about historical facts, and no one had any exclusive monopoly on the facts.[15]

In the Cold War era, textbooks' immutable and essential facts all pointed in the same direction. American history was proof that dialectical materialism was bad history. Certainly Marx's condemnation of the exploitation of the masses did not apply on this side of the Atlantic. It was as if the progressive historians had never picked up their pens. Textbooks that did not conform to the Cold War version of consensus history, including books such as the Beards' that had been inspired by the progressive critique of consensus history and had long been in use, were driven from the market. Their sales dropped as the books were assaulted by patriotic groups or by conservative local and state school boards. Publishers did not want to put themselves at risk by introducing new books that would incur the same kind of criticism. One of the leading textbooks, Ralph Henry Gabriel's *Exploring American History* (1955), actually encouraged students to assist the authorities in ferreting out hidden Communists. Gabriel, an intellectual historian teaching at Yale, informed his readers, "The FBI urges Americans to report direct to its offices any suspicions they may have about Communist activity on the part of their fellow Americans."[16]

Consensus textbook authors were both conservatives and liberals. Nevins, a conservative, always believed that "our destiny is to preach liberty and free enterprise," and his admiring biographies of men of industry and finance sent that message. Commager was a liberal—but he still adhered to the basic consensus program. Never an apologist for the industrial moguls or the forces of fascism, a strong advocate for freedom of speech, an opponent of the red baiters, and certainly no racist, Commager nevertheless insisted that the United States had "escaped" the contentiousness of "parties which represent particular sections, particular classes, particular interests." Even the Civil War, he believed, demonstrated shared values in the North and South. From his own liberal perspective he too embraced the united front that he believed was needed if Americans were to ward off the Communist menace.[17]

Growing up in the fifties, my generation didn't know all the ramifications of the menace of the second "Red Scare," but we were told that something evil was nearby and had to be defeated. Doris Kearns Goodwin has said that during her childhood in suburban Long Island, nothing seemed safe.

In the larger world, the apprehension that communist subversion was undermining America . . . was intensified enormously by news that the Soviet Union had exploded an atomic bomb. It seemed inconceivable to many that the Russians had mastered nuclear science on their own. Traitorous spies must have provided the secret. The search for communist sympathizers in the government spiraled into a nationwide hysteria.

Even teachers in New York City, in Beard's day the haven of radicalism, were subject to screening and dismissal if their political views were too far left.[18]

By the beginning of the 1950s, leftists and radicals all over academia were on the run. The House Un-American Affairs Committee was investigating historians who wrote from a left-wing perspective; cross-examinations of witnesses by a young lawyer named Richard Nixon, and later a Red Scare fomented by Senator Joseph McCarthy of Wisconsin, had driven many scholars to cover, including those who had no connection to the Communist Party. Historians who could not hide lost their jobs and faced blackballing. A study of college teachers in the 1950s (over a third of whom were historians) that was published in 1958 reported, "Broadly speaking, from either the long- or short-range point of view, American social scientists felt in the spring of 1955 that the intellectual and political freedom of the teaching community had been noticeably curtailed, or at least disturbingly threatened."[19]

Not all proponents of consensus history were inquisitors, but the Cold Warriors assumed "a healthy unity" of American history that had no room for left-wing radicalism. It was "the heyday of consensus history." Looking back on the 1950s a decade later, the Columbia University historian Richard Hofstadter saw the triumph of anti-intellectualism in a nation "filled with people who are often fundamentalist in religion, nativist in prejudice, isolationist in foreign policy, and conservative in economics," a fearful and fearsome combination of prejudices that consensus history fed.[20]

The High-Water Mark
of Consensus History

The most brilliant advocate of consensus history in this troubled time, and on the surface the most uncritical of its purveyors, was Daniel Boorstin. A Harvard college undergraduate and a Yale Ph.D., as well as a Rhodes Scholar at Oxford, a lawyer as well as a historian (twenty-five years at the University of Chicago), Boorstin raised the theme of one people, one nation, one history to a new level of persuasive power. In his sweeping, heavily anecdotal trilogy on the rise of the American people, the first volume of which was published in 1958, he insisted that a shared American experience structured and molded the way that Americans viewed their world and themselves. The series title, *The Americans,* and the titles of the volumes—*The Americans: The Colonial Experience* (1958), *The Americans: The National Experience* (1965), and *The Americans: The Democratic Experience* (1973)—announced a consensus ideal fitting a nation trying to find psychological comfort in conformity and social harmony in celebration of its unity. But some Americans did not share in this experience and, as with previous consensus histories, they did not gain their proper share of space in his pages.

In *The Americans: The Colonial Experience,* Boorstin introduced his readers to colonial southern planters, who prized an "aristocratic camaraderie," and whose "localism" and "political activity" would become part of a national way of life. In the southern colonies, Boorstin found a Negro problem but few slaves. (They did not even make it into the index, despite the fact that some colonies had a black majority and slaves were everywhere in early America, North and South.) The only time his dusky hewers of wood and drawers of water appeared was in a discussion of whites' "slave patrols" in South Carolina. Boorstin was even able to discuss tobacco cultivation in Tidewater Virginia without mentioning the men and women who did most of the planting and harvesting of crop. Planters had the onerous task of "looking after the health of the slaves," as if the slaves were valuable livestock, and Virginia society, which in fact depended on slave labor, was instead for Boorstin, "a republic of neighbors" all of whom were white and most of whom, to judge from his account, were propertied males.[21]

The Indian got more space than the slave only because "the Indian was omnipresent; he struck without warning and was a nightly terror in the remote silence of backwoods cabins." Boorstin ignored Indians' genuine grievances and their repeated expressions of dismay at the expropriation of their hunting and farm lands by European interlopers, and he concluded:

> . . . the Indian menace, which haunted the fringes of settlement through the whole colonial era, remained a terror to the receding West well into the 19th century. Not until ten years after the massacre of Custer's force in 1876, when the few remaining Indians had been removed to Indian Territory or to reservations, did the Indian threat disappear.

For him, as for Parkman, Indians did not fit into the pantheon of "undifferentiated Americans" whose achievements, thoughts, and story really mattered, a judgment that led him to ignore many unpalatable facts about Indian-colonist relations.[22]

Women only got parts of six pages, and the picture Boorstin painted of them was one-dimensional, as he noted "the new and more diversified role of women in American life. . . . Evidence suggests that women in colonial America were more versatile, more active, more prominent, and on the whole more successful in activities outside the kitchen than were their English counterparts." Of course, colonial women's work included food preservation and preparation, but to describe women's work—including childbearing and -rearing, taking care of livestock, domestic manufacturing and nursing—as primarily related to the kitchen is more a caricature of the 1950s suburban homemaker than an accurate depiction of the female colonial settler. Moreover, Boorstin's blithe generalization did not include the slave woman, the Indian woman, or the servant woman, who together made up about 75 percent of all colonial women.[23]

Boorstin's second installment, *The Americans: The National Experi-*

ence, ranged even more broadly and confidently over the historical
terrain, avoiding, as had its predecessor, the sloughs and troughs of
the oppressed minorities and women.

> Between the Revolution and the Civil War the young nation flour-
> ished not in discovery but in search. . . . It lived with the constant
> belief that something else or something better might turn up. A by-
> product of looking for ways of living together was a new civilization,
> whose strength was less an idealism than a willingness to be satisfied
> with less than the ideal.

This was a picture-perfect description of America in the 1950s, a time
of consumption and conformity rather than idealism, but not of the
1850s, when wildly idealistic schemes of socialists, religious sectari-
ans, and free-love advocates competed for adherents; naturalists like
Henry David Thoreau told their neighbors to live simply; philoso-
phers like Ralph Waldo Emerson told them to dream great dreams;
and radical abolitionists and women's rights leaders plotted to change
the world.

But Boorstin's Americans were made of different stuff: they were
men who schemed to get rich, joiners and boosters, the "new *Homo
Americanus . . .* who began to dominate the scene," assaying all manner of devices to promote all manner of new enterprises. The new
men crowded into the cities, the railroad cars, and onto the roads, all
of which helped "ease the genteel distinctions of social class. . . . In
their present anxiety to arrive someplace in a hurry, passengers forgot, ignored, or abandoned the distinctions of other places and other
times." As a result, "new formed loyalties and enthusiasms, shallow-
rooted, easily transplanted" took the place of older, less voluntary alle-
giances to ethnic group or place of origin. Again, Boorstin's depiction
better fits the 1950s than the antebellum years.[24]

In the meantime, Boorstin's Southerners still obstinately failed to
fit into the overall story. He could not leave them out, nor could he
ignore that they refused "to think of the Negro as fellow-seekers after
the opportunities of the New World, who had an equal claim on its
benefits." Slavery (not slaves) played a crucial part in the coming of

the Civil War, but slaves still did not speak for themselves in his pages. Instead, they were the source of constant terrors and nightmares for Southerners, who here as elsewhere were assumed to be white only, and occasional participants in "bloody slave insurrections," like the 1831 Nat Turner uprising in Virginia.

The events surrounding the Turner rebellion are the subject of the first of two brief discussions of slavery in the volume. The second and more important section focuses on slaves' beliefs and customs. Boorstin saw slaves as helpless victims. They had no agency, hence no real humanity (another reason to ignore them). He argued that slavery "tended to destroy *his* African culture and to denude *him* of *his* traditions as he was deposited in the new world" (italics added). Not by accident or grammatical convention did Boorstin use the male singular when he could have used the plural. His discussion is confined to slave men; the separate roles, feelings, and experiences of slave women do not appear in the book except by subtraction. The "African immigrant was a *man* without a family. . . . Among the dehumanizing effects of slavery, none were deeper than the obstruction and diversion of maternal affection" (italics added). Boorstin must have known that this was just not true. Slave women nurtured their children, comforted their menfolk, engaged in affectionate marriages (with or without the consent of owners), and celebrated sentimental family ties in the face of loss of kin through sale and forced separation. Similarly, to write that "the slave was a man without a community" was to ignore facts. Anyone who reads the Works Progress Administration's interviews with elderly black people who had been slaves in their youth—materials readily available to Boorstin when he was writing—will see that slaves recreated communities to replace those lost through forced migration.[25]

Rather than belabor the repeated historical mistakes in an otherwise magisterial essay, one should keep in mind the utility of these falsities and fabrications. They served an important purpose. If the basic elements of social and emotional experience as I have described them were true of the slaves, and the slaves were such an important part of our history before the Civil War, then they would be entitled to as much attention as any other of Boorstin's subjects. Yet moving slavery and slaves to the center of the story would undermine the themes of progress and harmony essential in a consensus account, indeed replace them with prejudice and oppression. This Boorstin was no more willing to contemplate than were earlier masters of the consensus genre.

It was thus entirely appropriate (if somewhat ironic) that the first volume gained one of the Bancroft Prizes, given by Columbia University, and the second volume earned the Francis Parkman Prize, awarded by the Society of American Historians (the prize is funded by a grant made to the society by Allan Nevins). Boorstin's work more than ably carried on the consensus-building labors of Bancroft and Parkman. In fact, in *The National Experience* Boorstin discussed both Bancroft and Parkman. Boorstin found that Bancroft's history transcended the bounds of mere annals because "for many Americans he was less historian than prophet. . . . He used the national past as testimony of the nation's mission . . . the mission of mankind . . . confined not by political boundaries but only by the hopes of all mankind." Was this Boorstin's purpose too? In any case, it was a powerful message, and one entirely appropriate to the defense of American values and American foreign policy at the height of the Cold War. Parkman provided a different kind of inspiration to his time—and Boorstin's as well. No one could read Parkman's xenophobic and racialist typecasting and assert that he was a "prophet," but Boorstin believed that Parkman's works demonstrated that "the peculiarity of American history could hardly fail to give a special character to the national rites." Thus did Boorstin subtly but powerfully imply how a history like his own might bring a nation together during its most trying times.[26]

The truth was that Boorstin had been tried in those times and had been found wanting. In the 1930s he had briefly joined the Communist Party, but in the 1950s he readily recanted the beliefs of his radical youth. He even named names of other Communists when he testified before the HUAC, and agreed with its members that no Communist should be permitted to teach at the college level. In this light, one might see the first two volumes of *The Americans* as a kind of intellectual apology for a misspent youthful fling on the wrong side of the political fence. But the qualities in Boorstin's writing were much more complex than such a motive would imply. His vision was both deeper and narrower. In his third volume, *The Americans: The Democratic Experience* (1973), Boorstin called the story of America a "destiny" and a "mission." But in bringing the story to the present in the third volume of his trilogy, he left out any mention of the red scare of the 1950s, and the only McCarthy in the index is Patrick McCarthy. Thus he sidestepped any mention of the circumstances of his own shift to the right. His trilogy was sweeping in its conception but tunnel-visioned.[27]

Boorstin had given the general American reading public what it wanted, a popular history by an honored academic satisfying all its patriotic conceits and ignoring all its past sins. Long after the Red Scare of the 1950s had faded, Boorstin continued to publish with trade presses, sell books, and win popular favor and honors. *The Democratic Experience* won the Pulitzer Prize, and his later works on *The Discoverers* (1983), *The Creators* (1992), and *The Seekers* (1998) were best-sellers. In 1975 he left his teaching post at the University of Chicago to become Librarian of Congress, arguably the highest public honor an American historian can hold. As his successor, James H. Billington, said of him and millions of readers would confirm, "Dan's writings lift the reader up to a higher standard and direct us outward to look at aspects of life that we may have overlooked before."[28]

Boorstin had come to regard himself as an amateur historian—at least, he claimed this status. "One of the advantages of being an amateur," he said, somewhat tongue in cheek (as was his habit), "is that you don't get trained in the ruts." Eric Foner had already seen through Boorstin's pose, and in 1998 explained, "[Boorstin] prides himself on not paying a lot of attention to the trends of historiography." Consensus history, popular history, meant never having to apologize for not keeping up with the newest literature in the field.[29]

Neo-Consensus

In the McCarthy Era, consensus history reassured a people frightened by foreign demons and their supposed domestic sympathizers. It homogenized American experience, drawing a clear boundary line between what was, again supposedly, truly American in our history and what was not. The times seemed so fraught with peril and consensus history had proved itself so secure a haven that few could escape its magnetic field—not even so supple a thinker and fluid a writer as Daniel Boorstin.[30]

Boorstin's work was the high-water mark of the old consensus history, capturing its confident vision and authoritative narrative flow. But Boorstin's work did not have much of an impact on professional historians; indeed, as Foner implied and others said outright, it seemed old-fashioned in its style and its indifference to shifting trends in scholarship. It was not held up as a model for graduate students to follow. (Surely Boorstin was aware of all this when he called himself "an amateur historian." It was less modesty than sarcasm, a shot across the bow of the academics.) Instead, a variant of consensus history dominated the readings in seminars in the early 1960s. One could best describe it as "neo-consensus," for in the hands of four of the most brilliant of historians of the era, Richard Hofstadter, Perry Miller, Oscar Handlin, and one of their students, Bernard Bailyn, consensus got a new twist—irony.

Hofstadter, a radical in his youth and a New York City intellectual never friendly to the anti-intellectualism of the Red Scare mongers, explored the uniformities in American history with a jaundiced eye. In 1948, in *The American Political Tradition, and the Men Who Made It*, his study of American political ideologies, he insisted, "However much at odds on specific issues, the major political traditions have shared a belief in the rights of property, the philosophy of economic individualism, the value of competition; they have accepted the economic virtues of capitalist culture as necessary qualities of man." All of these, he continued, "have been the staple tenets of the central faith in American political ideologies," though it was plain that he did not subscribe to these values himself.[31]

Sometimes cynical, and always aware of the oppressive capacity of consensus, he became its disaffected chronicler. In *The Age of Reform* (1955), a Pulitzer Prize–winning study of reform movements from 1880 to 1940, he punctured the "disjunctions—between perception and actuality, words and behavior, actions and consequences" in a way that made history both a more problematic and a more vital guide to present politics "from the perspective of our own time." In *Anti-Intellectualism in America* (1963) he revealed the unpleasant face of consensus. It gained him his second Pulitzer Prize.[32]

Perry Miller, an intellectual historian teaching at Harvard, was Hofstadter's contemporary, though the two could hardly have been more different. Miller was a demanding and sometimes difficult mentor, rarely loved though always respected, a man of letters first and foremost, as far from a radical in his politics as one could get. His two-volume intellectual history of puritanism, *The New England Mind* (volume 1: *The Seventeenth Century;* volume 2: *From Colony to Province*), remains a classic of consensus history. For him there was a single "puritan mind" in early America, and its "declension," like the decline of piety itself, lay in the "apostasy, ingratitude, and corruption" of generations who did not know the founders of New England or share their fixation that God had remade Israel's covenant with them. Instead, by the 1730s, their grandchildren had to concede that "reality—all the complex, jostling reality of this anxious society—demanded new descriptions" of the world. It was still one people and one history, but a tortured people and a terrifying history.[33]

Early in the 1960s, Miller had completed the first part of his *Life of the Mind in America* (published posthumously, in 1965, a year before it won the Pulitzer Prize). As he had in his earlier studies of puritan thought in America, Miller concluded that there was in America one mind—an "American Protestantism"; "the evangelical heritage"; the "American mentality"; a "legal mentality"; and a "search for an identity"—but again that mind was tormented by self-doubt and multiple personalities. (Indians, women, immigrants, Catholics, Jews, and African Americans did not take part in these mental exercises—at least not in his pages.) "Almost universal" among the lawyers was a "deepening spiritual unrest" as law confronted religion; an "apprehension" as law came face to face with political parties; a "background of anxiety" as law dealt with labor; and a "mood of hopeless sounding pessimism" as law contemplated the violence of democracy and anti-slavery that legalizing slavery had "precipitated." This was consensus history, but seen from its underside—the world falling apart.[34]

Oscar Handlin was Miller's colleague at Harvard, where he was as
dedicated a teacher as Miller; unlike Miller, however, Handlin was the
son of immigrant parents. When I audited his course in American
social history, I was awed by his grasp of the subject and the lyrical,
almost rhapsodic manner in which he portrayed ordinary life. All
American historians of my generation read his study of immigration,
The Uprooted (1951). Plainly, he had not swallowed the one people–
one nation story line—he was a student of Irish and Eastern European migrants and their experience in the metropolis—but his deeply
moving story of the poor white immigrants, a group often omitted or
shoved to one side in the mainstream accounts, nevertheless adopted
a holistic approach and accepted the homogenization of experience
that characterized consensus history. To it he added a profound and
moving sense of the ultimate irony of the immigrant experience.

From whatever village in the Old World the immigrants came,
"The family [was] never . . . isolated. Its concerns were those of the
entire village. . . . The community stood ready with sanctions of its
own to make sure that children were obedient, that parents were
good, and that relatives were helpful to each other." En route to
America, "the mere going was disruptive. . . . When so many new deci-
sions were to be made, they had to be made alone. . . . In America also
the economic unity of the common household enterprise disap-
peared. . . . In the characteristic immigrant employment, the individual was hired as an integer. He was one line in the ledger, one pair of
hands on the floor, one pay envelope at the window, with no reference to who was there at home."

For Handlin's immigrants, the disappearance of the old ways came
in a single generation: "Steadily the relatives dropped away; the husband, wife, and children were left alone. . . . The bonds to those left at
home also disintegrated." The children of the immigrants departed
from the Old Country's mores, language, and habits of thought, and
away, therefore, from their parents. "In the face of this whole development the immigrants were helpless. . . . Often it was necessary for the
fathers to turn for enlightenment to their sons." At the end of the
tale, sadly but inevitably for all concerned, "the old couple were left
alone. Looking back over across the years, they realized they had

been incapable of controlling the course of events." They had achieved a near-impossible feat—transporting themselves to a new world and enabling their children to enjoy its fruits—only to find that they were left behind.[35]

The last of the pantheon of neo-consensus historians is Bernard Bailyn, a student of both Miller's and Handlin's. He has, I think rightly, been described as the greatest living American historian. In his work one can find Boorstin's sense of the wholeness of American experience tempered by Hofstadter's critical detachment, Miller's brooding irony, and Handlin's gift for poignant empathy. There can be no doubt that he is a consensus historian (though he denies it), nor that he sees its ambiguities and ironies.[36]

In his Pulitzer Prize–winning *Ideological Origins of the American Revolution* (1967), one reads,

> It is the meaning imparted to the events after 1763 by this integrated group of attitudes and ideas that lies behind the colonists' rebellion. . . . The colonists believed they saw emerging from the welter of events during the decade after the Stamp Act [of 1765] a pattern whose meaning was unmistakable. They saw in the measures taken by the British government and in the actions of officials in the colonies something for which their peculiar inheritance of thought had prepared them only too well.

Such shared presumptions transformed the meaning of the colonists' struggle, and it added an inner accelerator to the movement of opposition.

In his *Voyagers to the West* (1987), an examination of migration patterns from Britain to the American colonies on the eve of the Revolution, Bailyn states:

> The provincial emigration [from the British Isles to the North American mainland] was predominantly the transfer of farming families, whose heads were men of some small substance, or at least to some extent economically autonomous. These were families, therefore, likely to contribute quickly to the growth of the American popula-

tion. And they would contribute quickly too to the growth of the American economy, not only by their constructive enterprise but by the demand they created, the markets they enlarged, as consumers. Above all, they were eager from the start to take advantage of opportunities created by the opening up of new land in America.[37]

If Bailyn's revolutionaries and voyagers seem the stuff of consensus history, he believed that they set in motion forces they did not anticipate and perhaps never did fully understand. For the revolutionaries it was the irony of what he called their "contagion of liberty." They wanted a return to older liberties and ended up freeing the slaves, replacing state religions with liberty of conscience, writing constitutions that had no precedent in history, and fashioning a great republic whose boundaries and aspirations exceeded all their expectations. For the voyagers it was a profound and unanticipated transformation in people who began their lives in Britain as subordinates in a system of indentured servitude and ended with them in America as free men and women.

As Bailyn judged in a 2003 essay, the "logical, ideological, and conceptual problems" the revolutionary generation faced in founding a new nation were daunting. "There was no end to the problems, and there was never any certainty in the outcome. Some of the problems in the course of time would be solved, some persist to this day and will never be fully resolved. But what strikes one most forcefully in surveying the struggles and achievements of that distant generation is less what they failed to do than what they did do, and the problems that they did in fact solve." For Bailyn, unity and achievement as themes in our history could not be understood without also understanding the tensions and ambiguities of history. This is the essence of the neoconsensus persuasion.[38]

The End of Consensus

If such complex thinkers as Hofstadter, Handlin, Miller, and Bailyn could be placed in the consensus camp, surely consensus history had come a long way from the patriotic fables of Bancroft and the poetic falsehoods of Parkman—even from the self-satisfied cant of Boorstin. But the Hofstadters, Handlins, Boorstins, and Bailyns differed from Bancroft and Parkman, and even the first professionals like Wilson, Hart, Turner, and Beard, in another way: they did not come from the social or ethnic elite that had been the cradle of earlier consensus historians. By the end of the 1950s, history writing was no longer the exclusive preserve of a handful of white Protestant men from middle- and upper-class backgrounds. Consensus historical writing did not end with the 1950s, but the consensus within the historical profession was rupturing because the profession itself was changing.

Consensus history's underlying strength derived from the ethnic and religious homogeneity of its craftsmen. By the end of the 1950s, the uniformity within the historical profession that was reflected in consensus history was disappearing. Historians of America were no longer, as Turner wrote in 1910 of his first class of history students at Harvard, just "New England boys, with names that spell eastern conservatism." Nor were they, like Turner himself, sons of the pioneers of the western movement, men "of the 'Western Waters'," where "freedom . . . developed inventiveness and resourcefulness . . . [and] the American spirit—the traits that have come to be recognized as the most characteristic—was developed."[30]

Hofstadter, Handlin, Bailyn (and Boorstin, too) were all Jews. To be sure, there is no such thing as a Jewish view of American history, any more than there is a racial determinant of any scholarly enterprise. If that particular form of insult to human intellect unfortunately still thrives in some quarters, it has no merit. Nevertheless, the newcomers had a different take on American history, and some members of the historical professional fraternity with ethnic backgrounds of the more traditional sort watched the arrival of the newcomers with unwelcoming eyes. As the Brown University history professor Carl Bridenbaugh put it, ungenerously, in his 1963 AHA presidential address, American history had been swarmed over by "younger practitioners . . . and apprentices . . . who are . . . product[s] of lower middle-class or foreign origins, and their emotions not infrequently get in the way of historical reconstructions. They find themselves in a very real sense an outsider in our past and feel themselves shut out. This is certainly not their fault, but it is true. They have no experience to assist them, and the chasm between them and the Remote Past widens every hour."[40]

Contemporaries recognized that Bridenbaugh's not-so-veiled reference was to the Jewish historians in the profession, though he by no means limited his vitriol to any one ethnic group. Anti-Semitism was nothing new, of course. Oscar Handlin may not have known that his mentor, Arthur M. Schlesinger, had written to potential employers that his student had "none of the offensive traits which some people associate with his race," nor did Boorstin know that in his quest for the Rhodes scholarship, Schlesinger had to inform the master of Balliol College that the applicant, "is a Jew, though not the kind to which one takes exception." (Ironically Schlesinger was also Bridenbaugh's Ph.D. director at Harvard.) In 1953, Howard Beale publicly chastised the profession for its anti-Semitism—but such general bias should not have been a surprise when elite schools like Yale and Harvard still had either formal or informal quotas on the number of Jews who might be admitted.[41]

In the 1960s, the next wave of newcomers—the students of Bailyn, Hofstadter, and Handlin—did for American history what the progressives could not and the neo-consensus historians would not: they paved the way for an entirely new paradigm for American history, called the new history. They called for and themselves created new histories—inclusive, diverse, self-critical—and this new history did battle with consensus orthodoxies. As Warren Susman, one of the younger Jewish historians that Bridenbaugh so feared, wrote in 1964: "History is often used as the basis for a political philosophy that while explaining the past offers also a way to change the future. History thus operates ideologically. But by the very nature of its enterprise and the kind of society that calls it into existence, historical interpretation cannot be effectively monopolized for long by any special class or group." The America of the 1960s would be profoundly different from the America of all previous eras, and its history writing would reflect the new openness and cultural diversity of the society and culture. The new history would also feature a quarrelsomeness, suspicion of pandering to the public, and demand for methodological sophistication that profoundly widened the divide between academic and popular history.[42]

CHAPTER 3

The New History
and Its Promoters

T HE 1960S WERE AN ERA IN WHICH SCHOLARS DIS-
cerned an essential relationship between the writing of history and current events, an era when Americans found lessons in
their history to respond to crisis. Younger scholars and teachers in
these years began a profound redirection of the profession, and
within it, the crafting of American history. I and others have called
this view new history, combining under that term many different
strands of writing and thinking. All of them diverged from the way
that consensus history was conceived. Sometimes practitioners of new
history were driven by a relentless intellectual curiosity, but often the
motive behind new history was reformist. As three of these new historians, Elizabeth Fee, Linda Shopes, and Linda Zeidman, wrote in
their history of Baltimore, Maryland: "This book is admittedly partisan. The authors were nurtured in the dissident politics of the 1960s
and bring to their work both an appreciation for the dignity of working lives and a vision of social justice and equality."[1]

Outraged by the Viet Nam War and inspired by the civil rights movement, this new generation of professional historians set themselves the task of dismantling consensus history. Some of them were political radicals, and they gave renewed life to the progressive critique of consensus. Others were more concerned with black history and women's history and were determined to move the story of these groups to center stage. Liberal textbook writers carried these programs forward in new kinds of surveys, adding social and cultural highlights to political narrative. In the process, the new history and its promoters in colleges and universities attracted recruits, and young people flooded into graduate programs seeking entry to the profession.

But the new history was not just a leftist version of relativism, in which praise for the working poor replaced praise for the moguls of industry. Its acolytes aspired to a history that did not glorify their own kind or their own time so much as force readers to read less passively. "Our purpose is to look at [history] in a new way . . . [to] develop a deeper appreciation of . . . crisis, conflict, and change, and failure to change." Above all, the new history was critical—critical of older interpretations, easy generalizations, and even of its own conclusions. It made all historians more aware of the dangers of resting on the convenient and self-serving platitude. The remodeled profession was consequently highly sensitive to criticism from without, though equally quick to find fault within its ranks. Though it proclaimed its intention not to tolerate unethical conduct on the part of historians, it had yet to define what such conduct might be.[2]

The New Left

The rise of historical radicalism in the 1960s had been anticipated by the progressive historians. They argued that historians should recognize conflict as well as consensus and tell the many stories of people ignored in the older histories. As Richard Hofstadter told an assemblage at Harvard's Charles Warren Center, and later wrote in his *Progressive Historians* (1968), the progressives had understood that there were times when the dominant party or faction or interest in America refused to recognize the right of its opponent to exist.

The so-called New Left, a cadre of radical historians that emerged in the 1960s, not only made groups that had been marginalized or omitted from consensus history the centerpiece of their historical writing; they also made it impossible for anyone in the profession to ignore them. In the jargon of the time, they "walked their talk," making the "personal into the political" as they carried the message of the new history into classrooms, street demonstrations, and professional meetings.[3]

By the middle of the 1960s the United States had backed into a land war in Asia. President Lyndon Johnson feared that a Communist takeover of all of Viet Nam would lead to Communist expansion throughout the region. When President Johnson upped the ante in Southeast Asia by sending more and more troops to Viet Nam, younger academics not only questioned our participation in what they regarded as a Vietnamese civil war, they objected to the jingoistic rhetoric by which the U.S. government justified its war effort. The antiwar movement and the civil rights movement became rallying points for young teachers and students. Teach-ins and protest marches took place on campuses across the country, turning colleges and universities into the locus, at first unwillingly to be sure, of student radicalism, a phenomenon that the New Left encouraged.[4]

Borne on waves of student unrest, the New Left coalition in the colleges and universities grew in numbers throughout the decade and stretched across the country from the University of California at Berkeley to the University of Wisconsin at Madison, Ohio's Kent State University, stolid Yale, red-brick Rutgers, and the City University of New York. The New Left's leaders founded journals, sponsored conferences, published critiques of existing scholarship, and generally raised hell. Sometimes the hell-raising went on within the radical ranks. In one such imbroglio, in many ways typical of them all, Jesse Lemisch, an assistant professor at Roosevelt University in Chicago, and Eugene Genovese, of Rutgers, clashed over what Genovese regarded as "an unprincipled and scurrilous attack" on him immediately before the 1969 annual convention of the American Historical Association, and what Lemisch saw as a threat in Genovese's reply. Lemisch had written of his intention to protest at the convention against the Viet Nam War. Genovese had responded, "There are an enormous number of people who have taken full measure of the situation, your intention and the spirit of your enterprise"; their combat, added Genovese, would be "to the knife." Genovese's somewhat overblown statement was chilling nonetheless. In another war of words, Genovese and Yale's Staughton Lynd bashed one another over whether to take radicalism to the streets (Lynd) or to write more radical histories (Genovese).[5]

New Left folk memory has the mainline organizations of the profession and the elite publishers looking askance at these boisterous and often quarrelsome newcomers, and there is some evidence to support this view. On the other hand, radical leaders like Warren Susman, Genovese, and Christopher Lasch were publishing important work in prestigious venues during the 1960s. At a 1967 session of the Organization of American Historians devoted to assessing the first fruits of New Left scholarship, Irwin Unger had decried the New Left's use of history as a political weapon and called the movement "bad tempered," yet even he admitted that the New Left historians had to be taken seriously, for what they said and the intensity with which they said it[6]

In 1968, the New Left historians, led by Barton Bernstein, a historian of American diplomacy, published a collection of essays entitled *Towards a New Past.* The idea was to showcase the variety of New Left thought. The essays ranged from the Revolutionary era to the 1960s, and from the inflammatory to the conventional. More important still, the collection was widely reviewed.[7]

The *American Historical Review* devoted a "Review Note" to the collection in which two reviewers were assigned the task of assessing the contributions of the movement. One of the reviewers was Aileen Kraditor, a radical historian working on abolitionism and women's rights. Despite finding that the essays had "no common thread" and "vary greatly in their scholarly and literary merit," she was delighted with the collection as a project, for, "To a radical the very diversity is welcome, for it is a refreshing contrast to the simplistic, unimaginative,

and dogmatic uniformity with which most earlier—and a few modern—anti-establishment historians read the historical record and
guaranteed its opacity."[8]

The other reviewer, Johns Hopkins University's David Donald, had
harsher words for the book. He judged that radical history was "not of
sufficient consequence to merit extended consideration in the pages
of our major professional journal." But he inadvertently conceded
that the New Left point of view could not be ignored: "Here, then, are
the voices of the New Left—mostly neither new nor left. On the basis
of this collection of essays it would be easy to conclude that the historical profession has already paid these writers more attention than they
deserve." He concluded, "Let them . . . end their plaintive laments that
the 'power structure' of the historical profession ignores them."[9]

The profession as a whole could not dismiss the New Left. Its devo-
tees saw to that. In December 1969, for the first time, the AHA presidency was contested, the radical historian Staughton Lynd getting
nearly 30 percent of the vote. At the convention, Lemisch read a
paper to a session summarizing the New Left's professional concerns:
The "radical voice on campus . . . is suppressed. . . . Radicalism will
always be defined by those in positions of power within established
institutions as passing over the line, . . . defining the point at which
permissible dissent becomes impermissible." The business meeting
was heavily attended, and the crowd of young scholars there insisted
that the AHA openly condemn the Viet Nam War. Typically, the radicals could not agree on the next step. Lemisch demanded a repudia-
tion of the Viet Nam War; Genovese, though he opposed American
participation in the war, argued against requiring the AHA to take
sides. Any position the organization took would deny to those not
present their chance to voice an opinion.[10]

The disputatiousness of the radicals, especially within their own
ranks, was a symptom of their determination to integrate personal
experience and commitment into their professional conduct and
writing. As one of the radical historians, Howard Zinn, recalled much
later:

Before I became a professional historian, I had grown up in the dirt and dankness of New York tenements, had been knocked unconscious by a policeman while holding a banner in a demonstration, had worked for three years in a shipyard, and had participated in the violence of war. Those experiences, among others, made me lose all desire for "objectivity," whether in living my life, or writing history.

Even allowing for some romantic exaggeration in Zinn's confession of "where he came from," his memoir is a perfect example of the way that radicals legitimated the incorporation of personal experience in scholarship. Genovese made the same point in somewhat less personal fashion in his 1971 essay, "On Being a Socialist and a Historian." He explained, "No one on the left would deny that every man and woman ought to be politically active. . . . In fact what we stand for is the realization that all historical writing is unavoidably political intervention."[11]

Such activity did not mean departing from the professional responsibility of writing good history—in Zinn's words, "a responsibility to struggle for maximum objectivity." He continued: "Ideologically motivated history is bad history and ultimately reactionary politics. . . . Scrupulous honesty in reporting on the past would be needed. . . . There would be no incentive to distort the past." Zinn was confident that he would find the same basic "values, ends, and ideals" in history as in his own experience. Those values not only dictated that he ask the right kind of questions about the past, about "social change . . . equality, liberty, peace, and justice," but about how to get the message across to the reading public. He decided that his textbooks, "people's histories" of the United States, could revise the consensus account by simple addition: "The chief problem in historical honesty is not outright lying. It is omission or deemphasis of important data." So Zinn added to the conventional story what he judged had been left out of it: episodes like the massacres of striking miners by hired gunmen, the decimation of the native populations by the colonizers, and the cost in noncombatant life in the dropping of two atomic bombs on Japan.[12]

Radicals "walking their talk" could have serious professional consequences. In 1968, David Green was a first-year history professor at the sprawling and densely populated Ohio State University main campus in Columbus. During the sad and angry days following the assassination of Martin Luther King, Green burned his draft card in front of one of his classes. Although he had terminated the regular session and announced that he was acting as an individual rather than as an instructor, his act nevertheless led to his dismissal. The Ohio State University faculty committee that reviewed the case had recommended that he merely be castigated for poor judgment, but the president and the board of trustees imposed the harsher penalty. Perhaps they feared the escalating violence would spill onto High Street and then down the hill to the state capitol; or that it tarnished the image of the university in a conservative city (the mayor of Columbus at the time had little use for student radicalism and said so); or that the antiwar demonstrations in which Professor Green had participated were too visible to both state legislators and important alumni.[13]

When I arrived in Columbus in the summer of 1970 to take up an assistant professorship at OSU opened by Green's dismissal, troops of the Ohio National Guard involved in the shooting of students at Kent State University not three months before occupied the campus. Student protest simmered in a broth of fear and animus. Some in the history department, hardly a bastion of radicalism—its only other left-wing historian had resigned and taken a job elsewhere in protest against Green's dismissal—felt that Green's academic freedom had been violated, but said nothing loud enough for anyone outside our offices to hear.[14]

The cost of demonstrations was not borne only by the dissidents. Descriptions of the student demonstrations at Columbia University in 1968 and the police response to student demonstrations I witnessed in Harvard Yard on April 9 and 10 the next year—both of which involved history professors and graduate students—convince me that the radical historians were no more astute in their political choices and tactics than other activist groups. When they laid down the shield of academic freedom and picked up the spear of violent confrontation everyone paid a price. Radicals who trashed their professors' offices and went to jail; liberal administrators who called in city police forces to arrest students who were occupying buildings on campus; conservative scholars who misread the purposes of the demonstrations and became targets of abuse—all shared this tunnel vision. One elderly and out-of-touch Harvard historian was so incensed and baffled by student protest in the tumultuous days of 1969 that he stood guard at night inside Widener Library, lest radical graduate students whom he saw as berserk destroy the books. Little did he realize that the radicals saw themselves as the historical descendants of Wendell Phillips and William Lloyd Garrison, uncompromising abolitionists whom he had discussed in his own lectures.[15]

By the end of the decade, the New Left, sure that its time had come, was poised to rewrite American history. But in hindsight even the most sympathetic observer will conclude that their effort has failed to achieve its objective. Radical historians are still around, to be sure. At the 2004 AHA meeting one could stop in the lobby at the makeshift MARHO (Marxist Historical Organization) kiosk to pick up a copy of the *Radical History Review* and join the group. The *Review*'s "teaching radical history" section, celebrating its tenth anniversary, lauded the "remarkable range and richness of radical history not only in the classrooms but also in community museums, union halls, and elsewhere." But the original project of rewriting all American history, a truly revolutionary goal, was never reached.[16]

In part the reason for the marginalization of radical history may be that the movement ran out of ideas and started to repeat itself. If there is anything that sells in American culture, it is novelty. By contrast, the stale, no matter how nutritious, is left on the shelf. In 2003, *Radical History Review* published a talk that Lemisch gave in April 2002 in which he said more or less what had said in 1968. To three hundred conference attendees at Columbia University he insisted that academics must support the unions at the university, in particular the Graduate Student Employees United. Graduate student unions were not new (the formation of one at Harvard was discussed in 1969), and their demands—better pay for long service, medical benefits, and other practical matters—were as old as unions themselves. They did not seek to remake the world in a more equitable way, only to aid themselves and their families.

Lemisch did not see that. Instead, he offered the gathering a sermon right out of the 1960s.

We're all here *because* [emphasis in original] we're in favor of bridging the gap between activism and the academy. . . . Being an activist is a necessary prerequisite for historians who want to see through the reigning lies. . . . Activist experience gives the historian experiential understanding of the power of the state, repression, social change, agency, surprise in history, the distortions peddled by authority, and the depth of commitment of those with power to maintaining the standing order.

In a peroration presumably directed to the graduate students in history he concluded, "You can't *begin* [emphasis in original] to understand how history happens unless you have this basic training as a historian/activist. A good dose of tear gas makes us think more clearly as historians." That is nonsense.[17]

The worn edges of New Left activism were only one reason that the promise of radical history remained unfulfilled. Maurice Isserman and Michael Kazin, writing in *America Divided: The Civil War of the 1960s,* offer another:

As the New Left grew larger, it also grew more internally divided. . . . Whites were no longer welcome in the black movement, save as outside supporters. . . . The early 1960s vision of the movement as a "beloved community" in which all those committed to social change could join together in common effort and fellowship had come apart at the seams by mid-decade.

The battle of words between activists like Lynd and ideologues like Genovese was tepid compared to the division between the academic radicals and terrorist groups like the Weathermen. Todd Gitlin, one of the founders of the Students for a Democratic Society, recalled his own realization that other, more radical, young people were taking the movement beyond persuasion and demonstrations into the void of mindless violence. If that was where the New Left led, he, and many other young scholars, did not want to follow.[18]

A third reason was the co-optation of some of the most productive radical historians and the incorporation of their insights into the mainstream of historical scholarship. As one reliable commentator,

John Higham, recalled, by the end of the 1960s, "In professional journals and meetings the current intensification of moral commitment among historians has been received with remarkable indulgence." Lemisch might still be out in the cold, but other radical historians long before 2003 had taken seats at the head table of the profession. Their table manners became more conventional, too. Christopher Lasch, once one of the young radicals, lamented in 1989 that "radical historians came to be admitted as partners in the scholarly enterprise only when they signified their willingness to observe the prevailing conventions and to write books that were just as narrow, tedious, and predictable as the books written by their ideological opponents." Most of the New Left had, gradually and perhaps inevitably, slid toward the liberal center. By accepting membership in the professional community—indeed, by becoming officers and board members of the very mainstream organizations they had once attacked—the radicals had won a prize they had not sought.[19]

Or perhaps some radical historians simply became conservative as they got older? Higham had considered Genovese one of the foremost of the radicals. Reviewers of *Towards a New Past* agreed. Historians of all stripes concede that his work on slavery will always be a standard in the field, whether they buy his arguments or not. But by the 1990s, Genovese's intellectual journey had taken him far from his leftist origins. In 1994, again mixing the scholarly and the political as he had in "On Being a Historian and a Socialist"—though in quite different proportions and with new ingredients—he wrote:

Only a strong dose of institutional authority and hierarchy [today] could preserve the distinctiveness essential to the preservation of freedom—and even democracy, sensibly construed—in the larger society. . . . The perspectives offered by southern conservatives [in the defense of slavery among other southern peculiar institutions], which I have hastily sketched, remain alive, if at bay: opposition to finance capitalism and, more broadly, to the attempt to substitute the market for society itself; opposition to the radical individualism that is today sweeping America; support for broad property ownership and market economy subject to socially determined moral restraints; adherence to a Christian individualism that condemns personal license and demands submission to a moral consensus rooted in elementary piety.

Shorn of the modern tone of some of the language, it was a reading of the antebellum South's elite philosophy that sailed awfully close to Paul Buck's and Woodrow Wilson's views. Certainly it evoked the old aphorism that the far right touches the far left in its ideology.[20]

Did the rise of the New Left then prove what Beard and Becker had proposed—that all historical scholarship is relative to the experiences of the historian, and the time and place in which the historian writes? Did the conformity of the 1950s give comfort and credibility to the consensus view, and did the tumultuous conflicts of the 1960s then breed the new history of the radicals? Was the demise of radicalism itself the inevitable product of the politics of the me-first generations of the 1980s and 1990s?

Not really. First of all, the New Left was hardly the first cadre of radical historians to confront consensus history—their progressive predecessors had made a similar case for refocusing our story on conflict and oppression. Second, although the New Left was surely a product of its times, its message transcended those times. Indeed, it had a kind of otherworldly timelessness—seeing all things fresh, out of their time and place. Only Genovese among the New Left lights insisted that history must remain totally historically minded, however much the radicals might want to bash the bosses and the slave owners. Third, the radical historians as a group might have lost their light, but the radical message echoed in the rise to prominence of certain formerly neglected areas of historical inquiry and the introduction of these, along with their chroniclers, to the profession. Finally, the brutally sharp-edged critical skills that radicalism honed became a hallmark of the entire profession. No more powder-puff reviews; no more (well almost no more) good-old-boy networks protecting substandard work and promoting weak candidates to high offices; no more get along, go along career paths—not as long as the radicals were watching.

(Relative) Newcomers to the Canon—Black History and Women's History

R adical historians and the radical historical vision opened a door wider to nontraditional historians and history that, before the 1960s, had barely let in a sliver of light. A relative handful of African American and women historians had written about America before the 1960s, but their contributions had little influence on the public or inside the profession. By the beginning of the 1980s, however, no one trained in the 1960s or 1970s could ignore black history or women's history. The shift in the scope of our historical writing and the demography of our profession was profound.

Although a handful of historians—even those who grew up in the midst of the segregated South and went to school or taught at bastions of racism like the University of Mississippi and the University of Georgia—did not see the impact of racism all around them, other historians had seen the need for inclusiveness long before the 1960s. As Oscar Handlin wrote in *Race and Nationality in American Life* (1957), racial segregation sapped American strength in the struggle against the Communist foe, which made "millennial promises" which we could not match, not so long as we were divided into two nations, one abusing the other while "hoping for the purity of their own race." His plaintive question was simultaneously a rebuke: "Is our belief in democracy coupled with the reservation that it is workable only in favored climes and in the hands of favored men, or is this a way of life open to all?" Segregation had to end, and historians of all colors— over 40, in fact—marched with Martin Luther King Jr. from Selma in March 1965. They included John Hope Franklin, who is black, and William Leuchtenburg, who is white. They linked arms and looked ahead, following John Higham, whose furled umbrella, held aloft, bore a placard with the hastily lettered words "U.S. Historians."[21]

Many of the young black scholars of the 1960s had become interested in history because their exposure to the civil rights movement had raised their consciousness. The same events that motivated younger white scholars to concern themselves with the injustices done blacks in history (and in the historical profession) motivated black scholars to claim pride of place in writing the stories of their own people. If one of the more progressive aspects of the New Left emphasis on minorities was the increasing attention that young white scholars gave to subjects in black history, some black historians found it galling that whites would attempt to hijack black history just as numbers of black scholars were moving into the profession. A turf war erupted. A number of the younger black scholars, led by Sterling Stuckey, Vincent Harding, and Julius Lester, insisted that only blacks could teach black history. Black students jeered, picketed, or absented themselves from classrooms when whites lectured on the black experience. Even noteworthy white historians who had been pioneers in revising our understanding of the oppression of blacks, such as Kenneth Stampp, C. Vann Woodward, and August Meier, came under attack. In 1969, Eric Foner, a newly minted Ph.D., was hired to teach African American history at Columbia, his own school in his hometown. He recalled, "Inevitably and understandably, many of Columbia's black students felt that the first such course in the College's two-hundred-year history ought to be offered by a black scholar." With some difficulty—black students picketed his course and denounced him—he managed to convince his class otherwise. "Teaching and writing in black history should be held to the same standard as in any academic discipline. The race of the instructor" should not matter, he asserted. But it did.[22]

The most tragic event in this controversy concerned Robert Starobin. Like Foner and many of the other younger white historians who wrote on black history, Starobin was Jewish. He saw social injustices keenly, and wrote with sympathy of those that blacks faced. His "The Negro: A Central Theme in American History" was intended to refute the "traditional" view that blacks were passive (and unimportant) victims of history—happy "Sambos"—and go beyond the "elitism" and "conservatism" of "revisionist" views from the 1930s through the 1950s. He championed the radical view that put racism in the center of our history, and lauded the work of Lynd and Genovese as well as less radical historians like William Freehling, Leon Litwak, and

Joel Williamson for making that point. But all of the latter happened to be white. When Starobin read a paper on black history at a 1969 Wayne State University conference on the subject, Vincent Harding walked out of the lecture hall while Starobin was speaking; Stuckey and Lester gave blistering criticisms from the rostrum, after which they followed Harding to the exit. Starobin, shattered, committed suicide the next year.[23]

Lester later wrote a kind of confession that demonstrated the underside of the connection between politics and scholarship.

> It was one of those situations that are unavoidable when blacks and whites come together in post-Black-Power America, a situation in which people are not individuals, but historical entities, playing out a drama whose beginnings are now so submerged that we will never find them. . . . any white man who devotes himself to teaching and writing about black history must have the fortitude and strength of a bull elephant, because blacks will let him know that his presence is unwanted and undesirable . . . That day at Wayne State University my heart ached for Bob, though I didn't know him, but I knew what I had to do to him. He had to be attacked and I did so. . . . I bowed to the demands of history.

In other words, history made Lester do what he did. He played to the black audience, and regretted it later, writing in 1971, "History makes its demands, but one does not have to accede to them." Harding put it differently, in 1986: "Black scholars! Black, green, white, yellow human beings! Come then comrades! It would be well to decide at once to change our ways. We must shake off the heavy darkness in which we were plunged and leave it behind." He did not mention Starobin.[24]

For a time the black power movement within the profession also put older black historians, including those who had led the way for the incorporation of black history into American history and the integration of the main-line historical associations, in a bind. Historians such as John Hope Franklin had gained much for their brothers and sisters by a policy of partial accommodation combined with their continuing insistence on equal treatment of black historians. They had convinced the ruling bodies of the Mississippi Valley Historical Association (the precursor to the Organization of American Historians) and the Southern Historical Association not to hold their conventions in any hotel that discriminated against blacks. Still, for any signs of accommodation or compromise in their professional posture or their work, they faced the obloquy of the young Turks.[25]

A more enlightened stance to their colleagues was adopted by the younger generation of black women historians such as Nell Irvin Painter and Darline Clark Hine. Painter has long argued that historians must cross "the color line. . . . How much richer history would be," she recently mused, "if historians of all races followed [John Hope Franklin's] lead and peered beyond their own allotments!" In an essay reviewing the accomplishments of historians of black women, Hine asked for historians to step beyond their race and class, insisting that "Black women historians must begin to research and write histories of white women." It was Foner's argument in reverse. "Why?" asked Hine. "Because we need to know more about them. We need to break down these intellectual and professional boundaries in order to develop and refine our methodologies for comparative and intersectional analysis." The implications of her proposal profoundly transformed the relationship between new history and consensus history. Once again there would be one history of one people in one nation, but that people would have many faces and the chroniclers of their experiences would reflect that diversity themselves. "I suspect that many already over-burdened and over-extended black women historians will chaff at this exhortation to cross the racial lines in their scholarship. . . . I hear their questions. Won't writing about white women undermine and/or impede progress on the black women's history project?" The answer lay in Hine's own studies of white women in the South: her account of their view of their world enabled her to better understand how they saw black women.[26]

As Painter's and Hine's thinking shows, women historians found ways to express a sense of their own mission within traditional frameworks of professional cooperation. The rise of women's history in the 1960s and 1970s was striking but not divisive and it has changed the working patterns of our craft. As one of its leading practitioners, Joan Wallach Scott, wrote in 1983, questions over feminism and the relation between women's history and gender studies "have established the framework for debate and discussion among historians of women during the past fifteen years. Although there are clear lines of difference discernible, they are better understood as matters of strategy than as fundamental divides."[27]

The first graduate program in women's history was introduced at Sarah Lawrence College, in 1972, by Gerda Lerner. There are now over 700 women's studies programs worldwide. Lerner herself was a spark plug in the organization of women in the profession, chartering the Coordinating Committee of Women in the Historical Profession (CCWHP) organized at the AHA in 1969. She was a true radical, having walked her talk long before she became an academic. As a Communist, a union organizer, a refugee from Nazi Germany, and a victim of the Red Scare of the 1950s, she was by 1969 a "post-Marxist" honest enough to admit that she had fallen "uncritically for lies I should have been able to penetrate and perceive as such," and then strong enough to continue to battle for social and gender justice, "even if the particular vision I had embraced has turned to ashes. . . . Like many persons of the Old Left I retained my class analysis and my deep commitment to racial equality, which I brought into my understanding of Women's History at a time when such ideas were new to most of the young women then building this new discipline."[28]

The next generation of women historians were grateful for her gift to them. As Linda Kerber, Alice Kessler-Harris, and Kathryn Kish Sklar recalled in 1995, in the years between 1969 and 1972, "trekking through unfamiliar terrain" of graduate studies,

> . . . each of us encountered Gerda Lerner: sometimes it was through something she had written; sometimes it was at a political meeting; sometimes it was on a scholarly panel. She seemed to be everywhere. Her authoritative voice . . . cajoled, persuaded, encouraged and demanded changes in the way we wrote history and in the way the profession treated women. We responded because her words resonated with what we were thinking and because she was radical and brave.[29]

And also because, I think, the women, from the old hands to the neophytes, preached and practiced sisterhood. Kerber, Kessler-Harris, and Sklar handed on to the next generation Lerner's dedication and mentoring. My wife, Natalie Hull, began her graduate education in history at Columbia University in 1974, and she was buoyed by the mutual support she found among the women in the profession. Kerber, for example, took Natalie aside after her talk at the first Berkshire Conference on Women's History and encouraged her to finish her graduate degree.

The women's coordinating committee would sponsor ad hoc and then standing committees on women's status in the profession in the AHA and the OAH. These committees, inaugurated in 1970, opened employment opportunities for female scholars, helped women to get on the boards and the programs of the major organizations, and generally created a spirit of common interest so strong that some men began to joke about an "old girls' network" to rival the "old boys' network" that had dominated training and hiring in the profession from its inception. In 1969, women received a little over 10 percent of all doctorates in history. By 2002, they were receiving about 38 percent of the Ph.D.s awarded each year in history. In 1959, women made up less than 5 percent of history faculties. By 1988, this had risen to 17 percent, and by 1998, according to AHA data, to 27.6 percent. About 25 percent of the tenured and temporary faculty are women. Women slightly outnumber men among the untenured on tenure track—suggesting that in the past five years, departments are hiring slightly more women than men.[30]

Women's history is also increasingly well represented in publishing statistics: In 1968, Aileen Kraditor lamented that women's history was still left out of "'real' history." An ABC-Clio bibliography of articles and anthology entries on women's history from 1964 to 1977 showed 3,395 entries, or about 260 a year. By contrast, the second volume of the bibliography, covering the period 1978 to 1984, listed 3,700 articles and anthologized essays on women's history, equivalent to 612 per year. After selecting a small number of these for inclusion in the second edition of their own anthology, *Women's America*, the editors, Linda Kerber and Jane DeHart, concluded that "the new research is not only quantitatively extensive but qualitatively impressive." One example: in the first edition, in order to include a contribution on household labor in early America the editors had to rely on an article written in 1938, by Julia Cherry Spruill. By 1987, they could take an excerpt from Laurel Thatcher Ulrich's recent *Good Wives* (1982), the forerunner to her magnificent, multiple-prize-winning *A Midwife's Tale* (1991). *Women's America* has gone through five editions, the last in 2000, and is still going strong—a sure sign that it is being adopted for use in classrooms.[31]

That Ulrich could win the Pulitzer, Bancroft, and Dunning prizes for a book about a Hallowell, Maine, midwife in the late eighteenth and early nineteenth centuries would have been highly unlikely in earlier years. Even more unlikely was Ulrich's subsequent hiring by Harvard University. The Harvard History Department, which had only one female member for much of the 1960s and 1970s, in the 1990s and early twenty-first century added Lizabeth Cohen, Nancy Cott, Joyce Chaplin, Jill Lepore, Drew Gilpin Faust, Ruth Feldstein, Lisa McGirr, Rebecca McLennan, and Susan O'Donovan to teach American history. The incorporation of women's history and gender studies into the larger corpus of historical writing and the inclusion of growing numbers of women in the profession have been a model of what the radicals wished without the stridency of radical rhetoric.[32]

Revising the Textbooks

With radical, black, and women's history pouring forth, the stage was set for revision of the textbooks. At first the authors of the older books and their publishers proved remarkably unwilling to incorporate the new history. They clung to the older consensus model, adding, as the 1960s progressed, token women, Indians, and blacks to their pages. Perhaps this was because teachers were content with the coverage in books they had long used and were wary of adopting books that had new and innovative content, or because publishers did not respond quickly to altered patterns of scholarly publishing.

The illustrations chosen for textbooks tell the story of this lag better than words. The 1968 edition of *The National Experience*, the work
of six of the leading historians of the day—John M. Blum, Bruce Cat-
ton, Edmund S. Morgan, Arthur M. Schlesinger, Kenneth M. Stampp,
and C. Vann Woodward—was replete with images. Volume I featured
portraits of almost all the presidents before 1876—only William
Henry Harrison, John Tyler, James Polk, Zachery Taylor, Franklin
Pierce, and James Buchanan were omitted—and depictions of every
major politician, along with battle scenes and factories, even Fulton's
steamboat. But there were only four illustrations of people of color: a
reproduction of John White's drawing of Roanoke Indians in a canoe;
"John Smith had the nerve to take command"—a highly fanciful ren-
dition of John Smith holding a gun to the head of the Pamunky chief
Opechancanough; a sketch of "indigo drying in South Carolina" that
did not mention the fact that the people shown working were slaves;
and a group picture of "Southern freedmen" (without, appropriately
given the caption, any women in the picture).

There were three depictions of women, but their presence was not
noted in the captions: a picture of French ladies surrounding Benjamin Franklin during his diplomatic stay in Paris entitled "Franklin
played his role to the hilt"; a sketch of women working in a textile factory captioned "weaving by power loom" (the power loom was more
important than its female operators); and a photograph of two
women miners in the California gold fields captioned to spotlight the
Gold Rush, not the women miners. The only women identified as
women in the first volume's illustrations appeared in a pen and ink
drawing of "The reform crusade; Women's Rights Convention, New
York." This kind of tokenism reflected a resistance to change rather
than its embrace by the publisher or the marketplace.[33]

An alternative, more progressive series of textbooks was published
by Dushkin Publishing of Guilford, Connecticut, in the 1970s. Their
relatively inexpensive readers in American history stressed the clash
of views among historians and the stories of people left out of the
major textbooks. The Dushkin readers, revised every year, were not
widely adopted, however; today the Dushkin Group is part of
McGraw-Hill and provides on-line supplements and *Annual Editions*

composed of excerpts from popular history magazines and other print media.

A better-financed and more prestigious effort to write and market an American history as seen from the bottom up was *Who Built America?*, a collaborative two-volume effort of the American Social History Project. In 1981, Herbert Gutman, a professor of American social history at the City University of New York, secured funding from the National Endowment for the Humanities, the Ford Foundation, and CUNY, "to produce a wide range of accessible educational materials" on labor history for all levels of students. Gutman died in 1985, but the project continued under the direction of his coworker Stephen Brier. The book, two volumes totaling over 1,300 pages, was truly history from the bottom up and told the stories of white- and blue-collar workers, immigrants, minorities, farm workers, and factory workers. It attempted to explain changes in politics and diplomacy as a function of the rise of industrial capitalism. The book is a wonderful resource for lectures, but its unwieldy size and topical organization made it unsuitable for classroom use.[34]

Two more mainstream works led the development of modern college textbooks in American history. The first, a book for a so-called "small market" course in early American history, was Gary Nash's *Red, White, and Black* (1974). Nash was not a New Left radical, but his sympathies were left of center. As a graduate student at Princeton in the early 1960s he got involved in efforts to improve the lot of New Jersey's many migrant-worker communities, and at the University of California at Los Angeles (UCLA), where he spent his career, he helped with job training programs. The experience redirected his interests, from Quaker politics in colonial Pennsylvania, the subject of his dissertation and first book, to the "evolution of racism in America." The result was *Red, White, and Black*, which appeared in Prentice-Hall's History of the American People series (Prentice-Hall is a major textbook publisher). Leon Litwak, the series editor, called the book a first. It gave agency to the "'historically voiceless'" poor and to "those who struggled and lost . . . an altogether different perspective and approach."[35]

By focusing on ordinary rhythms of life rather than particular political events, Nash could explore the diversities within cultural groups without imposing arbitrary judgments about winners and losers. He imagined himself living within each group (a feat that Parkman never attempted), and was thus enabled to see the world as that group saw it, making the text far more historically minded than were other treatments of the colonial era. To be sure, there were some exaggerations and distortions in his innovative account. At times it simply seemed to reverse the old consensus polarities, celebrating what the traditional accounts denigrated. For example, the statement "Throughout the colonial period European observers stood in awe of the central Indian traits of hospitality, generosity, bravery and the spirit of mutual caring," is not quite accurate about either the Europeans' attitudes or the Indians' conduct. Nor was it quite correct to say that the Indians had "a kind of innocence that beckoned destruction." Still, the work was an instant classic. A second edition appeared in 1982, and a third in 1991.[36]

The second book to put the new history at the center of textbook publishing was *A People and a Nation,* which came out in 1982. It had five authors, something of a novelty in itself, including Cornell's Mary Beth Norton. Not since Mary Beard's collaboration with her husband had a leading women's historian been a coauthor of a history textbook. Norton recalled that she was asked to join the team to write "a new kind of book" in late 1975, and she agreed to write the chapters dealing with the Colonial and Revolutionary eras.[37]

A People and a Nation, the first textbook on the market to embrace a social-history, many-voices approach, made an important contribution to the textbook world. Houghton Mifflin deserves much credit for taking a chance on the new concept, and even more credit for waiting seven years for it to come to fruition, especially when the editors and production staff knew how far ahead of the curve the book was. The authors stated their purpose in the preface:

Into this traditional fabric [of political and economic history] we have woven social history, broadly defined. We have investigated the history of the majority of Americans—women and of minorities. And we have sought to illuminate the private side of the American story:

work and play, dress and diet; entertainment; family and home life; relationships between men and women; and race, ethnicity, and religion.

Where earlier generations of textbook authors had defined history as a parade of public events, the authors of *A People and a Nation* set out to blur the distinction between public events and the private, intimate, domestic events that are "the stories of real people."[38]

While the Norton team was waiting for her to finish her chapters, Nash joined with five other authors to write a survey textbook entitled *The American People: Creating a Nation and a Society* for Harper & Row (it is now published by Longman). It would appear two years after *A People and a Nation*. Like the textbooks of the 1950s, it bridged the gap between popular history and works written by and for professional historians, but it did this in the tonalities of the new history. It celebrated not a narrow consensus but "a rich and extraordinarily complex human story . . . a convergence of Native Americans, Europeans, and Africans . . . a magnificent mosaic of cultures, religions and skin shades." The authors' commitment to inclusiveness, to "a history that treats the lives and experiences of Americans of all national origins and cultural backgrounds, at all levels of society, and in all regions of the country," not only indicated the new-history ideological orientation of the authors but also signaled that the Norton et al./Nash et al. formula might be the wave of the future.[39]

The two publishers were betting a large pot of money that the new-history textbook formula would be attractive to younger college teachers. Launching a new textbook costs half a million dollars. Textbook publishers are risk-averse, and they would have not invested the time and money in the two projects if they had not had some evidence of the likelihood of their success. The long gestation period of major, multiple-author history textbooks—allowing for many years of revision based on reports from teachers who might, in future, adopt the book for their classes, and dealing with the changes in the team of authors and editors—gives the publishers time to assess the changing demands of the market as well as to promote their forthcoming products.

In both teams, coauthors came and went, as did in-house publish-

ing staff. Randall Woods, one of the historians originally signed to
work on Nash's *A People and a Nation,* recalled that by the time the
book appeared the project had lost all but two of its original authors,
including him. James Henretta, lead author of another major social-
history survey first published in 1987, confided that the book would
have been out "four or five" years earlier but for "quite a remarkable
series of setbacks." Woods's and Henretta's experiences were not
unusual.[40]

The wide adoption of the social-history, many-voices books by college teachers rewarded their publishers' faith in the project. Moreover, the success of Norton et al. and Nash et al. set off a chain
reaction as the other major textbook publishers scrambled to assemble groups of authors who would focus on the new-history perspective—stressing social as well as political history and inclusiveness and
diversity. The publishers' gamble had paid rich dividends, for by the
middle of the 1980s, the new generation of historians wanted the
many voices/diversity books for their students.

The new-history persuasion in the textbooks was not simply another
version of consensus, with critique replacing celebration and diversity
supplanting uniformity. Instead, the new history promoted a self-con-
scious, experimental approach to pedagogy. Some of the new-history
textbooks were narratives, while others were social histories, or social-
political, or political-social, or textbooks that desired "to integrate
social and political history" or to "perfectly blend the structure a
political narrative provides and the insights gained from examining
social and cultural experiences." New, imaginatively designed aids to
comprehension included features such as sidebars and boxes, and
set-offs of whole pages. The variety of these features was striking as
well: "The People Speak" and "American Views" (excerpts from primary sources), "The American Mosaic" (topical issues set off in separate essays), "The American People Gather" (essays on leisure and
entertainment), "A Place in Time" (essays on localities and their populations), "An American Album" (historical photographs), "Counterpoint" (selections from historians disagreeing about an issue), and
"Diagraphics" (combinations of maps, charts, and pictures to explain
changes in technology and population). Pedagogical approaches bor-

rowed from other disciplines included focus questions at the beginning of each chapter; review questions at the end; and student "toolkits." The diversity of the design and approach came to match the diversity of content.[41]

Despite the diversity of presentation, one fact remained indisputable in the American history textbook industry: the new history was there to stay. College students were guaranteed exposure to it, by their assigned textbooks as well as by the lectures of their professors. The new history spoke to all of them, as inclusive in its audience as it was in its coverage. The need to be inclusive meant losing the fabrications of exclusion and the falsification inherent in the old consensus history. What was more, the increasingly fierce competition among the growing number of textbooks for market share, and the need to revise and republish books every four years (so that publishers and authors did not lose market share to used books), drove the textbook authors to master the most recent professional literature and the publishers to send sales representatives to every campus in the country, further spreading the new-history gospel.

Because the textbooks had to be revised periodically, the "facts" in them were never immutable or fixed, another way in which the textbooks of the 1980s diverged from the textbooks of the 1950s. The new history had always preached that facts were not bricks ready to hand, but imaginative constructs, little arguments composed of bits of evidence, and one historian's "fact" was not necessarily another's. This in turn meant that the precise language that historians used to express facts was not fungible—one could not just borrow one's predecessors' language and formulations. The new textbooks thus began to include huge bibliographical sections, indicating the secondary sources that the authors had used. Although the new textbooks still borrowed ideas and formulations from earlier writers, their authors took great pains not to reproduce unique phrases or key ideas without some form of attribution. In sum, the new-history textbooks moved the profession ever further and further away from the content and the form of consensus history, including its habit of leaving out inconvenient or unpleasant facts and its inclination to borrow from other books.

The Jobs Crisis

Unlike many of the leading consensus historians' works, the source of the new historians' authority lay not in the bookstores but in the classrooms. The new-history teachers had found that refashioned history was enticing to students. It spoke in the language of relevance and tied current problems to past events. It opened the door even wider to people with diverse backgrounds and heritages, inviting them to join in the scholarly enterprise. It democratized graduate study in a way that proponents of consensus history had never contemplated.

But at first the invitation to young people to join the ranks of college-history teachers brought the profession to the brink of anarchy. From the end of the 1960s into the 1980s, a "jobs crisis" hung over the historical profession like a sword of Damocles. Graduate programs in history proliferated faster than jobs for the graduates appeared. While this process democratized graduate history teaching, breaking the monopoly of the elite schools, it held out the false promise of employment to those entering graduate programs.

The G.I. Bill, passed during World War II to aid veterans seeking a college education, had flooded colleges and universities with students—college enrollments grew from 1.4 million in 1946 to 2.7 million ten years later—and many new campuses had been opened to fill the demand. Jobs for history teachers seemed sure to open everywhere. Established graduate programs increased their intake of applicants, and new programs appeared. Although there may have been a genuine commitment to broaden opportunities for young men and women who could not gain entrance to the elite programs, every state school's administration knew that there was money and prestige in a Ph.D. program, and some of the new programs were borderline (the AHA called them "marginal") in terms of the resources at their command for training graduate students.

When I went to Ohio State in 1970 I was surprised to learn that the state legislature, in a fit of what can only be called academic populism, had allowed many of the smaller state schools to begin Ph.D. programs in history. In the formula for funding these programs, called the FTE or full time equivalents, the department benefited directly from the size of its graduate program because twice as much weight was given to graduate students taking courses in the departments of history as to the undergraduates. Whether the graduate programs were accommodating the demand or creating it, democratically inclined or just greedy, the result of the new programs was a flood of young people seeking history jobs at the end of the 1960s that stayed high into the early 1980s.

The statistics are staggering. At the height of the jobs crisis, in the spring of 1975, the AHA began collecting data on graduate history programs. Clearly, the largest programs had gorged themselves on new applicants. Over the course of the 1973–74, 1974–75, and 1975–76 school years, the University of California at Berkeley admitted 53, 78, and 63 new students, respectively, to add to a total of 190 full-time graduate students in 1976. UCLA admitted 78, 92, and 99, to its total of 301 full-timers. Wisconsin let in 80, 61, and 65, and had 411 full-time grad students in 1976. UC Berkeley produced 20; UCLA, 42; and Wisconsin, 51 Ph.D.s in 1975.

Other state universities were almost as active: The University of Illinois at Champaign-Urbana admitted 37, 35, and 32 graduate students in history over these years; the University of Illinois at Chicago Circle admitted 62, 57, and 55. But the latter's graduate students were different from those at Champaign-Urbana and the leading California universities, for over half of the Chicago Circle graduate students were part-timers. Other state universities had significant numbers of part-time graduate students: Rutgers (164 full-time, 65 part-time), Indiana University (89 full-time, 154 part-time), University of Kansas (90 full-time, 39 part-time), University of Connecticut (82 full, 44 part time), State University of New York at Binghamton (68 full-time, 51 part time), SUNY at Stony Brook (77 full-time, 45 part-time), and CUNY (84 full-time, 95 part-time time).

No one seemed concerned about the fact that job opportunities had not materialized in the anticipated numbers, although the outcome of the shortfall was predictable—a growing backlog of unemployed job seekers. In the meantime, the grad students lived on their stipends, when they could get stipends. Although many students received aid, most often in return for teaching classes or serving as graders, many large programs such as Columbia University's (351 students enrolled full-time in 1975–1976), the University of Chicago (111 full-timers), Duke (89 full-time), Georgetown (101 full-time, 102 part-time), Harvard (159 full-time students), and the University of Pennsylvania (170 full-timers), did not fund every student.

Graduate students facing the crisis prolonged their studies. In Ohio, graduate schools were bursting at their seams, but students were delaying completion of their degrees. The University of Akron had admitted 21, 23, and 22 new graduate students during the years 1973, 1974, and 1975, joining those already in the program, for a total of 58 full time and 97 part time, but turned out only one Ph.D. in 1975. The University of Cincinnati added 29, 23, and 16 over these years to its graduate student body, for a total of 101 full timers in 1975, but also produced only one Ph.D. In the years 1973–75 no one at Bowling Green State University got a Ph.D., though the school had admitted 44 students during the period. By 1981, when the new admissions of the middle 1970s should have been finishing at the marginal Ohio programs, the numbers of dissertations had not increased. The pattern of the middle 1970s persisted in the new decade. The University of Akron admitted 21 new students in 1979, 32 in 1980, and 25 in 1981, but only had one Ph.D. in 1981; Bowling Green State let in 7, 11, and 10, but produced only three Ph.D.s; and the University of Cincinnati improved slightly, to seven Ph.D.s, after admitting 17, 13, and 11 new students.[42]

The stories of a "lost generation" of young scholars were heart-rending and unending. At the 1970 AHA meeting, according to a report in the New York Times, 2,481 applicants registered for 188 available teaching positions. The AHA itself surveyed departments and discovered that "less than half" of their finishing graduate students had found "satisfactory employment." In 1971, the AHA counted over 800 job candidates who found no jobs. And the "job gap" continued to widen. In the early 1970s, on average 1,100 history Ph.D.s were produced each year but only a mere 700 positions opened. By the end of the seventies, the number of Ph.D.s sent out into the world had declined to match the number of new slots (both figures would

dip into the 500s in the mid-1980s), but there remained a huge sur-
plus of unemployed or underemployed Ph.D.s seeking full-time jobs.
And most major history departments only slightly downsized their
graduate programs in the 1980s. UCLA, for example, dropped to 269
full- and 5 part-time, Berkeley had 165 full-time, and Wisconsin was
training 207 full-time and 31 part-time.

The demand for teachers in history did not exceed the supply until
the beginning of the 1990s, by which time 20 years had passed for
some of the first victims of the jobs crisis. History departments noted
the finally rising demand but ignored the backlog, and so they started
accepting more new graduate students. In 1990, Berkeley was back
up to 192 full-time, UCLA to 273 full-time, and Wisconsin had 233
full-time and 21 part-time students. Worst hit by the crisis were individuals whose funding or teaching at their own universities had
ended, but did not yet have their doctorates. Some continued to pro-
long their schooling, hoping that association with a program, even if
they did not complete it, would help them find employment.[43]

The crisis continues. The historian Jacqueline Dowd Hall wrote in
the on-line newsletter of the OAH, "I am a mentor to graduate students who face . . . a shrinking proportion of full-time, tenure-track
positions and an alarming increase in the number of contingent
[part-time and adjunct] workers." In fact, the number of part-time,
adjunct, and temporary history positions has mushroomed. In some
community colleges and branch campuses over 75 percent of the history faculty are contingent. No wonder that Hall, who is a tenured
professor at University of North Carolina, Chapel Hill, was experienc-
ing a "professional version of survivor's guilt."[44]

———————

The job crisis created a gulf between tenure-track and tenured professors on the one hand and job seekers and temporary instructors on
the other. The gap seemed to send a message of a heartless and grim
profession. Although the new history promoted diversity, it also questioned old assumptions about professional harmony. Certainly its
aggressive, almost gleeful embrace of the themes of conflict and

incompleteness matched the growing fracturing of fields and subfields into tiny specialties. As they tried to find some small patch of
uncovered ground to farm, for new-history dissertations still had to
provide new information, more and more of the younger scholars
seemed to be writing for one another rather than for the general
reader. In 1989, the intellectual historian Peter Novick lamented that
"as a broad community of discourse, as a community of scholars
united by common aims, common standards, and common purposes,
the discipline of history had ceased to exist."[45]

Novick's eulogy for the profession was wrong in one important
respect. No one within the profession could doubt that a revolution
had come and gone, leaving the profession forever altered. Never
again would it be the preserve of white men of a certain kind of
breeding and attitude. With its broadened membership base, including for the first time large numbers of women, the corps of professional historians for the first time closely resembled the makeup of
the people whose stories it tried to tell. None of these men and
women could or would ever want to go back to a time when historians
fabricated and falsified and uncritically parroted one another's claims
that ours was one people, one nation, and one history.

Still, there was a subtle danger for the profession as its new, diverse
description became a prescription for diversity. By the end of the
1980s, every professional committee and every session at the major
national historical conventions had to have "balance"—defined as
equality of numbers of men and women and, if possible, representatives from a variety of major ethnic groups. In their formal "calls for
papers" for the national conventions, the OAH and the AHA program committees required groups submitting proposals for sessions
to demonstrate this balance. At the same time, the national professional associations were gaining a distinct ideological cast. They were
moving to the left. At first, very likely only those inside the profession
saw this shift, but it did not take long for conservatives in politics,
media, business, and other areas of public life to notice what was hap-
pening. The shift in the internal politics of the major professional history associations saw certain individuals who had not published very
much rise to positions of genuine influence, suggesting that honors

and offices within the profession were not based on scholarly accomplishment but on interest-group representation. The change from elite to populist self-government was hardly unique to the historical profession—indeed it reflected trends in the academic world as a whole—but it would have profound consequences when historians professed to speak in neutral, objective tones on issues of general public interest.

At the same time, a gap was opening between historians who focused on major public events, political and military figures, and diplomacy and those who thought that the everyday life of ordinary people—birth, marriage, child rearing, and other demographic issues—was more important. Lemisch's "history from the bottom up" had taken root in the new history, but not as he expected. Instead of providing a radical critique of American politics, the new historians were radically shifting the angle of repose of all history in the direction of social and cultural life. The two sides in this debate—the major-events group and the everyday-life group—began to struggle for control of the programs at the major conventions, each accusing the other of intellectual imperialism.

Finally, Novick's plaint reflected a sobering but essential truth about the new history. If no safety valve could be found for its disputatiousness, no brighter side to its discoveries of oppression and betrayal in our past, no way to tie together its many valuable but often narrowly framed research findings, it might lose its most important audience—the American reader. For in their rush to overturn the falsities and fabrications of consensus history the new historians had forgotten what had made consensus history so successful all those years. General audiences wanted something from history that the profession seemed determined to withhold: proofs that American history could inspire and delight.

Compared to the prize-winning works of their consensus predecessors, many of the most honored contributions of the new historians shared the disheartening trait of excessive fault finding. In the 1950s and 1960s, the Bancroft and Parkman prizes had been captured by upbeat books such as Boorstin's *The Americans*, Merrill Peterson's uplifting *The Jefferson Image in the American Mind* (1961), William E.

Leuchtenberg's admiring *Franklin Delano Roosevelt and the New Deal, 1932–1940* (1964), Richard B. Morris's stirring *The Peacemakers: The Great Powers and American Independence* (1966), and Bailyn's *Ideological Origins of the American Revolution* (1968). But by the end of the decade and into the 1970s and 1980s these prizes were going to far more depressing studies such as Winthrop Jordan's searing indictment of American racism, *White over Black: American Attitudes Toward the Negro, 1550–1812* (1969); Eugene Genovese's radical analysis of slavery, *Roll Jordan Roll* (1975); Robert A. Caro's investigation of the evils of power politics, *The Power Broker: Robert Moses and the Fall of New York* (1975); Edmund S. Morgan's sad tale of the rise of slavery in Virginia, *American Slavery, American Freedom: The Ordeal of Colonial Virginia* (1976); Robert Gross's elegy for a dying New England on the eve of the Revolution, *The Minutemen and their World* (1977); William S. McFeely's less than complimentary *Grant: A Biography* (1982); William Cronon's sobering account of how the Puritans deforested New England, *Changes in the Land* (1984); Joel Williamson's study of the underside of southern culture, *The Crucible of Race* (1985); and last but hardly least, Eric Foner's troubling explanation of how Reconstruction failed, *Reconstruction: America's Unfinished Revolution, 1863–1877* (1989). Without the optimistic, celebratory self-confidence that the consensus history and historians exuded, the new history and its promoters could find themselves without any audience.

Or, worse—with a hostile audience. In what seemed to be its moment of triumph, the new-history revolution faced a conservative backlash against the leaders of the movement and the history they promoted. In the 1990s, a series of critical dialogues between leading members of the profession and critics of the new history would politicize—and brutalize—history and historians in a far more public way than the originators of New Left history had ever envisioned.

CHAPTER 4

In the Eye
of the Storm

BY THE END OF THE 1980S, THE PURVEYORS OF THE new history were buoyed by their apparent triumph in the classroom and the textbooks. The sweeping victory, in which consensus history was left to the popular historians (and a few notable academics of the old school), bred a mischievous arrogance. As the new historians grew a little older themselves and became leaders of the profession, they assumed that everyone accepted the basic tenets of the new history, or at least could be persuaded of their validity. They forgot what Warren Susman had written in the first years of the struggle to replace the orthodoxies of consensus: no group or party could control how history was used or monopolize its production forever.

Insofar as the new history was a liberal history, it reached out to many who had had no history in the textbooks or the classrooms under the consensus-history regime, but it also antagonized those who wanted consensus history of the most conservative and patriotic kind. No sooner did the new historians gain ascendancy in the academy, in the historical associations, and on the advisory boards of various historical institutions than they found all their gains in jeopardy. They did not master the lessons they should have learned from their contest with the consensus historians over the meaning of history. Instead, they took their ascendancy as "the opportunity (and perhaps the obligation), to bring historical scholarship to bear directly on policy issues, sometimes collaborating in the drafting of legal briefs or legislation." In other words, new historians were jumping into the public arena feet first, and, as it happened, with eyes closed.[1]

Why did the new historians not see this handwriting on the wall, when some of them had written the graffiti themselves years before? A characteristic of the new scholarship was an increasing technicality and specificity. Women's historians were drawn to close studies of family and community; ethnic historians demanded a new look at the minutia of culture, labor, and urban life; minority historians wanted more detailed studies of immigration, acculturation, and other sociohistorical phenomena. Method became more important, as historians eagerly borrowed theories and skills from social sciences and literary criticism. Professional historians lamented this compartmentalization but did little to make their research accessible to general readers. Though historians praised clear writing, few put elegance of style ahead of heavily researched documentation. The result was a widening gap between what gained applause as popular history, often the work of journalists or historians who had left the classroom, and minutely detailed, methodologically involuted professional monographs that few outside the academy read. In short, historians were so busy inventing newer kinds of history and trying to master newer methods that they did not see how far they had strayed from what most Americans wanted from history. The professors forgot that history had to service more than historians and their students.[2]

I suspect that the embrace of obscure methods and the miniaturization of history was not so much a result of the brash overconfidence of the new history as a retreat from contentiousness itself. Perhaps after so much of it, new historians had become tired of name-calling. But all that changed in the 1990s. Then, leading professional historians at the top schools found themselves at the center of the culture wars, assiduously promoting the importance of critical thinking in history and defending the expertise of the profession against a resurgent tide of celebratory chronicle on the one hand and the sniping of media pundits on the other. It was a role for which the best and brightest of history professors were not trained, and sometimes they performed it poorly.

It All Started with Christopher Columbus

"It all started with Columbus"—that is how I was taught American history in the New York City schools. Columbus Day was a school holiday, and once I went to the Columbus Day parade in Manhattan. It was a source of pride for Italian Americans and they looked forward with pleasure to the celebration. On Columbus Day, 1989, President George H. W. Bush prepared the way for a national festival commemorating the five hundredth anniversary of Columbus's arrival in New World waters. "On Columbus Day, we pause as a nation to honor the skilled and courageous navigator who discovered the Americas and in so doing, brought to our ancestors the promise of the New World." Little did the president anticipate that the quincentenary celebration would cast Columbus and his fellow European explorers in a wholly new light.[3]

On the eve of the jubilee, Native Americans objected to the celebration. Indian advocacy groups had never regarded Columbus as the discoverer of anything. Their ancestors were already here, living in villages and towns, cultivating gardens of corn and beans, worshipping powerful spirits who dwelt in forest, mountain, and celestial abodes when Columbus espied the greenery of the Bahamas. As a "First Nations" spokesman explained, "We do not call ourselves 'Native American,' because our blood and people were here long before this land was called the Americas." Other Indian observers noted, with some asperity, that Columbus brought with him cockroaches, rats, and a host of hideous diseases to which the natives had no natural immunities. The result was the near depopulation of the Caribbean and later of Mexico and the east coast of North America. As the Iroquois spokesman and historian John Mohawk wrote on the eve of the quincentenary,

> Can it be that the celebration of Columbus's "discovery" in full view of the historical context, is one of the great propaganda victories of history? The colonization is a story of military conquest carried out by a people possessing vastly superior arms against sometimes practically unarmed populations, of subduing and sometimes exterminating those populations, of appropriating their land and their labor to the ends of the conquerors.[4]

The strident tone and widening scope of the controversy showed how important history could be in the culture wars. For every parade with floats of Columbus's flagship, the *Santa Maria,* there were anti-Columbus vigils and protest meetings, including one on the steps of the Capitol in Washington, D.C. Charges of "Eurocentrism"—the assumption that civilization spread from Europe to the rest of the world—came from a wide array of sources, even the American Library Association. In June 1990, a resolution was passed by the ALA. It began: "Whereas Columbus's voyage to America began a legacy of European piracy, brutality, slave trading, murder, disease, conquest, and genocide . . ." The librarians did not remind their readers that Native American peoples like the Maya, the Aztec, and even John Mohawk's Iroquois forebears were pitiless imperialists, gobbling up their neighbors' territory and demanding tribute, omissions suggesting that the librarians were engaging in some propagandizing of their own. With an admirable but somewhat suspiciously timed historical-mindedness, the Knights of Columbus replied to protesters that Columbus's conduct and views had to be understood in the context of his times. The U.S. Congress's Columbus Quincentenary Jubilee Commission tried to quiet the dispute by changing the "celebration" to a "commemoration," but the shift in language mollified few.[5]

For all professional historians, Columbus's actions were part of a much longer and broader story than his four voyages, but the meaning of that story divided these historians. Some specialists in Native American history regarded the protests as proof that they had been right all along about Columbus. Francis Jennings, one of the premier historians of Native American life, titled his 1993 book *The Founders of America: How Indians Discovered the Land, Pioneered in It, and Created Great Classical Civilizations, How They Were Plunged into a Dark Age by Invasion and Conquest, and How They Are Reviving.* New Left historians were delighted that they had another opportunity to press their case against consensus history. In 1991, Howard Zinn told an audience that the context of conquest was far broader than Columbus's voyages and the subsequent Spanish dominion in the Caribbean. "What also marks these five hundred years—and that's why adding the facts about Columbus is important—is that they are five hundred years of conquest by the Western powers, represented first in that one instance by Spain, but very soon by many others. Five hundred years of conquest, of exploitation, of enslavement, of violence, of war, of colonialism . . . a generic truth about Western civilization." To some conservative scholars, this kind of critical interpretation of the Age of Discovery was an unacceptable bashing of American aspirations and ideals. They leaned far in the other direction. Lynne Cheney, then head of the National Endowment for the Humanities (NEH), later recalled that she had to override NEH panel recommendations that "charged Columbus with genocide, but portrayed the Aztecs—who practiced human sacrifice on a massive scale—as a gentle, peace-loving people."[6]

Most professional historians, standing on their reputations and expertise, observed the controversy as if they were above the fray. James Axtell, chair of the AHA's Quincentenary Committee, found merit in both sides' views. The controversy had led to "serious, ethnically sensitive, commemorative . . . advances into our textbooks, classrooms, and public media." At the close of a thoughtful and balanced review of the scholarly literature on Columbus, Delno West made a collateral point:

Since each generation asks its own questions about the past, it would not be surprising that Columbus studies continue to flourish. Today we are concerned with race and gender, environmental history, and comparative cultural studies. Columbus and the events of 1492 lend themselves to these inquiries. Much remains to be done to understand Columbus and his enterprise fully.

Axtell and West implied that a battle in the culture wars had been averted when the professional historians lent their expertise to the dispute. They turned a political donnybrook into a legitimate academic event.[7]

Though professional historians did not recognize it at the time, the tug-of-war over the Columbus quincentenary was a harbinger of turbulent times ahead for historians. It had lured academic historians into a public quarrel and convinced them that their expertise shielded them from criticism. That was a mistake. From the start of the cultural storms of the nineties—the controversy over the National History Standards (NHS) from 1992 to 1996; the tumultuous career of the planned *Enola Gay* exhibit at the Smithsonian Air and Space Museum from 1987 to 1995; and the impeachment and trial of President Bill Clinton—historians played a featured role, and before these storms quieted, the very right of professional historians to speak with authority about the past was called into question.

National History Standards

The saga of the National History Standards began innocuously enough. In 1986, a Columbia Teachers College education professor, Diane Ravitch, reported the findings of the National Assessment of Educational Progress. She and Chester A. Finn, Jr., a professor of education at Vanderbilt University, characterized the results of the history section of the assessment as appalling. Although over 60 percent of schoolchildren tested knew the names of Columbus's first three ships, fewer than 30 percent had any idea why he sailed west. Second-semester history students in the high school classes selected for the test proved remarkably ignorant of other basic facts about American history. Over 60 percent did not know that the Civil War occurred between 1850 and 1900, 70 percent did not know what the Jim Crow laws were, and 30 percent could not even find Great Britain on the map. To Ravitch the lesson of the history assessment was clear: students did not know basic facts in American history.[8]

The complaint about basic facts represented a particular approach to the relationship between fact and interpretation. Professional historians—even those who still embraced some form of consensus history—no longer believed that any one set of facts was always essential. Conservative educators and their political allies nevertheless insisted that schoolchildren must be taught a certain core of key facts, because these facts proved the superiority of American history over all others. It was the same argument that George Bancroft had made over 100 years earlier. No need for Bailyn's ironies or Nash's multiple perspectives or Mary Beth Norton's focus on ordinary people. The inculcation of national character in new generations depended upon national adherence to a particular view of history. Widespread ignorance of these historical facts, by contrast, put the nation at risk.

The Heritage Foundation, the American Enterprise Institute, and other conservative think-tanks promoted this view of history, but not only conservatives were demanding more history in the schools. Professional historians of all persuasions agreed that high school students were leaving school ill prepared in history. Thus, although her findings had a conservative, consensus spin, Ravitch's report struck a chord with professional historians' associations. Their members joined with the NEH and the U.S. Department of Education to direct conferences and commissions to address the problem of historical illiteracy. Together the professionals and the teachers formed ad hoc committees and inaugurated programs to reach out to history teachers in the schools, and to support existing events like National History Day.[9]

In 1987, the Lynde and Harry Bradley Foundation, whose mission is to be "devoted to strengthening American democratic capitalism," funded a commission, named the Bradley Commission and headed by the Columbia University historian Kenneth Jackson, to lay out the grounds for a nationwide secondary school history program. The teachers and professors of history on the commission created a platform, much as would a major political party. Of necessity, the planks in the platform were general, for (as the commission's report conceded) there was not agreement on every item.[10] First, the commission arrived at a set of broad curricular goals: "The study of history" should be considered "indispensable to the education of citizens in a democracy" and therefore should be "required of all students." Context as well as factual material and "training in critical judgment" should accompany "memorization." The curriculum should include American history, world history, and western civilization "to reveal our democratic political heritage and its vicissitudes."

A closer look at the offsetting terms in this initial section of the report hints that the commission was already split between traditionalist-celebrants and critical-thinking advocates. In particular, memorization of key facts was set against critical judgment. The phrase "democratic political heritage" and the word "vicissitudes" balanced one another in what was obviously a set of uneasy compromises.

The commission's list of "perspectives and modes of thoughtful judgment derived from the study of history" paired opposite stances. There was a sop to the critical-thinking school: history teaching should "prepare [students] to live with uncertainties and exasperating, even perilous, unfinished business" and to "grasp the complexity of historical causation . . . and avoid excessively abstract generalizations." There was also a sop to those who preferred heroic chronicle: history in the schools must "recognize the importance of individuals who have made a difference in history."

In its draft enumeration of the "vital" themes in history, the commission again performed a balancing act, first appeasing the new historians with a bow to "the changing patterns of class, ethnic, racial, and gender structures and relations. . . . The new prominence of women, minorities, and the common people in the study of history, and their relation to political power and influential elites. The characteristics of multicultural societies." But students were not to neglect the "evolution of American political democracy." Some of the required subject matter—"the distinctly American tensions between liberty and equality, liberty and order, region and nation, individualism and the common welfare, and between cultural diversity and civic unity, and . . . the major successes and failures of the United States, in crisis at home and abroad"—itself mandated a complex balancing act.[11]

What held the commission together was a common sense that history had something vital to offer every school student. So long as the precise details of the curriculum could be subsumed in general terms, and the differences in approach cloaked by pairing opposites, a semblance of unanimity would reign. But lurking beneath the surface unity of the commission's report rumbled the battle between consensus history and the new history that had commenced in the 1960s.

Gary Nash, who was invited to address the Bradley Commission members and whose remarks were later included in its report, explained what he thought was needed in the schools: "The view that history is with the people is not only more fitting for a democratic society, in which it is assumed that an active citizenry is essential to the maintenance of liberty, it is more accurate." Nash gave this social history–many voices approach a pedigree, asserting that "the peculiar disjunction of fabricating an elitist history for a democratic society has been challenged for at least a century by a long but thin line of historians connecting the contemporary scene with past generations." From the 1960s, radical, black, and women's history provided the foundation for "inclusiveness." Nash's goal was not to label these groups as "victims," nor simply to add more names to the roster of heroes and heroines, but to reveal how contested and contingent, how painful, our history was. An echo of this goal was the commission's ultimate decision to supply topics for world history rather than just the history of Western civilization—a commitment to inclusiveness (and a rejection of Eurocentrism) that would return to haunt the framers of national history standards.[12]

The next step was the creation of an organization to fill in what the Bradley Commission had left blank. Linda Symcox, who became an assistant to the director of the National Council on History in the Schools (NCHS) shortly after its creation, recalled how it came into being. Her story began in California with the inauguration of a new statewide "History–Social Science Framework" that emphasized the importance of narrative chronology. Symcox judged the California plan an attempt to find a "middle ground" between the "assimilation" and the "pluralism" or, in terms of the most recent debates over American history, "traditional" and "multicultural" approaches. Symcox did not say that the framework entirely ignored the New Left critique of older histories, simply replacing celebration of consensus with celebration of diversity. But she did assess the result as "upbeat" history that rejected "victimization, divisiveness, and negativism."[13]

When Lynne Cheney, the head of the NEH, decided to underwrite the history initiative, she turned to Charlotte Crabtree, a social studies professor who had nursed the California framework program, and with Crabtree at its helm, Cheney's NEH funded a National Center for History in the Schools at UCLA, where Crabtree taught. "The center's mission would be to survey the state of history education nationally and to develop model programs for teaching history." An NEH grant of $1.6 million for the project was announced on March 22, 1988. Now all that remained was the work itself.[14]

Crabtree asked Nash, also at UCLA, to act as the associate director of the NCHS. No one could doubt his authority as an expert on American history. His particular view of American history was well known, and it hardly squared with Cheney's, but his prominence had led the Bradley Commission to invite him to address it and Houghton Mifflin to sign him on as the editor of a series of history textbooks for use in schools (including one on California history). Plainly, he understood the problems of history education in the schools. Symcox did not say so, but bringing in someone like Nash would also quiet any objections that other liberal professional historians might have about the work the NCHS accomplished.[15]

Nash himself recalled that the NCHS began as an agency to gather data, in part through convening teams of scholars to "work with a slate of appointed Teacher Associates, who met during the summers and produced model lesson plans built from primary documents." The push for national standards came later, in 1990, and from the very top—President George H. W. Bush's State of the Union Address. Among the president's "national education goals" was the objective that students understand the "diverse cultural heritage" of the United States. The president's reference to heritage, echoing the term's use in the Bradley Commission report, reflected the traditional celebratory role of history education, but inclusion of diversity in the formula was evidence that the new history could not be ignored. Nash understood the threat to both the new history and to the autonomy of experts in the national education program, and he was bound and determined not to let anyone reimpose an official consensus version of history on the schools.

Lynne Cheney wanted to turn the president's generalities into a program for uniform national testing, a goal that raised much contention on the National Council on Educational Standards and Testing they created to oversee the process. The council supported the idea of national assessments but not a single national test in any subject. In their view, such a test might be feasible in mathematics or the sciences, but in the humanities, particularly history, the creation of such a test (choosing appropriate questions and determining the correct answers to the questions) would depend on the existence of a standard content on which the test writers agreed. But by 1990, such agreement would be hard to find among professional historians. Even the multiple-choice test answers in the advanced placement history tests were being challenged along ideological lines, as one of my colleagues who wrote those questions for the Educational Testing Service in Princeton, New Jersey, has told me.[16]

In October, 1991, at the urging of Cheney, the NEHS submitted a proposal to fashion national standards. Nash thought at the time that "the prospect of national history standards represented both an opportunity to bring recent scholarship into the schools and a danger that this scholarship would be rejected by standards writers hostile to it." For Nash, the term "recent scholarship" was shorthand for the new history. But only occasionally requiring people to reassess what they believe is important is fraught with peril. Cognitive-dissonance theory tells us that people do not like to hear or see things that do not fit their existing notions—and the new history, while old hat to its practitioners such as Nash, was not so familiar or so accepted in the nation's schools. Still, if there were to be national standards, Nash wanted to be part of the team that wrote them. As he put it, "Those who were at first reluctant about the wisdom of this enterprise soon decided that they might compromise their own best interests if they failed to join in. If the cards were being dealt, why would historians or social studies educators not want seats around the big table." In 1991, the NCHS was the biggest table in the house.[17]

The first task was assembling the players. Crabtree and Nash decided to avoid spokesmen for the far right and the far left—too polemical and maybe too much at odds to sit down and work with one another. All 28 individuals eventually asked to serve on the national board did, many of them suggested and all approved by Cheney, along with Crabtree and Nash. A national forum brought in more advisers and associated the project with community and religious institutions, as well as the OAH and the AHA. The organizers recognized from the start the political nature of the undertaking and enlisted representatives of major interest and religious bodies in the drafting process. There would in addition be nine focus groups representing the major institutions involved in history education and three curriculum task forces of classroom teachers (one for K–4, one for grades 5–12 for U.S. history, and one for grades 5–12 for world history) to write the actual guidelines.[18]

The diversity of the working groups' composition fostered "passionate" debate. Some of the drafters wanted "to do a better job" than the textbooks—which to them meant more "multiculturalism." Not bits and pieces, patches and filler, but a focus on minorities throughout the standards. Defenders of the value of unity claimed that overemphasis on multiculturalism would "balkanize" the curriculum and worsen the divisions that already existed in America and in the classroom. Finn added that the curriculum must emphasize "the great unifying Western ideas of individual freedom, political democracy, and human rights," a prescription that had little weight with forum members who wanted the horrors of slavery covered more extensively. Ruth Wattenberg, representing the American Federation of Teachers, pressed for a combination of the traditional and the newer critiques. The AHA's associate director James Gardner threw down his own gauntlet: the AHA "would not be part of any standards project that did not address the multicultural aspects of our history." Commenting on the world history standards, the vice president of the AHA's teaching division, Robert Blackey, a professor at Cal State San

Bernardino, reported that his division was "adamantly opposed to the Eurocentrism" it found in the draft. For sixteen months this whipsawing of the NCHS staff—Nash and Crabtree were present at all of these exchanges—continued; one could have forgiven them if they had cried for mercy.[19]

Early in their deliberations over national standards, the NCHS published *Lessons from History: Essential Understandings and Historical Perspectives Students Should Acquire*, a curriculum guide that the center's scholars had prepared that could not, its compilers judged, "have appeared at a more timely moment." The 1992 work was right down the middle of the fairway (oh, maybe a little hook to the left), much like a condensed version of a standard current college text with summaries of what students should learn from the history of succeeding periods rather than the precise content of the lessons. It lauded the ideal of a "common core" of information in history courses centered on "the story of the long human struggle for liberty, equality, justice and dignity." But such a struggle was not linear, for its progress was never assured. "Americans need to understand the ideas, conditions, and people all over the earth that have carried the struggle forward and those that have hobbled, betrayed, or defeated it." So there were good guys and bad guys, and "if we are to secure and extend freedom, justice, and respect for each other in an increasingly diverse society . . . citizens need to know the forces that have shaped us."

Lessons from History had at heart a new-history message. Nash's guiding hand was apparent everywhere, if one knew to look for it. The manual called for an end to the "false dichotomy between facts and conceptual analysis." Democratic ideas were both real and visionary. History was not just narrative, but an "interpretation of narrative," a narrative with "depth," expressing "contingency and complexity." A simplistic notion of "progress" was a "trap that many survey history textbooks still lay for students," as was the older focus on "winners." A program of "active learning and critical inquiry" using primary sources would enable students to "write and speak their own minds" instead of passively absorbing what teachers or textbooks said. Major narrative themes were to include social; scientific and technological; economic; religious-cultural-philosophical; and political spheres. But the traditional content of schoolbook histories was not ignored. The Founding Fathers, pictures and all, made their appearance, and their achievements were featured and praised, as were the Constitution and the Bill of Rights.[20]

But Nash toned down the new-history pitch, and the body of the lessons contained only one speed bump that could slow approval from conservatives. The treatment of the Cold War and anti-Communism in the 1950s and 1960s made no concessions to the Cold Warriors. What was said was true; but much was not said that would have explained conservatives' ultimate dissatisfaction with the standards. There was no hint in *Lessons from History* that the Soviet Union or Communism posed a significant threat to American national security or way of life, or that anyone at the time honestly thought so and acted from those convictions. The Viet Nam War was not depicted in terms of a global struggle between capitalism and Communism, much less as the outcome of aggressive action by the North Vietnamese forces, but simply as an event "deeply unpopular and divisive" at home.[21]

Despite Nash's efforts at balance, the AHA and OAH focus groups complained that *Lessons from History* ignored conflict and the oppression of women, minority groups, and others, in effect "sanitized" history. With such strong criticism coming from the professional historians representing the AHA, the council of the NCHS "decided to . . . abandon" the *Lessons from History* framework and "start from scratch." Nash and a world-history expert, William McNeill, "were deputized to write a series of new organizing questions for American and world history that would guide the task forces in their first summer's work of developing standards."[22]

Because of the highly publicized nature of the project, Nash had to do double duty as publicist and draftsman. At the time, he insisted that the debate over the National History Standards was not among experts behind closed doors defending partisan stances or professional associations defending their own territory, but was "a *public* [emphasis in original] debate among educator-citizens." He was certainly right that the standards thus far were not the work of "high officials of state," nor were they ever meant by the NCHS to be imposed on districts, schools, and teachers who did not want their guidance. He was a little disingenuous, however, when he denied that the authority of the standards derived from the expertise of their framers. The members of the various panels were the best teachers, administrators, and historians that the NCHS and the NEH could assemble. Moreover, the decision to drop *Lessons from History* as a framework was based directly on the complaints of the professional organizations. Men like Gardner and Blackey were educators and citizens, but to call them "citizen-educators" rather than experts in their fields was spin to conceal the fact that the AHA had gained, in effect, a veto power.[23]

The AHA wanted "all cultures" to have "equal billing." Symcox, reading the internal correspondence and working closely with Crabtree, felt that Gardner suspected the NCHS of being Cheney's tool. With Blackey, Gardner had lobbied against any language that privileged Western ways or values over other cultures'; such a bias would perpetuate the cant that Western imperialists recited as they subjugated Africans and Asian peoples, he implied. Symcox hinted that NCHS had caved in to this pressure. The final version read, "Standards in world history should include both the history and values of diverse civilizations, including western civilization, and should especially address the interactions among them." But Gardner, a public historian, and Blackey, who taught European history, had won a pyrrhic victory. The concession was a self-inflicted wound from which the world-history standards as then written would never recover.[24]

The final version of the National History Standards should not have come as a shock to conservatives who knew anything about the project's shift in direction from 1992 to 1994. Conservative council members were upset with the decision to reduce coverage of Western civilization and shared these concerns with Cheney and Ravitch, who in turn spoke to Nash and Crabtree privately, but all of them continued to work on the project. Cheney in particular lauded the work as it progressed. Even when she stepped down as head of the NEH after the election of President Bill Clinton in November 1992, she announced that her most important act as director had been sponsorship of the NCHS. At the same time, one should note that her compliments were uttered in the fall of 1992, before the major rewriting of the standards began. Teachers nominated by the various organizations were at work on the revision from the summer of 1992, but it was not done when Cheney stepped down.[25]

In the meantime, Nash was busy coordinating the completion of the American history portion of the standards. In May 1994 a complete draft of the NHS was ready for internal circulation. Most of the affiliated institutions and groups were delighted with the task forces' achievement, though Finn warned the council that he saw "political correctness and relativism" in "too many places," and that local Chambers of Commerce and conservative media pundits like Rush Limbaugh would find "the usual manifestations of excessive attention to fashionable groups and obscure individuals." Nash later wryly noted that "some council members were more sympathetic to Finn's opinions than they indicated during the meeting."[26]

Charlotte Crabtree retired in June 1994, leaving Nash alone at the top of the NCHS to fine-tune the standards. There was still in-house criticism, but it was too late; by the end of September the *National Standards for United States History* were almost ready for public viewing. One can see how the standards differed from the *Lessons from History*. Even the illustrations were strikingly divergent. Unit IV of *Lessons from History*, entitled "Nation Building (1783–1815)," featured portraits of Washington, Hamilton, Madison, and Jefferson. In *National Standards for United States History* the unit titled "Era 3: Revolution and a New Nation (1754–1820s)" dropped every one of these illustrations and instead used pictures of the Boston Massacre, Molly Pitcher (a woman who helped load cannons in a Revolutionary War battle), the Marquis de Lafayette, the signers of the Declaration of Independence, the "Unite or Die" flag, New York City's Federal Hall, and Congressman Matthew Lyon of Vermont fighting with his colleagues. Anyone who compared the two books might easily conclude that the great white men had been omitted from the standards deliberately, for every other difference between the two leaned in the same direction.[27]

It was not the standards themselves that critics found most objectionable, but the sample exercises, called "Examples of Student Achievement," attached to each standard. Many of these, particularly for grades 9–12, lacked balance. Those accompanying the standards for U.S. involvement in Vietnam (Era 9, standard 3C), included: "Analyze the diverse groups and major arguments advanced against the war. Analyze why the war contributed to a generational conflict and concomitant lack of respect for traditional authority figures. . . . Assess the validity of the class basis of combat service in Vietnam. . . . Debate the proposition that national security during the Vietnam War necessitated restriction of individual civil liberties and the press." Students were not given the opportunity to explore whether there were positives behind the war effort or even explain its plausibility. Nash later concluded that the decision to publish the exercises alongside the standards, as if the two belonged together and the exercises were the best or the only way to teach the standards, was "fateful." A more accurate term would have been fatal.[28]

Cheney tried to torpedo the standards even before they were published. Years later, she recalled that she had liked *Lessons from History* but found that the *National Standards for United States History* "reflected the gloomy, politically driven revisionism" that had become "all too familiar on college campuses." In addition, she lamented that the heroes were all gone, replaced by minor figures. Enduring values were gone, too; only oppression remained. On October 20, 1994, Cheney's op-ed piece entitled "The End of History" graced the back pages of the *Wall Street Journal.* In it, she ridiculed the standards for elevating the National Organization of Women, the Sierra Club, and Harriet Tubman in importance above the Constitution, the U.S. Congress, and Ulysses S. Grant (though in fact she was taking her materials from the "Examples of Student Achievement," not the standards themselves). The result, she judged, was a "grim and gloomy" account of America that could only give comfort to the "politically correct." Cheney saw politicization as well: supposedly buoyed by Clinton's victory, the NCHS had pursued a "revisionist" agenda and discarded the older consensus under which the NEH had originally promoted national standards.[29]

The terms "politicization" and "politically correct" were soon flying right and left, their meaning changing dramatically according to who was doing the flinging. The first was an accusation that political advantage rather than some other principled and neutral purpose was behind one's opponents' view of history. Anyone could use it, and everyone did. The second term was an epithet invented in the 1980s by conservatives to attack certain kinds of curbs on speech and behavior that colleges imposed on students and teachers who used racially abusive language that harassed or demeaned an individual. The courts have struck down a number of these campus codes as violations of the First Amendment rights of the speakers. In any case, many liberals also opposed the speech codes from the outset, but the "political correctness" label had an adhesive quality that allowed its use outside of the campus. "Politically correct" came to apply to any political, pedagogical, or intellectual position that conservatives found distasteful. For liberals, the term's indiscriminate use echoed the accusations of "pinko" and "Commie symp" that red baiters had thrown about in the 1950s. As David Kennedy, a Stanford history professor and hardly a left-winger, noted, the *National Standards for United States History* did "have a tone, and a decidedly modern one. To call that tone 'politically correct' whether in its strident or deferential variations, is a cheap shot, incomplete and misleading."[30]

Nash was convinced that Cheney's op-ed piece was politically motivated: she saw a chance to help the Republican right in the election of 1994, a few weeks ahead. She—not he—had politicized the standards. Certainly Republican Congressman Newt Gingrich of Georgia, himself a former teacher of history, understood her message. Nash repeated a story that had Gingrich, on a limousine phone, helping the arch-conservative radio commentator Rush Limbaugh prepare his attack on the NCHS. Gingrich would later add to the *Congressional Record* his article from *U.S. News and World Report* entitled "History Standards Are Bunk." Echoing Henry Ford's infamous dismissal of all history as "bunk," Gingrich aimed his fire at the professional historians:

> The fiasco over the American and Western history standards is a reflection of what has happened to the world of academic history. The profession and the American Historical Association are now dominated by younger historians with a familiar agenda: Take the west down a peg, romanticize "the Other" (non-whites), treat all cultures as equal, refrain from criticizing non-white cultures.[31]

In his own snide commentary, Limbaugh, spurred by Cheney's demand that the standards be dumped, condemned the secret deliberations of academic bullies who had flushed American history "down the sewer of multiculturalism." Limbaugh replayed clips from Nash's description of the project, interrupting the out-of-context excerpts to insert out-of-place comments. To Nash's proposal that students must go beyond memorization of facts, Limbaugh sneered that Nash did not believe there were facts. When Nash suggested stepping back from the celebration of heroes, Limbaugh accused Nash of tearing down heroism. "History is what happened," Limbaugh puffed, in unconscious mimicry of the nineteenth-century consensus historians, not the incomplete complex and critical activity that Nash was trying to portray, which Limbaugh characterized as "a bunch of PC crap."

Limbaugh was no expert but believed he knew more than all the professors put together. The *National Standards for United States History* was a "stupid book." Limbaugh scored what he surely thought to be clever points by sleight of hand. He replayed a sound clip of Nash saying that Cheney was wrong about the absence of white males in the standards—that there was a white man on every page. Nash no doubt referred to pages that contained standards and examples. But Limbaugh snorted, "Well I've got the book and I turn to page two. Page two is right here. Not one white male mentioned on this page." It was a page in the introduction discussing the methods by which the task forces worked. Incidentally, on the same page are to be found the words "humankind," "human," "individual," "humanity," "peoples," and "citizens," all of which include white males. The *National Standards* argued that history was not what the powerful did to the powerless. It was the experience of all people. Hence, when the NCHS generalized about history, it did not use terms like men or rely on the masculine singular pronoun "he." Technically, Limbaugh was right—the words whites or white males or men were missing on page two.[32]

Where Limbaugh shotgunned Nash, John Leo, a conservative contributing editor to the *U.S. News and World Report,* mortared an entire army of aging academic radicals. Leo charged that the standards had been written "from the counter culture perspective by oppression-minded people who trashed the dean's office in the 1960s (or wished they had)." Although many of those aging radicals were white, in the *National Standards* "white ethnics more or less disappear." He was worried: "This won't do. The whole idea was to set unbiased national standards that all Americans could get behind." As it was, the project had been "hijacked by the politically correct."[33]

Nash worked overtime to help generate favorable publicity on the standards. By then he had been commonly accused of being the author of the entire work, and it became his job to save what he could of the task forces' labors. He woke the slumbering historical community and they rallied to the standards as much to defend the reputation of historians as to promote any particular view of American history. Democratic politicians seemed sympathetic, and even moderate Republicans asked for time to read the NHS before joining their critics. But Nash's hopes for a fair or at least an informed public debate were doused by the size of the Republican Congressional victory in 1994 and its forthcoming control of both Houses of Congress. Worse, at a meeting of drafters and critics, former supporters of the standards questioned the very first criterion for the study of history that the NCHS had adopted: active questioning and learning rather than simple memorization of facts. Now they insisted that facts came first.[34]

Republican Senator Slade Gorton of Washington could not have agreed more. He understood the political capital that an attack on the "Examples of Student Achievement" could raise. At the very least, it would embarrass Clinton as he prepared his run for a second term: if he supported the standards he risked being pilloried; if he attacked them and he would be abandoning the educators and professionals who were his strongest allies. On January 18, 1995, there was a main motion on the floor of the Senate for the unfunded mandates bill (a piece of legislation totally unrelated to the standards). During the debate, Gorton moved to amend the bill by adding a rider prohibiting federal government agencies from certifying the NCHS work and denying to it any further federal funding. His amendment stated:

If the department of Education, the National Endowment for the Humanities, or any other federal agency provides funds for the development of the standards . . . the recipient of such funds should have a decent respect for the contributions of western civilization, and United States history, ideas, and institutions, to the increase of freedom and prosperity around the world.

Gorton did not feel that the NCHS deserved any more time, or that changes to the document would be forthcoming or acceptable. "The standards are fundamentally anti-western and anti-American," he later wrote in the *Seattle Post-Intelligencer*. Democrats and one Republican, Senator James Jeffords of Vermont, objected, but they did not have the votes to prevent the rider from passing. A compromise resolution passed 99–1, the only dissenter having gone on record as opposing the standards.[35]

In February 1995, during the long and embittered denouement of the NHS controversy, Finn puckishly suggested that better standards would have resulted from a committee of "bus drivers, policemen, shopkeepers, engineers, preachers, and orthodontists"—in other words, rank nonexperts—rather than the experts on the NCHS. It was a classic expression of the anti-intellectualism Hofstadter had described. In 1923, a fundamentalist Oklahoma legislator had explained his opposition to the teaching of evolution in the schools in similar terms: "I'm neither a lawyer nor a preacher, but a two-horsed layman and I'm against this theory called science." In her October 20 *Wall Street Journal* op-ed, Cheney herself had written that the standards were the brainchild of "an academic establishment." As for Limbaugh, he was no yokel. He knew that if the expertise of the academics in the NCHS was suspect; if they were thought to be biased or represent an interest group rather than simply communicating objective and neutral knowledge, then the authority of the *National Standards* would be undermined. He too dismissed the idea that "experts" knew any more about teaching history than, well, Rush Limbaugh: "Well, anybody who's had a child knows . . . that heroes are crucial to motivation, inspiration and pointing to the finer achievements and accomplishments in life . . . and if this stuff grabs hold . . . this is not the way to build a strong society."[36]

When all was said and done, a revised version of the standards, based on suggestions by a distinguished panel of educators, historians, and politicians assembled by the Committee for Basic Education, appeared in 1996. They proposed and the NCHS agreed to dump the "Examples of Student Achievement," revise some of the more provocative terminology in the standards, and make uniform the subject matter across the various chapters. The revised standards have been adopted in many school districts.[37]

In 1996, the dean of American historians, Arthur M. Schlesinger, Jr., looked back on the history standards controversy's impact on the profession. "Being a historian has almost become a dangerous occupation. The public seems to have few inhibitions about passing judgment on the inner business of the historical community." Why all the furor he seemed to be asking. "It would not seem unreasonable for historians to offer their informed judgment on the way history should be taught in our schools." Schlesinger thought that the "slant and spin of interpretation and emphasis" in the 1994 version of the *National Standards* was flawed, particularly the world-history standards. He dismissed the attempt to give equal emphasis to Asian and African origins of American institutions. "Democracy, representative government, freedom of speech and the press, due process, religious toleration, human rights, women's rights . . . are peculiarly European in origin. . . . Why pretend otherwise." (Actually, many of these have little discernible precedent in European history. They are uniquely American; Europeans conceded as much when they looked to us for inspiration, and we ought to be able to boast about that.) But whatever problems existed could be remedied "easily," said Schlesinger. There was an outcry and Nash and the NCHS "responded as scholars should. They took note of objections . . . and produced a redraft. The revised standards seem a sturdy and valuable document, sober, judicious and thoughtful." But then, Schlesinger was a well-known Democratic political figure, and his remarks might not have been purely disinterested.[38]

Schlesinger saved what he could of the professional historians' authority, but he could hardly deny that it had suffered. As Ravitch later recalled in her own postmortem on the debate, "In a model of democratic discussion and professional responsibility," the standards were refashioned. But that reframing was not left to the historians.

"Gary Nash and his colleagues at the . . . NCHS center responded professionally and enthusiastically to the Committee on Basic Education's report," but the professionals had gone too far in using "race, class, and gender" lenses to refocus their view of the past. Ravitch had little use for those historians who thought "the public" ill-informed.[39]

Enola Gay at the Smithsonian Museum

At the same time that the *National Standards for United States History* was undergoing fine-tuning, a controversy erupted over an exhibit that was planned to accompany the display of the World War II bomber *Enola Gay* at the Smithsonian Air and Space Museum in Washington D.C. The *Enola Gay* exhibit that Smithsonian curators contemplated and the script they prepared for it went beyond the restoration and display of a famous aircraft that carried the atomic weapon that destroyed Hiroshima. They placed the aircraft within the larger context of the dropping of the atomic bomb and the end of the war.

Since the 1960s, New Left historians had been vocal in their criticism of the destruction of Hiroshima and Nagasaki by atomic weapons, arguing that use of the bombs was unnecessary in military terms and primarily intended to awe the Soviets. In effect, their use was the beginning of the Cold War. Some military historians who had little use for the New Left interpretation of these events nevertheless agreed that Japan would have fallen without our dropping the bomb at all, or that the second bomb, at Nagasaki, was unnecessary, or that some demonstration of the potency of the bomb without killing thousands of civilians would have convinced the Japanese to surrender.[40]

But the planned exhibit unleashed a firestorm of criticism from conservatives. Once more they accused the experts of partisanship. This time the experts were the public historians at the museum. Public historians work for local, state, and federal government agencies as curators of museums, guides at national parks, and as interpreters at commercial historical recreations. They preserve historical records, sites, and artifacts. They are consultants to businesses and expert witnesses in lawsuits. Many train as academic historians but elect to work in the public arena instead of the classroom. The National Council on Public History, founded in 1980, had 850 members in 2003, and cooperates with the AHA and the OAH among other organizations. In fact, in that same year over 1,750 members of the AHA listed their primary occupation as outside the academy, presumably in public history jobs. Given the millions who visit the Smithsonian's museums and similar sites all over the country, it may well be that most Americans get their idea of our past from exhibits that public historians prepare and manage.[11]

From the moment that Martin Harwit took up his duties as director of the Smithsonian Air and Space Museum on Monday, August 17, 1987, until his resignation in 1995, his time was consumed by the Enola Gay controversy. Many individuals and lobbying groups wanted the *Enola Gay* exhibited, but with widely varying purposes. Paul Tibbets, pilot of the *Enola Gay* on its fateful mission, dropped in and asked that the bomber be restored to its former condition but left a monument without a message. The veterans of the 509 Bomb Group wanted a memorial to the B–29 fliers, and believed that the atomic bomb had saved many of their lives, as well as the lives of the troops who would have had to invade Japan. The Air Force wanted its wartime efforts shown in favorable light. Not to be ignored were aviation buffs who saw the restored aircraft as part of the history of wartime air technology. Peace groups wanted the exhibit to show the horrors of the war, in particular the devastation wrought on Hiroshima. Japanese politicians and private citizens wrote letters and followed with delegations. They wanted an exhibit that would show how they had suffered from the bomb. Members of Congress chipped in with demands of their own. The regents of the Smithsonian, with Chief Justice William Rehnquist at the helm, offered suggestions as well.

Harwit simply wanted the exhibit, with the *Enola Gay* as the drawing card, to tell a story. The issue was whose story was most important—the same problem that the drafters of the National History Standards faced. The *Enola Gay* had become a symbol whose meaning went beyond historical facts or interpretations. Depending on the way it was contextualized it could celebrate or denounce, excuse or indict, entire nations. In the end, on orders from the director of the Smithsonian, the original script for the exhibition was destroyed and employees of the museum were forbidden to circulate any copies in their possession.[42]

Professional historians were slow to see how this argument within the military history–museum fraternity affected the profession as a whole. But when the executive board of the Organization of American Historians awoke, it responded vigorously. On October 22, 1994, the board resolved:

> The OAH condemns threats by members of Congress to penalize the Smithsonian Institution because of the controversial exhibition on World War II and the dropping of the atomic bomb. The OAH further deplores the removal of historical documents and revisions of interpretations of history for reasons outside the professional procedures and criteria by which museum exhibitions are created.

On January 26, Brigadier General Roy Flint (ret.), the president of the Society for Military History, sent a letter to the Smithsonian regents saying much the same as the OAH resolution.

> While our members possess varying views about the history of World War II, we share a passionate commitment to freedom of speech and to providing the best scholarship with integrity. . . . The Smithsonian's prominence as the leading museum of our nation and its possession of the *Enola Gay* demand a full presentation of the context and history of those events. Even more importantly, the Smithsonian must stand publicly against the politicizing of scholarship in public discourse, and it must resist all efforts to impose conformity in the rendering of history.

It would be a "crippling blow" to public history, wrote the general, "if the institution conceals this exhibit, or directs the display of the artifacts without the history of [their] use or a discussion of the significance of the events."[43]

In 1996, a copy of the original script was published without the consent or assistance of the Smithsonian or any of its employees. It was controversial from its inception, in January of 1994, despite its authors' claims that the script was "the whole story" and it was just "reporting what happened." The assertion that any work of history could be "the whole story" and "reporting what happened" was one that consensus historians made all the time, and new historians laughed at its conceit. But in spite of the consensus-toned apologia, the script itself was not reflective of consensus history at all.[44]

The authors saw the war as one "marked by extreme bitterness. For most Americans . . . it was a war of vengeance. For most Japanese, it was a war to defend their unique culture against Western imperialism." In short, it was a war between two imperial powers. The authors took pains to avoid moral judgments, which in effect meant the omission of key elements of the Japanese war plans and conduct of the war. There was no hint that the Japanese routinely tortured and killed prisoners of war, subjecting some of them to chemical warfare experiments, or that the Japanese treated civilians in war zones with contempt at best and the utmost cruelty in some cases. In fact, the authors bent over backward to see events from the Japanese point of view, calling the bombing campaign against Japanese civilian centers like Tokyo "the ultimate demonstration of the destructiveness of strategic bombing . . . during which Japan would suffer incredible devastation" in violation of our own stated aims of avoiding civilian casualties. The Americans were racists, said the script's writers, and considered the "yellow peril" as a far more devious and dangerous enemy than the Germans. Yet the script made no reference to Japanese racism, a major facet of Japanese culture before, during, and after the war.

The script included a series of special segments called "Historical Controversies." Among these boxes was a discussion of the Japanese peace diplomacy of the spring of 1945. The authors concluded, "It is nonetheless possible to assert, at least in hindsight, that the United States should have paid closer attention to these signals from Japan." Most historians avoid this kind of editorializing. A second "Historical

Controversy" asked whether the United States could have ended the war in the Pacific sooner, without dropping the bomb, had Truman guaranteed that the emperor would not be deposed. The script proper continued along these lines, mentioning opposition from the scientists who invented the bomb and manufactured it, as well as from some of the civilians in the Department of War. A fourth box giving historians' answers to the question "Was the Decision to Drop the Bomb Justified?" concluded that the issue would "remain forever controversial." Fair enough—and certainly in tune with the way that new history regarded the historical process—but how did such a prediction fit with the authors' claim to have reported "what happened"?

The original script included a highly detailed and absorbing account of B–29 construction, the role of the new bomber in the war against Japan, crew training, the experiences of men on the missions over Japan, and how deadly Japanese air defenses could be—military history of a traditional, anecdotal sort that could not have raised the slightest objection from veterans. But the concluding portions of the planned exhibit were of an entirely different cast. Entitled "Ground Zero," with shocking photographs and sharply etched captions, it conveyed the horror of the bomb's impact. Anyone reading details like "People caught in the open within one kilometer of the blast experienced temperatures so high that the dark, heat-absorbing pattern of their clothing was burned into their flesh," would think twice about the mission's necessity.

The concluding section of the original script, "The Legacy of Hiroshima and Nagasaki," did not assess the legacy of the war as a whole, nor the legacy of Japanese imperialism, nor even the legacy of high-altitude bombing. It made ground zero rather than the *Enola Gay* the centerpiece of the exhibit. By implication, this section constituted a pointed condemnation of the decision to use the bomb. If "the bombing of Hiroshima and Nagasaki nevertheless played a crucial role in ending the Pacific War quickly," the necessity of the atomic attack was still "hotly contested." What was more, the script ended with the judgment that the use of the bomb started an atomic and then a nuclear arms race that continues to this day.[45]

The original script was amended in many ways during conferences with various interest groups in the winter and spring of 1994. A final, fourth version of the script omitted the final "Legacy" section entirely and left out much of the photography from ground zero. That was a part of the natural process of revision the curators encouraged. In their minds, the professional historian's expertise was not arrogant or exclusive. They welcomed the comments of those who condemned their work, and offered to discuss problems with their critics. But on January 30, 1995, when the new director of the Smithsonian, I. Michael Heyman, pulled the plug on the exhibition before it opened, he explained, "There are differences between a university and the museum world of the Smithsonian. Most people treat academic work as that of the professor—either as author or in the context of a presentation to a class or scholarly audience. Scholarly work, of comparable quality, translated into an exhibition in a museum, and in particular a national museum, however, is seen as an official statement and a national validation." In other words, the Smithsonian could only survive as a museum if it did not insist on academic freedom for its public historians. (Heyman did not note the fact he had waited until after the election of 1994—when the Republicans gained control of both houses of Congress and right-wingers dominated the party—to try to save the museum from its own historical professionals.)[46]

When the academic historians jumped into the fray belatedly, they found themselves, and the authority as experts that their careers in teaching, research, and writing history supposedly conferred on them, under attack. The professional public historians, in pressing the case for the new history's critical approach, once again became targets. They were called "cloth-headed" revisionists by the conservative columnist George Will and were berated by other conservatives who claimed to speak for the people. For these pundits, the exhibit seemed as anti-American as the National History Standards. David Thelen, the editor of the OAH's *Journal of American History* and a much published historian himself, offered a tempered response: "Our conversations with government, interest groups, and the public at large will be more candid if we acknowledge that scholars, like veterans, differ in their conclusions." The critics of the script and the exhibit retorted that the *Enola Gay*'s larger meaning was not supposed to be seen "from both sides," but from the right side. Gingrich explained why on February 6, 1995: "The same gratuitous touches that turned up in the *Enola Gay* exhibit text (for example, Japanese brave and noble, Americans racist and destructive) show up in many other Smithsonian exhibits now, and, to nobody's surprise, in the proposed history standards too."[47]

The conservative media portrayed a handful of experts too young to have seen combat and too preoccupied with political correctness to find fault with the Japanese opposed to thousands of veterans who knew first-hand about the horrors of war, and about who was really responsible for them. The *Wall Street Journal* editorialized that "academics" were "unable to view American history as anything other than a woeful catalog of crimes and aggressions against the helpless peoples of the earth," and the *Washington Post* warned that something must be done to counter "the carping of elitists [historians] dedicated to tearing down national morale." Next to the conservative pundits' commentary on the op-ed pages appeared angry letters to the editor condemning the relativism of the exhibit. Political cartoonists had a field day with the historical "revisionists" at the museum and their academic comrades.[48]

There is a last chapter to this saga. It has two verses. First, on August 18, 2003, at its annex in Dulles, Virginia, the Air and Space Museum unveiled a restored *Enola Gay*. The director of the annex, General Jack Dailey, said that the exhibit, opened to the general public in December 2003, would focus on the restoration project itself and the technological advances of the B–29 over other bombers at the time. There was to be no mention of the Japanese side of the story. The second verse: the phrase "*Enola Gay*" has become a generic reference to supposedly too-relativist historical exhibitions whose script is too critical of the United States. Thus, when the Smithsonian prepared an exhibit on sweat-shop workers in the American textile trades, a fashion industry spokeswoman called it "a diatribe against our industry . . . another *Enola Gay*."[49]

The Impeachment and
Trial of President Clinton

In the same troubled time for historians in which Nash acceded to
the revision of the National History Standards and Harwit stepped
down rather than go along with what he saw as a political decision
regarding the *Enola Gay* exhibit, President Clinton was laying the
groundwork for his own impeachment and trial. By engaging in
White House wantonness with an intern named Monica Lewinsky, he
compromised his own stature and that of his office; but in refusing to
admit to it under oath, was he committing impeachable offenses?

For scholars, the question required serious research into the historical records. But on a practical level, it was a question that would
be answered by the House of Representatives. The House is given
exclusive power by the U.S. Constitution to impeach officers of the
United States, including the president. In the past, members of the
House had claimed that an impeachable offense was anything that a
majority of the House said was an impeachable offense. In the case of
President Clinton, rather than insisting on such a broad and overtly
partisan definition of its own power, the House Judicial Affairs Committee held hearings on the scope of impeachable offenses, at which
leading constitutional and historical scholars testified.

I had coauthored a book on the Founders' views of impeachment
and was contacted by Sean Wilentz, a Princeton history professor,
early in October 1998. He was gathering signatures for the anti-
impeachment advertisement that he, Arthur Schlesinger, and C.
Vann Woodward planned to publish in the *New York Times* on October
30. I had no qualms about historians joining to protest publicly the
proposed grounds of impeachment, though I did share with Wilentz
my concerns about the petition's claim that this impeachment would
endanger the Constitution.[50]

Senator Max Cleland of Georgia, a trained historian, was concerned about the House Republicans' views of the open-ended scope
of their impeachment power, and at his request we conferred on the
historical precedents. I suggested that however the House character-

ized impeachable offenses, the Senators were supposed to be both judges and jurors in impeachment cases. What the lower house might see as impeachable, the upper must weigh according to different standards. Just as a prosecutor may be swayed by many concerns having nothing to do with the merits of the case, so the majority of the representatives might be swayed by their party affiliation and their antipathy to the person in the Oval Office. Senators Cleland and Tom Harkin, of Iowa, would later raise this point during the Senate trial of President Clinton, and Chief Justice William Rehnquist, presiding over the trial, confirmed its validity.[51]

In the meantime, Wilentz was not the only historian to involve himself in the final stages of the impeachment quarrel. The advertisement he drafted had over 400 signatures when it appeared in the *New York Times* on October 30, 1998. In it, "historians speaking as citizens" warned that "the theory of impeachment underlying these efforts is unprecedented in our history." Some of the signers were conservatives, most were liberal in their politics, but all agreed that partisan politics should not dictate the outcome of an impeachment vote. The open letter warned of dire consequences to the future independence of the presidency and begged Congress "to get back to the public business."[52]

Key signers, including Wilentz, Schlesinger, and the Pulitzer Prize–winning constitutional historian Jack Rakove, went the next week to Washington to testify before a subcommittee of the House Judicial Affairs Committee as Wilentz conceded during the hearing, —"at the invitation of the White House." On January 8, 2000, Rakove, too, admitted that he had volunteered to testify, offering his services to a law school colleague at Stanford on the Clinton legal team. Plainly, the anti-impeachment cadre of historians recognized that they were wagering their scholarship and expertise in a political contest.[53]

And what the historians who went to Congress said raised many of the same issues as the National History Standards squabble and the *Enola Gay* fight. Wilentz spoke at some length and his testimony captured the drama and reflected the essence of the anti-impeachment argument. He did not condone the president's conduct. He was there "to defend the institution of the presidency, the Constitution, and the rule of law" from being subjected to the same politicization process as had occurred in 1994 and 1995. He then made a historical (and as it turned out a historic) prediction: "Any representative who votes in favor of impeachment, but who is not absolutely convinced that the president may have committed impeachable offenses . . . will be fairly accused of gross dereliction of duty and earn the condemnation of history."

Politics had made strange bedfellows of the historians on this occasion. Wilentz, an acolyte of the new history, had nonetheless discarded the notion of how historians worked that emphasized multiple viewpoints and evolving understandings of past events, which Nash had posited during the NHS fight. Wilentz had also rejected David Thelen's notion that historians must tell the public that historians often disagree, in favor of an older, essential-facts-from-which-no-one-can-dissent view. Wilentz had adopted the tone of the impartial, objective consensus historian when he pointedly warned one pro-impeachment congressman, "Later generations of historians will judge these proceedings" and pronounce a verdict. Wilentz warned: were members of the House to "go through with the impeachment, disregarding the letter as well as the spirit, of the Constitution, defying the deliberate judgement of the people . . . you will have done far more to subvert respect for the framers, for representative government and for the rule of law than any crime that has been alleged against President Clinton."[54]

In abandoning the nuanced, self-critical approach of the new history, Wilentz had taken one step over the line from disinterested expert to expert witness in the adversarial legal sense. Historians are often called upon by law firms to serve as expert witnesses in litigation. Historians notably served in this role in civil rights cases. For example, C. Vann Woodward and Alfred Kelly helped the NAACP deal with historical questions in *Brown v. Board of Education* (1954). In the 1960s and 1970s, historians worked for lawyers representing Indian tribes in the effort to regain ancestral lands and for states quarreling with one another over boundary lines and water rights. More recently, they have provided research and testified in reapportionment (voting rights) cases and suits involving the dangers of tobacco products, lead paint, and asbestos. There is a corporation that recruits and trains historians for this occupation and supplies their names to law firms. More informal networks within the historical profession helped to recruit the over 50 historians who have assisted defendants in tobacco litigation. Corporate expert witnesses are paid well—$150 to $200 per hour is the low end of the scale these days.[55]

There is some question in some historians' minds as to whether supplying research and testimony for hire after being coached what not to say ("trained" is the word the lawyer-handlers of the expert-witness historians use) comes very close to violating our professional ethos. Jonathan D. Martin, who holds a Ph.D. in history, is a lawyer, and most recently served as law clerk to a federal district court judge, has written: "The adversary process requires lawyers to spin the law and facts to serve their clients; lawyers are not expected, or even permitted, to be balanced and impartial. Historians, by contrast, should be open to all evidence they might encounter, and they accentuate the very ambiguities, contradictions, and inconsistencies that lawyers work doggedly within ethical bounds to hide or to smooth over."[56]

The AHA's *Statement on Standards* requires that historians disclose "all significant qualifications of one's arguments" and must not "misrepresent evidence." What is more, professional historians are enjoined to "strive to bring the requests and demands of their employers and client into harmony with the principles of the historical profession." Some expert witnesses believe that they are doing just what the AHA requires. J. Morgan Kousser, who has spent the past two decades testifying for racial minorities in voting-rights cases, regards the experience as "affording opportunities to tell the truth and do good at the same time." William Stueck, another historian who has become a veteran expert witness for tobacco companies, has told me that in every case in which he was involved, the plaintiff, the plaintiff's family, and the plaintiff's counsel did not deserve a windfall monetary award, at least insofar as his research persuaded him. The plaintiff knew very well how dangerous cigarettes were and chose to continue smoking. As Stephen Ambrose, testifying for the tobacco industry in 1994, put it, one would have to be "deaf and blind" not to read the warning labels and still believe smoking was safe. The tobacco companies won the case. (Ambrose, a lifelong smoker, succumbed to lung cancer in 2002, but never brought a suit against the cigarette manufacturers.) What is more, expert historical witnesses are enjoined by their lawyer-handlers not to deviate from literal truth, and most lawyers (along with their witnesses) in public-interest cases regard historians' testimony as "pure."[57]

Even if the historical expert witness gathers and arrays information according to the best historical methods, the result is not the best history. James Mohr was one of the prime authors of the so-called "Historians' Brief," a friend-of-the-court brief in which he used historical arguments to defend the right of a woman to an abortion in *Webster v. Reproductive Services* (1989). Mohr has said that the lawyers did not want to hear about the complexities of the matter—they wanted a clear statement supporting their clients. In *Patterson v. McLean Credit Union* (1989), involving discrimination at the workplace, Eric Foner signed a "friend of the court brief" on the meaning of the 1866 Civil Rights Act that directly conflicted with the account he gave of the act's purpose in his prize-winning book *Reconstruction: America's Unfinished Revolution.*[58]

Indeed, the very purpose of expert-witness testimony is to establish the rights of one party to the litigation against the other, not to represent the uncertainty of historical findings. Surely the new history would have a hard time in a court of law. (Not by accident many of the expert witnesses for the tobacco companies are not supporters of the new history.) In any case, after listening to the war stories of historians who have done research, written briefs, and testified in voting-rights cases, I have come away struck by how different their attitude toward opposing expert-historian witnesses was from the collegiality one usually finds among historians who disagree in academe. Ordinarily, they bang heads with one another then go off to have dinner together. Not so historians in the adversarial system of litigation. They really come to dislike one another. In *Equal Opportunity Commission v. Sears, Roebuck, & Co.* (1981), a case involving equal pay for women that is now infamous among historians, the entire profession seemed to choose sides between the conflicting testimony of two women's historians, Rosalind Rosenberg (for Sears) and Alice Kessler-Harris (for the female employees). It may be a symptom of litigation fever or simply the result of losing a case after so much work, but whatever the cause, the entire process demeans the historians and subjects them to public scorn as well.[59]

Wilentz was vilified for posing as a neutral after his testimony. Congressman Henry Hyde of Illinois, the Republican leader most responsible for the impeachment, "revived the cluelessness-of-the-eggheads routine." He joked that an intellectual could be defined as "someone educated beyond their intelligence." The conservative author and lawyer Ann Coulter was even more vitriolic about Wilentz's comments, agreeing that "history would track down" the members of Congress—but only those who voted against impeachment, a crew of "gutless idiots." Ironically, in light of their expert-bashing rhetoric, Hyde and Coulter were joined by conservative academics such as Robert George, a Princeton professor of government and a colleague of Wilentz's. He lampooned the open-letter signers for their overdramatic pedantry. "The message is one that Americans by now should be very leery of: 'Trust us, we're professors.'" Bruce Schulman, a historian at Boston University, tried to put the conduct of historians in the impeachment episode into a more neutral context. Sympathetic to their role, he was forced to admit that "the public, for its part, greeted the erudite pronouncements of historians . . . with yawns. The nation ignored its scholars, viewing their research as irrelevant technicalities or partisan propaganda." But Michael Beschloss, a historian of the American presidency, commented, "Historians must be optimists—especially historians of America, a country and system with almost infinite capacities for regeneration and healing." If President Clinton could be forgiven, perhaps the public would also forgive the academics who supported him.[60]

What Next?

The historians of the 1990s found themselves in a public arena where image and spin control trumped nuanced, thoughtful scholarship, and terms like "politicized" and "politically correct" had no fixed meaning. Some historians, like Marc Trachtenberg, accused the AHA itself of becoming "politicized." Eugene Genovese agreed. The association was "specialized, careerist, bureaucratized, and politically conformist." The demand for more studies on race, class, and gender to the exclusion of other fields "uncomfortably resembles the McCarthyism of the 1950s," he said. "It is being imposed by presiding cliques that have made ideological conformity the primary criterion for holding office."[61]

When conservatives spoke of "thought police," they were referring to liberal professors in the classroom; when liberal academics spoke of the thought police they meant the American Enterprise Institute, the Republican-led corporate think-tanks, and conservative news commentators. Battles over curriculum escalated into wars over public relations. Conservatives responded to the liberal speech codes of the 1990s with demands for intellectual diversity and bills of rights for conservative students and professors. The historians had tumbled willy-nilly into this contest for control of language, a war of sound bites rather than sound reasoning.[62]

What did it all mean for the academic historians' reputations in the public mind? First and foremost, the history professors lost their mystique. As much as they had been lambasted for living in an ivory tower, distance had lent enchantment to the stories they told from that height. Now conservatives accused them of standing at the doors of the classroom and the gates of the college barring the way to conservative students and charged that they spoke with one highly partisan voice to anyone who would listen (a nice twist on the consensus theory that the leftist historians had so roughly handled). According to Alan Kors, a conservative historian at the University of Pennsylvania (and thus a self-confessed oddity), "This is one of the most difficult things. One is desperate to see people of independent mind willing to enter the academic world. On the other hand, it is simply the case they will be entering hostile and discriminatory territory." Robert George agreed: the conservative who wanted to be a humanities professor is "going to run into intense discrimination trying to find a job." Websites for students to report the bias on the part of their professors began to appear, and the reports on them invariably cited cases of liberal professors forcing their opinions on captive student audiences.[63]

Bewildered, furious, feeling betrayed, eager to punch back with no targets, many at the top of the historical profession keenly felt barbs like the free-lance journalist Christopher Shea's thesis that the "the professors [have] tin ears." But in a real sense, Shea was right. In September, 2003 the *Journal of American History* introduced a new feature, an on-line "interchange" on the "practice of history" among nine leading senior historians. All were liberals; some were a little left of liberal. All embraced the new history. Their topic was change in the practice of history since 1970. It is unfair to them to repeat only snippets of the conversation, out of context, to make a point, but the interchange inadvertently does make a point about the elite professionals of the generation that won their academic credentials in the sixties and after. One participant, Patricia Nelson Limerick, a historian of the West, wrote: "Our field may have been the most 'retrograde' of all, in terms of its racial and gender exclusivity. Now young scholars are engaged in all kinds of boundary-blurring investigations." Alan Taylor, a historian of the early American period, chipped in: "The new approaches have offered considerable gains: gender as a major category of analysis is now well established; race is understood as actively daily constructed rather than as a universal given; and most scholars now recognize the importance of native people in all colonial regions." Nell Irvin Painter opined, "We need some Karl Marx alongside our Foucault."[64]

Although the comments were not as polished as the texts of articles or books, and like all performances in the theater of academe, the contributors wanted to impress one another as well as to inform readers, one can imagine how an educated layman, not to mention an ordinary American, would respond to some of the contributors' phrasings. "Boundary-blurring"? "Race . . . actively daily constructed"? "Some Marx along with our Foucault"? After all they had been through, historians still did not get the message. There was a broad unfulfilled need to make the practice and the product more, not less, intelligible.

In 1994, David Thelen, then editor of the *Journal of American His-*

tory, warned that the "obscurity" of the professional historians' writing had made it "remote from everyday life." The scholars were too busy "dazzling" one another with "the unfamiliar and erudite." The editors of the 2003 interchange raised the same question when they asked the panelists: "Does the recent call to write for a broader public undermine the legitimacy of scholarly discourse among historians?" It was the obverse of the real question historians should have been asking themselves after a decade in the eye of the storm: Were they losing their most important readership and forfeiting their authority by writing more and more about less and less? David Hollinger, an intellectual historian, dismissed the question with a sharp retort: Don't "forget that the larger community of readers we call 'the public' is less able than our trained, learned colleagues to evaluation the truth of what we write." He was adamant. "We should be proud of the fact that our profession is a profession of experts, of people who know that they are talking about." Taylor and Painter were a little less antagonistic to general readers, but they too urged their (professional) audience to seek peer rather than popular applause. It was simply a matter, in Taylor's words, of "clinging to our principles." It would soon appear that even this was not easy for the professionals to do when confronted with evidence of fraud.[65]

PART II

Fraud

CRITICS OF THE NATIONAL HISTORY STANDARDS, the planned *Enola Gay* exhibit, and historians' role in the Clinton impeachment berated the historians involved in them as frauds, and hinted that the academics' bias had led them to knowingly misrepresent the past. By leaving out faith, heroes, and noble deeds, the new historians were concealing essential facts about American history. On the other side, historians like Gary Nash and Sean Wilentz implied that those who bashed professional historians had their own nefarious agenda. They wanted to swindle Americans out of their true history. However one couched or weighed these charges and countercharges, by the end of the 1990s no one could doubt that academic historians and their historical writings were in disarray. The public had lost confidence in the professors and they had lost faith in themselves. Historical scholarship faced a crisis.[1]

Even the prestigious American Historical Association could not hide a growing concern among its ranks for history's reputation. The decade of the 1980s had begun with Bernard Bailyn at the helm, calling for a "retelling of stories," a reunification of all the many highly technical findings of the younger generation of new historians. He was confident that this synthesis could be attained and in 1981 he devoted his address at the annual convention, "The Challenge of Modern Historiography," to a brief summary of the many highly specialized fields that needed to be incorporated into the story. In effect he was saying that his colleagues should bring consensus history up to date.[2]

In 1997, Joyce Appleby delivered a very different presidential address to the annual convention: "Today, we confront a challenge. . . . The static in our conversation with the public comes not from an inappropriately positivistic view of history but from its very opposite—confusion about the nature of historical knowledge and the amount of credibility it deserves. Such confusion can well incite indifference, even antagonism." And it had. Appleby desperately wanted the public to understand how the new history had changed the very foundation of how historical knowledge was acquired:

> You can't learn what history has to impart if you start with a false idea of what history is and how historians—amateurs and professionals alike—acquire knowledge about the past. Even worse, without this understanding, you become susceptible to rumors of cultural warfare and academic conspiracies. Doubts about the validity of historical knowledge having been registered, they must be addressed.[3]

The challenge, to Bailyn's mind, was to modernize consensus. He never doubted that history was discoverable or definite, nor that getting from facts to narrative was a problem that had to be explained. By contrast, in Appleby's thinking the crisis was not the indeterminacy of history (which she took for granted), but to explain to the public how we get "from facts to narratives." Bailyn was the last of the great neo-consensus historians, and he assumed that the public trusted him and the history he wrote because of who he was and the authority of his writing. Appleby had witnessed a public uprising against the new history's thoroughgoing rejection of master narratives like Bailyn's and all elite professional historians' claims of expertise and authority.

Appleby's earnest effort at damage control notwithstanding, it was clear that historians stood at the edge a chasm so deep and wide that no one could see its bottom or cross it. Public confidence in them and their product was at low ebb. If the authority and strength that internal unity once had given the profession was forever gone, a framework of shared ethical values might still hold the profession together and even, in time, enable it to regain its earlier prestige. But a structure of this type, imposed from above, crossing over all subfields and specialties, would stand only if it was rigorously maintained and courageously upheld. That, in turn, meant that a body of historians must draft an honor code and be prepared to enforce it. Then the true defrauders would be revealed.

The AHA had always regarded itself as the conscience of the profession. In the consensus era, this meant keeping a high moral tone in history and laying down criteria for membership in the profession. In the age of the new history, the term "professional" meant something quite different: ensuring that many voices were given an equal opportunity to be heard. In 1974, the AHA created the Professional Division, which was "specifically charged with responsibility for ethical concerns." At first, these included opening the doors of the profession to minorities and women. Then, in May 1987, after 14 years of drafting and revision, the American Historical Association published its *Statement on Standards of Professional Conduct*. The document is constantly evolving, but at its unchanging core is what can best be called an integrity code:

> Scholars must be not only competent in research and analysis but also cognizant of issues of professional conduct. **Integrity** [boldface in the original] is one of these issues. It requires an awareness of one's own bias and a readiness to follow sound method and analysis wherever they may lead. It demands disclosure of all significant qualifications of one's arguments. Historians should carefully document their findings and thereafter be prepared to make available to others their sources, evidence, and data, including the documentation they develop through interviews. Historians must not misrepresent evidence or the sources of evidence, must be free of the offense of plagiarism, and must not be indifferent to error or efforts to ignore or conceal it.[1]

The elevated moral tone of the code and the generality of its strictures reflected the varied interests of the many individuals who crafted it and the even more diverse concerns of the historians whose work it covers. It is inspiring rather than punitive and holds aloft a standard for all historians to follow. At the same time, the drafters of the code knew that even the most honored historians are not always so willing to admit their own biases or so swift in "disclosing . . . all significant qualifications" of their arguments. Errors of fact creep like sneak thieves into otherwise exemplary works of scholarship. Histori-

ans are only human, their task is never really finished, the publishers
are impatient, and the demands of colleagues and students for new
discoveries and fresh interpretations is unrelenting—but the fact
remains that with the code and the Professional Division in place,
professional historians had the means to reply to their many critics.

Poised to make the AHA the conscience of the profession by policing it, its leaders faced an immediate test of wills. It would have been
hard to find an American historian in 1991 unaware of the accusations that had been leveled against Stephen B. Oates, a University of
Massachusetts history professor. Oates was a prolific biographer and a
widely respected one. His 1977 biography of Abraham Lincoln, *With
Malice Toward None,* was something of a classic, and had often been
called the best one-volume assessment of a very important and very
complicated man. Then, starting in December 1990, a series of Lincoln scholars accused Oates of plagiarizing liberally Benjamin
Thomas's 1952 *Abraham Lincoln—A Biography* (Knopf). They brought
the matter to the Professional Division, and under its vice president,
Susan Socolow of Emory University, it investigated.[5]

In the meantime, all the parties involved, and even some not
directly affected, began giving statements to the newspapers. While
Oates and his accusers fired volleys at one another, friends of Oates's
gained the support of 22 other Lincoln and Civil War scholars,
including C. Vann Woodward, who had been an AHA president, and
Eric Foner and James McPherson, future AHA presidents. The newspapers reported that the 22 had independently examined the evidence and exonerated Oates. That was not entirely accurate, as some
among their number signed on because they knew and trusted Oates.
However they reached their opinions, the 22 signers of a letter to the
AHA stepped in between the AHA and the warring parties, which
undercut the AHA's professional and moral authority.

Exposed on all sides, the AHA Professional Division sought the
assistance of scholars in the field, sending them portions of both
books and asking their opinion as to whether Oates had plagiarized
Thomas, and then took nearly a year and half to reach a decision in
the case. The division found that Oates should have been more careful in citing passages from Thomas's book. Oates's work had been

"derivative to a degree requiring greater acknowledgment of Benjamin Thomas's earlier biography." People close to the matter were not sure whether the division had found that Oates was a plagiarist or had exonerated him. How were those further away to make sense of the ruling? At first, Oates gave interviews in which he said he was pleased that the AHA found no plagiarism (it did not use the word in its statement), but as the matter dragged on, Oates threatened lawsuits, and denied that the AHA had any jurisdiction over him. He was not a member, and he never did cooperate with the inquiry; all his defenses were made in public forums or to the media. Finally, after another AHA investigation of his use of secondary sources in his other biographies, he accused it of being "an Orwellian body" that was "harassing and persecuting him."[6]

There had been some missteps in the handling of the case, and recognition of this resulted in important procedural reforms in the way that the division heard cases. One issue was confidentiality. In response the AHA promulgated a confidentiality rule, whereby none of the parties to the inquiry nor the AHA would release any information on it during the inquiry. Nevertheless, the Oates case was still an embarrassment to the Professional Division when I joined it in April 2002. Mentioned as a plagiarist in an aside by a *New York Times* reporter, Emily Eakin, in a January 2002 piece, Oates once more protested his innocence with a posting on the History News Network. He insisted that the AHA was a "self-appointed policeman," and added a new defense to those he had made originally: Oates said that Benjamin Thomas, a popular historian, himself did not have notes—merely a bibliography—and much of what Oates supposedly took from Thomas actually was their common use of the same primary sources. Oates added in his HNN post that the AHA definition of plagiarism was too broad, particularly when the standard used was Lincoln biographies, many of which had no notes at all. Finally, how could he be found guilty under a definition of plagiarism promulgated in 1987, when he crafted his Lincoln book in 1977?[7]

In effect, Oates took refuge from the attack of professional historians and the Professional Division in the shibboleths of the old consensus history, reworked to fit the genre of popular history. What he said came down to the argument that if a work was popular, not academic, and if it did not lay claim to originality of research findings, it ought to be safe from attack. Facts were facts, and one could not be censured for relying on the same facts as one's scholarly predecessors—especially popularizers such as Thomas. Popular writers writing for popular audiences could not be held to the same self-righteous and inflexible standards as the integrity code proclaimed, even if authors did hold day jobs as university professors.

The Professional Division authorized Arnita Jones, executive director of the AHA, to publish a reply to Oates, which she posted on the History News Network in April 2002. In it she explained that the AHA "is not and cannot be the historical profession's police force," but added that it would continue to "uphold the standards of our profession." The AHA would not search for infractions, but it would investigate meritorious complaints brought to it. Robert Zangrando, formerly a member of the Professional Division and deputy director of the association, and a coauthor of the *Statement on Standards*'s passages on plagiarism, published his own response to Oates. Unlike Jones, who had to moderate her tone because she spoke for the association, Zangrando issued a stern rebuke to Oates, which was also posted on the History News Network: "Scrutiny in the best sense of that term is our surest guarantee for preserving the quality of our work and findings. . . . That again speaks to the need for an AHA response when a victim of plagiarism, a chance reader who spots misuse of sources, or any diligent practitioner wishes a review of possible abuses." Zangrando praised good faith and collegiality where Oates decried a "star-chamber" mentality.[8]

But for all Jones's careful wording and Zangrando's moral outrage, the fact remained that Oates's logic could shield any ethical misconduct, so long as it occurred in the context of popular history. The new history might have banished consensus from the academy, but consensus, wearing the garb of popular history, had proved itself to be armored against the integrity code and its would-be enforcers. At least that was the lesson the Oates affair seemed to teach. Leap across the chasm from the academic to the popular and no committee of inquiry would dare follow.

And a number of professional historians were making that leap. Helped by aggressive literary agents and savvy trade editors, a few historians were making it big in the popular book ranks. They joined the ranks of journalists and free-lance writers who got to see their books on the front table at Barnes & Noble, read their reviews in the national newspapers and journals of opinion, and wait for the royalties and prizes to roll in. In the meantime, stung by Oates's article and fearing that even more controversial major cases would come its way, the AHA announced the end of its 15-year experiment in adjudication. Who could blame the academic-turned-popular-writer if he or she concluded that the integrity code was pious humbug, and that popularity itself, like consensus in the old days, was proof against accusations of misconduct.

In law to defraud is to misrepresent or conceal with the intention of deceiving and the aim of gaining from that deceit. In historical scholarship, falsification, plagiarism, and fabrication were devastating types of fraud. They might not be indictable in a court of law, but they undermined the vary foundations of scholarly authority. What was more, they tested the profession's ability and willingness to police itself. The four cases that I trace in the remaining pages of this book cast their shadow over the Professional Division and the elected ruling council of the AHA as it decided to end adjudication. And they became symptomatic of the crisis that history faces.

CHAPTER 5

Falsification: The Case of Michael Bellesiles

I N 1985, MICHAEL BELLESILES WAS A RISING STAR among the second generation of new historians. In May of that year we shared the rostrum on a panel on early New York legal history, and I came away impressed with his passion for his subject, Revolutionary era Vermont, and his strong new-history convictions. Later, from down the road in Athens, Georgia, I watched with pleasure as Emory University in Atlanta rewarded his teaching and scholarship with tenure and promotion to full professorship, and sponsored the Institute on the Study of Violence in America, which he founded in 1987.

By the early 1990s, I was aware that his second major research and writing project, on early American gun culture, had taken on one of the most powerful political lobbying groups in America, the National Rifle Association. In its campaign against gun control it had adopted a take-no-prisoners attitude, but sometimes a scholar, like David facing Goliath, gets a chance to bring down a more powerful foe with a well aimed piece of work. Federal, state, and local gun control laws had gained some ground in the face of the NRA's implacable opposition. What a coup if a historian as passionate about research as Bellesiles could find evidence that the historical claims of the gun lobby, in particular its insistence that the widespread ownership and use of guns were necessary for the foundation of the American nation and were codified as rights in the Second Amendment, were made of straw.

Bellesiles's students have told me that he inculcated in them the ethical standards for research embodied in the *Statement on Standards of Professional Conduct*. They were not to falsify or misrepresent their findings; they were to keep accurate records of their visits to archives and libraries; and they were to fully document all the evidence they gathered. Falsification may have been systemic, systematic, and ingrained in consensus history, but it had no place in the new academic history, the history that Bellesiles taught. If consensus historians of yore could be excused because their biases were those of their time and place, the new history demanded a far more self-critical stance and willingly opened itself up to criticism by the scholarly community. Deliberately misrepresenting one's findings with the intent to deceive had no place in today's profession, and one would think that falsification would not for long escape discovery and censure.[1]

But if the target of a new historian was big and bad enough, and if the potential reward for bagging that target was great enough, even the best-trained and most honorable of new historians might be tempted to fudge research findings here and there. I imagine that Bellesiles, at some time early in his research into the gun culture in early America, faced this dilemma. Perhaps, as one of Bellesiles's most consistent supporters believes, he was merely "in the grip of a powerful insight." Bellesiles would later regard himself as a martyr to an unpopular opinion: "to question the American myth is to step outside of the mainstream." But there is no doubt that, in the end, he misrepresented his findings in his work, and when questioned about his findings, misrepresented how he obtained them.[2]

Bellesiles was not the first and will not be the last scholar to falsify his research. But his case is the most egregious of our era, and the way it played out came near pulling down the entire new history edifice. For Bellesiles used the assumptions of the new history against it, playing the professors against the NRA in a high-wire act of arrogant bravado. He knew that many in the liberal academic community strongly supported a gun control position, but a new history–style book that simply raised questions, refocused our thinking, and offered alternative interpretations of the conventional wisdom of gun ownership would only be read by a handful of other scholars and would not have much impact on the national debate.

There was another way to sell the message, however. Publish the book with a trade press so as to claim the kind of immunity from close professional scrutiny that the popular history authors enjoyed, but pack the book with pages and pages of endnotes, to display the skills of a professional historian. Cover lots of ground, from the colonial period to the Civil War, and lots of topics—hunting, probate records, militia service, gun repair, and marksmanship. Dazzle the reader with erudition and hammer the opposition with arguments. When conservative critics raise questions about the veracity of the research and the validity of the conclusions, accuse them of lacking expertise and exhibiting an excess of partisanship. When fellow professionals begin to raise similar questions about the work, claim that the NRA and its stooges are out to get him.

Bellesiles almost got away with it.

Smoking Guns

In the summer of 1996, I served on the panel on individual fellowships of the National Endowment for the Humanities' Division of Research Programs; our panel evaluated Bellesiles's project on gun culture in early America. He wanted to examine probate records at local courthouses (principally inventories of estates) and militia records to determine the number of guns in early America. I gave it my highest rating. It was not approved by my colleagues, however. I do not think the decision was political. My colleagues on the sitting panel were all supporters of the new history, and most of what we voted to approve had its stamp of approval. I wonder, however, whether this chapter of our professional history would have turned out differently if we had voted to support his work, giving him a full year of fellowship support to travel to collections and take careful notes.

Bellesiles told a committee of inquiry empaneled by Emory University in the spring of 2002 to examine his historical research that he had begun looking at Vermont probate records in 1983 as part of a study of the distribution of consumer goods and consumption patterns on the early national frontier. At the time one of the most controversial topics among early Americanists was the extent to which the market and consumerism reached into the frontier. Guns were among the items he had proposed to inventory, if he happened to see them, but his focus was not guns. Over the course of the decade, he expanded the geographical scope of his study to western New England, Pennsylvania, and North Carolina and at the end of the decade he narrowed the focus of his research to guns.[3]

Though Bellesiles did not point this out to the committee of inquiry, the battle over gun control and the debate over the Second Amendment had taken a new turn in 1989. In that year, a University of Texas Law professor, Sanford Levinson, had published a seminal article in the *Yale Law Journal* entitled "The Embarrassing Second Amendment," in which he argued that the Second Amendment could be read as a guarantee of the individual right to own and bear firearms rather than as concerning militia service—the latter being the position of gun control advocates. The article was widely cited and spun off dozens of law review pieces supporting the individual-rights, or standard view, of gun ownership. Some of the jurists who read the amendment in this fashion, including Levinson, favored some kind of gun control, but the National Rifle Association warmly embraced the new scholarship because it could be used to oppose all gun control. Bellesiles had already founded an interdisciplinary program on violence in America, at Emory University, which concerned itself with gun control, and he could not have missed the impact of Levinson's article.[4]

Bellesiles counted guns in probate inventories by dividing pages of yellow legal pads vertically, tallying the inventories he looked at with a tick mark on the left of the page and then noting which of those inventories had a gun in it with a tick mark on the corresponding right side of the page. There does not seem to have been a systematic sampling design. Instead, he would find an archive with a run of records and read them. When he reported these methods to the committee, he had already lost (about which more shortly) all of the records of his visits to the courthouses and other research locations and could supply the committee with only a few "loose papers" documenting his findings. The committee report noted with some asperity his lapses of memory and his disorderly manner of keeping records of his research. Ordinarily, historical researchers keep account of their travels, including the archives they have visited and the records they have viewed. At the very least, the Internal Revenue Service requires either receipts or a travel ledger if one is to claim itemized occupational expenses. For whatever reason, Bellesiles could not recollect nor had he retained a written log of his travels and his findings, save for the yellow pads themselves, and he claimed that they were ruined by a flood in his office in April 2000, long before his work came under scrutiny by the committee.[5]

Professional historians often present specific pieces or overviews of their research at conferences. These presentations are similar to filing a claim on a gold mine or recording a land purchase in the courthouse deed book. They issue a public notice of the work and stimulate interest in it. Bellesiles presented his early findings in a paper at the annual conference of the Organization of American Historians, in April 1994. At that time he handed out sheets listing guns he found in estate inventories from Massachusetts, Vermont, Westchester County, New York, and Indiana. Thirty-five percent of the Westchester County inventories had guns. I was not at that session, but folks I knew told me they came away excited by what he said and its potential impact on the debate over gun control.[6]

In September 1996, Bellesiles published a stunning article on gun ownership in early America in the OAH's *Journal of American History* (*JAH*), titled "The Origins of Gun Culture in the United States, 1760–1865." Most of the articles in the *JAH* are exhaustive in their detail. Bellesiles's had a different quality; a Da Vinci–like sketch for a full dress painting to come, striking in its clarity of argument:

> Before we accept an individual right to gun ownership in the Second Amendment, we must establish who were "the people" who were allowed to "keep and bear arms." Did they in fact own guns? What was the popular attitude toward firearms? Did such perceptions change over time? We will find that gun ownership was exceptional in the eighteenth and early nineteenth centuries, even on the frontier, and that guns became a common commodity only with industrialization, with ownership concentrated in urban areas. The gun culture grew with the gun industry.

If Bellesiles was right, then the Framers of the Bill of Rights had not foreseen the necessity of an armed America—only the value of arming the militia. Individual gun ownership was not an inalienable right.[7]

Bellesiles's reference to the Second Amendment placed the article at the center of the ongoing debate about the Framers' intentions for the Second Amendment. The article supported those who favored gun control, and who read the Second Amendment as referring to the militia (the preamble to the amendment is "A well regulated militia being necessary to the security of a free state") rather than individual gun owners. Bellesiles's piece was recognized as a powerful disproof that the frontier experience and the Revolutionary War were inseparable from widespread gun ownership. The article also claimed that militias were poorly armed and that neither the danger of Indian attack nor the allure of hunting persuaded Americans to buy or maintain firearms.[8]

In his article Bellesiles elected to display crucial numerical evidence in tables and use these tables to generate graphs. It was an appropriate decision. One of the major subfields of American history that blossomed in the same years Bellesiles was studying history at the University of California at Irvine was quantitative historical methods. Derived from the innovative work of historical demographers, economic historians, and political scientists, the movement had spread widely in fields as diverse as occupational studies, urban history, family history, electoral voting studies, and legislative bloc analysis.[9]

Bellesiles embraced the quantification methodology, with some limits:

> There are problems attached to the use of statistics in history. . . . The most thoughtful critics of quantitative methods agree that there is no real alternative to employing these records, with the proper caveats inserted. Without such efforts at quantification, we are left to repeat the unverifiable assertions of other historians, or to descend into a pointless game of dueling quotations—matching one literary allusion against another. Far better to match an entire collection of documents with other primary materials; for instance, probate and militia records. . . . In other words, the aggregate matters.[10]

Nevertheless, in Table 1 of his *JAH* article, "Percentage of Probate Inventories Listing Firearms," Bellesiles violated one of the most basic of quantitative design principles. He did not provide the total number of cases (conventionally symbolized by the letter N). In any table one should always report the true, raw figures. For Table 1, N would have been the exact number of probate inventories Bellesiles looked at, and he should have given smaller subtotals for the number of cases represented by each of the columns and rows of his table, although some authors neglect this step.

It does not matter whether one is simply summing probate records that mention guns (counting 1, 2, 3, and so on and adding up the result), or computing percentages of ownership by dividing the number of inventories listing guns by the total number of inventories consulted, or entering the numbers in some highly sophisticated computer program—one always tells the reader the raw number of cases. They are the raw numbers from which the percentages are calculated in the first place. Bellesiles only had to add up the tick marks on his yellow pads. Indeed, he must have already done this to calculate the percentages in each column.[11]

Another reason for Bellesiles to provide the total number of cases he viewed was to demonstrate that there were a sufficient number of cases in his sample to make the percentages a reliable reflection of guns in all probate records. He had not looked at every probate record. But had he looked at enough of them for his findings to be reliable? Bellesiles's Table 1 showed that on average, only 14.7 percent of inventories in the period 1765–90 included firearms. This supposedly rose to nearly 31 percent in the period 1849–50, when factories were turning out guns with interchangeable parts. But without knowing the totals who could say if he had looked at enough inventories to make his percentages trustworthy reflections of gun ownership in the entire society, much less to recheck his calculations?

In fact, Bellesiles's percentages were clearly wrong. Randolph Roth, a historian at Ohio State University, has been studying court records and tallying homicides for many years. He noted that according to Bellesiles's count, the "national average" percentage of probated estates with guns in the period 1765–90 was 14.7 percent. But the individual percentages in three of the four regions in this column of his table—"northern urban coast"—16.1 percent; "northern rural"—14.9 percent; and "South"—18.3 percent—were all higher than the national average he had calculated for the entire column. Only the "frontier" cell for that period had a lower percentage, 14.2 percent, than the national average. To pull the national average down to what Bellesiles said it was, more people would have had to die with probated estates on the frontier than in all of the other three areas combined. But in fact the frontier population was neither so wealthy nor its deceased so old as the populations in the other three regions; hence the frontier cell would have had far fewer total probated estates. (The more settled the region, the greater wealth of its individuals, the more likely they were to have probated estates. This is not only theoretically true, it reflects the findings of everyone who has studied early American probate records.)[12]

There were other anomalies in his data and computations. Westchester County, New York, was not one of the counties he named in his source note. In fact, no New York counties were named. But the 35 percent figure that he reported for Westchester in his 1994 OAH paper would have changed the percentage in his "rural north cell." There is no explanation why this data, on hand in 1994, was not included in the *JAH* article. Also, the one secondary source he noted on the probate records in the text and in the accompanying footnote 7 was Alice Hanson Jones's *American Colonial Wealth*. It is based on 919 sample inventories from the year 1774 weighted to resemble the population of the various colonies at the time. He suggested that he had integrated "Alice Hanson Jones's valuable probate compilation into the study." He did not note that she had found much higher rates of gun ownership in the 1776 era than he had. Over 54 percent of estate inventories she examined listed guns. Had he actually incorporated her inventories into his Table 1, the calculation of the "national average" for 1760–90 would have been even more improbable than it was. In fact, when questioned about his use of her figures, in 2002, he explained that he had not actually used her figures.[13]

Bellesiles committed a second serious methodological error in the way he noted the sources for the data in Table 1. He claimed to have based his calculations on data taken from various counties' courts records. Under Table 1, as its "source," he wrote, "probate records for the following 38 counties (modern names)" and listed various counties in New England, the Middle Atlantic region, and the South. In addition to not giving the actual number of inventories, either the overall total or the totals of the probate records, for each of the courthouses he visited, he neglected to say which courthouses or historical societies or state libraries he visited to see the records. In order to avoid the very confusion that Bellesiles's source note creates, scholars using manuscript court records always cite the title of the record and its year(s) in their source reference notes. All proper modern professional reference notes are supposed to allow a reader to go directly to the source, but reading the list of counties at the bottom of the table, one could not tell exactly what Bellesiles had found or where he had found it.[14]

Bellesiles was neither a quantitative expert nor a trained legal historian, but he knew better than to omit the size of his data sample and he knew how to give correct references to court records. In his Pelzer Prize–winning article on violence in Vermont in an earlier issue of the *Journal of American History*, published in 1987, he had been meticulously correct in both respects. He knew how to report actual numbers and how to cite country court records.[15]

One can only speculate on Bellesiles's motives in not including the actual figures and the precise court record citations his 1996 article. Other articles in the same volume of the journal in which his article was published included raw numbers in their tables and full references to the legal materials, just as Bellesiles had in 1987.[16]

It is not clear why the journal allowed Bellesiles to publish the piece without supplying this information. Editors are the first and last readers of submissions to journals, and editors have the authority to reject articles without sending them out for readings. Editors read all submissions and make a preliminary decision on whether they are good enough to send to outside referees for a final judgment. Why did the editor of the journal at this time, David Thelen, not spot these problems? Bellesiles later thanked Thelen for his "enthusiasm." One can see why Thelen might have been especially eager to publish it. Thelen's interest in the relation between past and present is well documented in his own words. Overturning received wisdom on a subject of such historical and present-day importance was a sure-fire attention getter for the journal.[17]

Why did none of the journal's outside referees catch the omissions and require that the information be included? All articles submitted to the journal are "blind-refereed," meaning the reader does not know the identity of the author and the author does not know the identity of the outside reader. The referees are specialists on the subject and sometimes members of the editorial board. On occasion, the editor solicits comments from four or five scholars who know the subject well. On September 29, 2001, one of the referees, Don Hickey, of Wayne State College in Nebraska, went public with the substance of the report he had written. Hickey recalled, "In the mid-1990s, the *JAH* asked me to referee B's article-length manuscript. I was not much of a student of early American guns but was probably asked to evaluate the manuscript because I'd written on the military history of the early republic and the War of 1812. The manuscript appeared to be based on massive research and it made a compelling argument." In fact, the article went on to win the 1996 Brinkley-Stephenson award for the best article in the journal that year, apparently ratifying Thelen's judgment and Hickey's recommendation.[18]

The journal's cite checkers might still have saved the day. All articles accepted for publication in the journal are "cite-checked" by graduate students at Indiana University working on the staff of the journal. Bellesiles went out of his way to note the "careful reading" his article received at the *Journal.* But it is almost impossible for cite checkers, no matter how diligent they may be, to double-check manuscript or archival reference notes. They would have to go to the archive. The alternative, requiring some sort of photocopy or other copy of the originals, would have been unwieldy and expensive. But the cite checkers, could, however have asked that Bellesiles be more precise in citing where he got the numbers. Belatedly, Thelen's successor at the *JAH* conceded, "Our editors, peer reviewers, and staff could and should have noticed the flaws in Table 1, such as the failure to include the sample sizes in each of the table's cells, to indicate which counties were used to construct each regional category, and to note the exact locations of the country records used." But if the journal had insisted on such information, could Bellesiles have provided it?[19]

Recounting

When Bellesiles's book, *Arming America* (Knopf, 2000), was published four years later, Table 1 appeared in the first appendix, on the probate records, and Bellesiles simply cited the article as his source for the data in the table without further elaboration. The table did not provide the totals of probate records he consulted or the subtotals for any of the rows or columns. The table in the book was almost exactly the same as the table in the journal article, with the same percentages in every row and column of the table, except some changes were made to the last column, for the years 1830–32, and a new column was added, for the period 1849–50. The source note now said "probate records of forty counties" instead of "probate records for 38 counties." The location of the probate records for Los Angeles and San Francisco was not given (and remains something of a mystery to this day), nor was the precise origin of the court records for the other counties added.[20]

The actual numbers of probate records Bellesiles allegedly consulted appeared in only three places in the text of the first hardcover
print run of the book, on pages 13 and 266 (frontier inventories) and
page 109 (inventories from Providence, Rhode Island). On page 13,
Bellesiles wrote that "an examination of more than a thousand probate records from the frontier of northern New England and Western
Pennsylvania revealed that only 14 percent of the inventories
included firearms." By page 266 the number of inventories for the
same frontier counties in the same time period had grown to 1,200.
Moreover, round numbers are always suspicious; the researcher who
actually counted should have an exact number at hand.[21]

A sound design for collecting this data, based on the actual total
numbers of surviving probate records, would require that the sample
for the other three regions in the early period have even more cases
than the frontier, because more people with estates lived in the Middle Atlantic region, New England, and the Southern region than on
the frontier. Even if Bellesiles simply stopped at 1,200 cases for each
region, it still would give a total of 4,800 probate records for the first
column.

A sound sampling design would also take into account the larger
number of probated estates in later years. One could thus expect that
columns two through six would have progressively more cases in
them than in column one. Still, if Bellesiles limited his research to
4,800 cases per column, he should have had a total of 6 x 4800, or
32,800, probate records.[22]

The paperback edition of the book, published in 2001, finally revealed the total of probate inventories Bellesiles allegedly examined:
11,170. This was less than half the number one would expect with any
appropriate sampling design. Still, it was a solid number. The paperback edition had gone into production sometime in 2000, so he must
have been able to provide this exact number of cases to Knopf's production staff at that time. Either he tallied the tick marks or he consulted his notes and found the exact number. It was appropriate if
somewhat late in the day for him to introduce the raw figures,
although he still did not break them down by county or region.[23]

Still, one wonders how he could supply the totals in time for the

2001 paperback edition of the book and not for the original print run. Bellesiles had told the committee of inquiry and various other inquirers that a flood in his office at Emory University had covered his yellow pads with water and ceiling plaster and destroyed the original data tallies. That flood occurred in April 2000, after his book went to press, so it should not have prevented him from including the 11,170 figure in it. On the other hand, if he simply did not total up the tick marks for the first edition, he could not have gone back to the water-soaked pads and totaled the tick marks for the second edition because by his own account the flood had destroyed all but a few loose papers of his data. It was a mystery how supposedly lost original data could reappear to enable him to add the number of cases to the 2001 paperback edition, then disappear once again when the committee of inquiry sought the data from him.[24]

The second actual count of cases Bellesiles provided in the hardcover edition, on page 109, came from Providence, Rhode Island. He listed 186 probate inventories "for property-owning adult males" from 1680 to 1730. Ninety of these "mentioned some form of gun." In the 2001 paperback, these inventories had declined to 181 "property holding adults" (no longer restricted to men), of which "eighty-eight mention some form of gun." In both editions, note 133 on page 110 gives the source of these figures as Horatio Rodgers et al., *The Early Records of the Town of Providence*, a 21-volume compilation. The interesting fact about this easily checked published source is that in it Bellesiles found that 48 percent of the inventories included guns, a figure much closer to the conventional wisdom of early American gun ownership and wildly at variance with Bellesiles's own figures for inventories in unpublished records during the same period for the same region. (Recall that he found 16.1 percent for the "northern urban coast.")[25]

The citation in the paperback edition of *Arming America* indicates that between the first publication and the reissue of the book a year later Bellesiles either consulted or decided to include five more of Rodgers's volumes of court records in his computations, but the result of adding these was a decrease in the number of inventories, from 186 to 181, even when women were included in the latter count. How the

addition of more source material on more people can result in a
smaller absolute number of inventories with guns is hard to imagine.

The Controversy

B ellesiles's answers to queries about these problems raised questions about not only his methods but his honesty. Either he went
to the courthouses and looked at the originals, or he examined
microfilm of the docket books, or he sent a research assistant to do it,
or he did none of these. Falsification of data is about the most serious
offense a historian can commit, but poor methods and worse memory
may lead to inadvertent errors that do not amount to intentional falsification. The fact is that scholars attempting to follow Bellesiles's foot-
steps when he admitted that he could not recall where he went would
either fail to find his tracks or discover that the sources he said he
used and the counties he said he visited (or the microfilms of country
records he said he used) did not provide evidence to support his
claims.[26]

Bellesiles had to expect that his work would be controversial. A
piece of research that turned so much received wisdom and conventional narrative on its head could expect to attract attention, both
favorable and critical. In fact, the book started attracting attention
before its publication, and much of the dialogue took place in cyber-
space, on the History Net, or "H-Net."

The H-Net was born on June 24, 1993, when Richard Jensen, a historian at the University of Illinois, Chicago, announced the creation
of an electronic message board. It would allow everyone interested in
history to post queries, comments, and announcements, "to easily
communicate current research and teaching interests; to discuss new
approaches, methods, and tools of analysis; to share information on
access to library catalogues and other electronic data bases." In short,
it tied historians to the revolutionary changes in information storage
and access on the web. There were thirteen original H-Net listservs in
various historical specialties. Anyone could sign on and gain access to
postings as well as post items themselves. Each listserv had a modera-

tor or editor and an editorial board. Defamatory and nonhistorical submissions are not posted. (By 2004, the H-Net had grown to over 100 listservs, each with a "discussion log" that allows anyone to review past postings on particular issues. Like membership, these were open to all, not just professional historians and their students.) The H-Net helped bridge the gap between the professional and the amateur historian.[27]

Revisiting the discussion logs for H-Law, H-OIEAHC (the early American site sponsored by the Omohundro Institute for Early American History and Culture), H-SHEAR (overseen by the Society of Historians of the Early American Republic), and H-South between 1996 and 2003 reveals that Bellesiles's assertions were soon targeted by amateur historians with an interest in American gun culture.

Clayton Cramer, a software engineer and gun enthusiast who received his master's degree from Sonoma State University in 1998, was the first to post his concerns about Bellesiles's conclusions on the H-Net, in 1997. Cramer and Bellesiles knew one another before the 1996 article was published. In 1995, Cramer was doing research for his master's thesis in history and wrote to Bellesiles for assistance. In the course of the correspondence, Cramer was able to supply Bellesiles with some sources on gun laws. Early in 1997, their contact was still friendly, with Cramer as graduate student seeking advice and Bellesiles as senior scholar helping out, but soon thereafter their relationship changed.[28]

When Bellesiles's "The Origins of Gun Culture in the United States, 1760–1865" was published in 1996, Cramer wrote a letter to the *JAH* questioning the typicality of Bellesiles's anecdotal evidence. Cramer's letter was little more than a list of antebellum travel accounts showing the presence of guns and controverting Bellesiles's quotations, but Cramer did hint, "If the probate data shows that guns were owned by a small minority of white males, then I conclude that the data suffers some serious selection bias problem."[29]

Bellesiles was shown a copy of Cramer's letter before its publication, as is the *Journal's* standard procedure, and published his reply in the same issue as Cramer's letter: "I could add a few more quotes to Cramer's list. Such would be an easy task, since my source would be the same as his: the 'Firearms Alert' internet site run by the National Rifle Association." When I happened on this exchange, in 1998, I was struck by the fact that Bellesiles did not refute, indeed did not attempt to refute, the substance of Cramer's criticism; he belittled it by associating it with a partisan, nonscholarly Internet source, and dismissed Cramer as a gun nut and crank. Bellesiles then suggested that all the anecdotal evidence the NRA members assembled would not shake his views, for

> The whole point of my article, which I may not have made clear enough, was to get beyond random anecdotes. . . . Cramer does not address any possible weakness in my use of probate records, nor does he cite any specific bias which such records may introduce into the final statistical base—both of which are issues worthy of discussion. Instead, because the results of the research call into question some underlying ideological perspective of his, he dismissed the statistics, and me as a scholar, out of hand. Such an approach is not only ill-mannered and illogical, it is also highly unprofessional.[30]

Each man accused the other of politicizing history (hardly a novel claim for historians to make in 1997), but in this and in subsequent H-Net exchanges, the issues shifted from politics pure and simple to historical expertise versus partisan amateurism—a framing of history and historians that characterized all of the controversies of the mid-1990s.

Cramer targeted Bellesiles's probate evidence in a posting on the H-Net:

> I used to think Bellesiles' claims about the scarcity of guns in early America were simply wrong, either because his sources were atypical, or that Bellesiles was engaged in wishful reading of his sources. After looking up a number of his sources, especially the official papers, ones that are easy to find out here on the West Coast, I have changed my mind. He's not just wrong; he's intentionally deceiving people.

To display his evidence Cramer set up a website. Bellesiles, watching for comments on the lists, replied immediately. (In fact, throughout the first year of these H-Net exchanges, Bellesiles replied to just about every posting on every list within a day or so of the posting's appearance.) "Clayton Cramer hates my research, and has for some time," Bellesiles wrote, reprising the tone of his December 1997 response to Cramer's letter in the *JAH.* "In the months before the appearance of *Arming America,* Mr. Cramer has flooded the web with condemnations of the book, many of which completely misrepresent my work." Bellesiles insisted that Cramer's attack was based on his NRA affiliation, and reminded subscribers that the book did not even mention the NRA until the next-to-the-last page. "There is of course no pleasing Mr. Cramer unless you agree with him entirely. . . . I remain confident that any fair-minded and unbiased scholar who looks at the complete records will be satisfied that I reported the material accurately."[31]

The distinction that Bellesiles made between Cramer, "a long time advocate of unrestricted gun ownership," and himself as a pure scholar was overdrawn, given Bellesiles's recognition of the impact of his findings on NRA and other lobbyists against gun control, but clever. The new history allowed for advocacy pieces, so long as they were based on sound scholarship. The book might not dwell on the Second Amendment or the NRA, but his *Journal of American History* article began with the debate over gun control, and before *Arming America* appeared, Bellesiles contributed an essay on gun control to Saul Cornell's anthology on the Second Amendment. Bellesiles's introduction to his own edited volume on violence in America, *Lethal Imagination: Violence and Brutality in American History,* published in 1999, also commented on the danger of guns in modern society. In a message he posted on H-South a week after he replied to Cramer, Bellesiles said, "I make no apology for being a political activist as well as an historian. I also make no pretense that I am completely dispassionate about the issue of current public policy. I do not expect an historian to be completely unaffected by the linkage between history and current policy." Bellesiles also made what he called a "sales pitch" for the Study of Violence program at Emory that went beyond disinterested scholarship.[32]

Hounded by Cramer and the NRA, Bellesiles had taken refuge in

his status as a scholar, and implicitly called to his side the entire profession. Whether or not they agreed with his stance on gun ownership
(and I suspect most did), surely academic historians would not let
their expertise be impugned by a rank and partisan amateur like
Cramer. In fact, historians had taken strong public stands on violence
in our society and its relation to gun control. The debate over the
meaning of the Second Amendment blurred the line between scholarship and advocacy, but nothing in the AHA integrity code bars a
professional historian from advocating what he or she believes to be
sound public policy. I have been a contributor to the gun control
movement since the inception of the Brady Bill, and in 1999 I signed
the friend-of-the-court brief that the Brooklyn Law School professor
David Yassky prepared for *United States v. Emerson* (a gun-control case
making its way through the federal courts) arguing for the constitu-
tionality of federal and state gun control. Fellow signers included
both Bellesiles and Stanley Katz.[33]

When Bellesiles placed his own advocacy of policy on a higher
plane than Cramer's by arguing that "an historian has certain obligations of accuracy that transcend current political benefit, especially
because it [is] so easy to get away with misquoting or misrepresenting
the past to a larger audience that has not a clue how to determine
what the truth is," he stood on the professional side of the chasm,
looking across at the amateurs and partisans. He treated Cramer, a
"non-historian," to an "introductory history lesson" of how historians
must "analyze events and ideas while providing the contexts for documents." Perhaps unintentionally, Bellesiles's two-pronged appeal to
expertise—he was an expert; Cramer was an amateur; experts had to
be accurate because "readers" did not know what was true, whereas
interest-group zealots had no such obligation—read like the same
sort of elite academic snobbery that opponents of the NHS and the
Enola Gay exhibit attributed to the entire history profession.[34]

Over the course of the two years after publication of *Arming America*, postings on Bellesiles's findings appeared on the early American,
southern, and legal-history listservs. The submissions were not contin-
uous, but had a punctuated, episodic quality. When Cramer, or, later,
the Northwestern University law professor James Lindgren, or other

contributors made further discoveries about Bellesiles's research, they posted it. A flurry of responses followed, led by Bellesiles himself. Then the *Arming America* correspondence on the H-Net died down, until the next discovery and volley of accusations and answers. A handful of individuals who were working on guns, or militia, or some related topic—in effect a crew of regulars—dominated the conversation.

Most of us just read along, until the debate spread from one book and its author's trustworthiness to the ethical limitations on criticism of another's work. Academic freedom—the freedom to express opinions on our and others' work—is essential to all scholarship. Truth arises from collective examination of one's work by others, a civilized give and take within the community of scholars, and that cannot happen when scholars are threatened with violence. Bellesiles reported that he was receiving "hateful, threatening, and expletive-laced telephone calls, mail, e-mail, and faxes." He charged that "dedicated individuals flooded my e-mail with hundreds of copies of the same message. Others sent repeated viruses from anonymous web addresses that drove me from public e-mail and 'hacked' my web site, altering and deleting material." So bitter and personal had the exchanges become that some critics of the book publicly accused Bellesiles of fabricating the attacks to gain sympathy for himself and immunity for his book.[35]

Richard Bernstein, a legal historian and law professor, led the charge to reestablish civility of discourse and protect academic freedom. Another scholar chipped in, "Whatever merit this discussion has for us, as scholars, vituperation and exaggeration do not add to that merit." However controversial a work of history might be, however politicized the debate might become, however committed the polemicists might be to their side of the story, nothing justified personal attacks. In the meantime, Bellesiles had become concerned that he could not give a paper without being harassed, nor could those who wished to hear him safely attend. When the Omohundro Institute for Early American History and Culture, based in Williamsburg, Virginia, received word that he and his family had been personally threatened, the council of the institute met and resolved "personal attacks upon or harassment of an author, as we have seen directed at Michael A. Bellesiles following publication of *Arming America* . . . to be inappropriate and damaging to the tradition of free exchange of ideas and the advancement of our knowledge of the past." H-Law immediately endorsed this resolution, as did the OAH and the AHA. No historian can work effectively in an atmosphere of suspicion and recrimination.[36]

In December 2000, Bellesiles announced that he was putting up a website on which he would answer questions about his use of the probate records. Bellesiles's website at Emory, www.emory.edu/HISTORY/ BELLESILES/Probatehome.htm, in mid-2001 offered probate materials allegedly from San Francisco, North Carolina, Ohio, Rhode Island, Maine, Massachusetts, Vermont, Tennessee, and New York (the long-lost Westchester County) records. None of these exactly duplicated the materials lost on the yellow pads. In September, he closed down this site, claiming that a hacker had planted on it unsuitable materials, but James Lindgren, a Northwestern University law professor, had accessed it shortly after it was created, and he did not find any evidence of hacking or hackers. As I write this, the website is listed by Emory as a "broken link."[37]

One of the central defenses that both Bellesiles and his supporters made in the course of the dueling postings on the H-Net was that the probate records only constituted a small portion of the entire book— some 13 pages more or less, depending on how one counted references to probate. Should the rest of the work, over 600 pages with endnotes and appendices, be thrown aside because of the errors in some numbers? As Emory's interim dean, Robert Paul, put it, "The question of the validity of the overall theses in the book . . . still remain to be settled by scholarly debate." On April 28, 2001, the constitutional historian Jack Rakove, of Stanford University, earlier a strong supporter of Bellesiles and his thesis, commented on the H-Net, "If [Bellesiles] has really screwed up, or distorted the evidence, then he should be held accountable, and if he can't defend his use of sources or rebut and refute the criticisms, then his work should be discredited." But Rakove was hosting a conference on the Second Amendment at Stanford that same weekend, and he included Bellesiles as a panelist. Rakove did not feel that defects in Bellesiles's statistics undermined his general point. Nor did Johns Hopkins's Michael Johnson, who found "much of his general argument is sound and is supported by impressive evidence." Paul Finkelman, a law professor and historian at the University of Tulsa, made the strongest case on the H-Net for the utility of the book's "overall argument," whatever problems might mar individual bits and pieces.[38]

The Reviews

Running parallel to the conversation within the scholarly community was a body of more public commentary on the book, the author, and the issues. The publication of *Arming America* by a high-quality house such as Alfred A. Knopf in the late summer of 2000 was a major publishing event. Bellesiles had calculated well when he choose this distinguished press. The Second Amendment's meaning was at stake, and perhaps gun control as well. As Sandy Levinson wrote in October 2001, "The marketing of *Arming America* very definitely emphasized its relevance to contemporary issues of gun control." The academics solicited for blurbs by Knopf were ecstatic in part because the book knocked the gun lobby. It was "a book for scholars and above all citizens," a "myth-busting tour de force. Bellesiles moves to the front rank of American historians with this deeply researched, brilliantly argued, energetically written and timely book. It is an instant classic"; "This is stunning history, brilliantly argued"; "At long last a superb book that systematically dismantles one of our most cherished and dangerous national myths"; "an astonishingly original and innovative book"; "This book changes everything. The way we think about guns and violence in America will never be the same." Michael Zuckerman of the University of Pennsylvania's history department pronounced the book's research scrupulous and the evidence overwhelming that the gun culture was the invention of the gun manufacturers in the years before the Civil War. Over a year before, Charlton Heston, then president of the NRA, had warned its members against the book and suggested that the author had "too much time on his hands." Bellesiles shot back that Heston needed to earn a Ph.D. in history before he began commenting on scholars' work.[39]

The early reviews ran from favorable to ecstatic. Two prize-winning senior historians, Edmund Morgan and Garry Wills, reviewed the book for the *New York Review of Books* and *The New York Times Book Review*, respectively. In fine, reviewers understood the policy implications of Bellesiles' work. So did Bellesiles, as he repeatedly indicated in his own defense. The gun lobby was out to get him, but within the circled wagons of the community of scholars he was safe.[40]

Roger Lane, a criminal justice historian at Haverford College, was one of the last of the favorable reviewers. He noted that the book was already much controverted when he completed his review for the *Journal of American History* in September 2001, and that the book had "added new ammunition" to the debate over gun control. He commended Bellesiles for shattering the myths and taking on the NRA and the gun lobby. Lane conceded that the book was overlong, repetitive, strained to make its points, and exhibited minor errors of fact, but

> . . . if these are the small bones to pick, the skull, spine, and ribs of this powerful book will all stand up. If specialists may argue with some of it, one reason is simply its great sweep. . . . If Bellesiles is sometimes careless in citing outmoded authorities in support of peripheral points or sets up scholarly targets made partly of straw, his own research is meticulous and thorough.

Lane was particularly impressed by the probate data.[41]

The only similarity between the favorable reviews and the unfavorable ones was the authors' obsessive use of gun metaphors. Criticism of the book first appeared in conservative journals, newspapers, and at first was the work of gun control opponents. Cramer's response was predictable, and his venue, *The National Review,* a conservative opinion journal, seemed an obvious place to debunk Bellesiles. Over time, however, other negative reviews began to surface whose authors were academics publishing in places that other academics could not ignore. For example, Robert Churchill, a young historian whose field was the early militia, and Joyce Lee Malcolm, a senior historian, published critical assessments in *Reviews in American History* and the *Texas Law Review*, respectively. They not only thought the analysis flawed, they doubted the validity of the research.[42]

By May 2001, the main tenor of the reviews had shifted from the admiring to the critical. Daniel Justin Herman's review, in H-Pol, suggested the direction the public debate was beginning to take. "There's been a count, there's been a recount, and there will be recounts of recounts, no doubt, yet no clear winner has emerged." Herman admitted that the book was "polarizing" and that the magnetic field conformed to the poles of the gun control issue. He judged the book "both mighty and flawed. . . . Given Bellesiles' recitation of gun censuses, gun manufacturers' reports, militia and army records, and probate records, *Arming America* seems practically, uh, bulletproof." (To his credit, Herman winced at his own gun metaphor.) But "able and reputable critics" had convinced Herman that something was wrong with Bellesiles's probate figures. What was more, "his use of anecdotal evidence was even more questionable for being half analyzed"—that is, Bellesiles would quote or cite a passage that made no mention of guns and thus seemed to support his view, while observations of the abundance of guns and Americans' skill in using firearms could be found a few pages away in the same source. Overall, Herman considered the argument too thesis driven and too hyperbolic in its claims, and Bellesiles too unwilling to admit anything of his opponents' case. In the end, Herman found the book "generated questions" and "issued challenges" for further research— two of the polite death notices that reviewers pass on books that are mightily flawed. The tide was now running against Bellesiles and the undertow was fierce.[43]

The hit-or-miss quality of the H-Net exchanges and the dueling book reviews left many readers bewildered, and thus everyone welcomed news that Bellesiles and other experts in the field would be joining combat in a special forum in the *William and Mary Quarterly*, scheduled for the winter of 2002. Richard Bernstein, writing to H-Law, suggested that "all interested parties ought to wait for the appearance next month of the January 2002 issue of the *William and*

Mary Quarterly, which will feature a full and careful examination of *Arming America*, as well as a response by Prof. Bellesiles." The *Quarterly* is the premier journal in early American history. Like those published by the *Journal of American History*, articles published in the *Quarterly* are refereed by outside scholars and editorial board members and cite-checked by graduate students at the Omohundro Institute for Early American History and Culture in Williamsburg, Virginia, the *Quarterly*'s sponsoring organization.[44]

In the forum, Gloria Main, an expert on Colonial probate records, found "something is amiss here." Ira Gruber, a military historian looking at the treatment of militia, concluded that Bellesiles "regularly uses evidence in a partial or imprecise way." Randolph Roth, focusing on homicide and guns, noted that he agreed with Bellesiles's policy aims but "the thesis of *Arming America* is wrong, and wrong in ways that will make it more difficult to persuade the public to back policy measures its author supports. . . . It is impossible to know what went wrong in Bellesiles' study, because he does not discuss his sample size or his sampling technique."[45]

Bellesiles replied in his contribution to the forum by retreating from some of the more fulsome claims he had made for the importance of the probate records: "Probate records alone cannot supply an entirely useful portrait of gun ownership. Other sources must be brought to bear on the problem. . . . I minimized reliance on probate materials in *Arming America* and canvassed a diversity of sources on America's gun culture. . . . At no point [in the book] do I state or even imply the centrality of probate records to this study." He repeated this qualification in *Weighed in an Even Balance*, a pamphlet he prepared to answer his critics on the occasion of the Soft Skull Press edition of *Arming America*, in December 2003: "As I presented my findings at historical conferences over the 1990s, I was persuaded that probate records are deeply flawed as a source."[46]

Neither his piece in the *Quarterly* nor the *Weighed in an Even Balance* statement agreed with the stance he took against Cramer in the 1997 *JAH* exchange, where he had touted his probate record statistics as the way to escape dueling quotations, nor with what he had written in the course of a 2000 H-OIEAHC exchange. "While some historians have expressed skepticism about probate records," he wrote at that time, "many historians, me included, have made use of these materials as a way at getting at the dynamic nature of the early American economy and the structure of the household economy." What was more, throughout the original edition and paperback version of the book he based important substantive points on the probate records, for example, "As the probate records of the [colonial] period evidence, gun ownership was far less widespread than is generally assumed."[47]

Vexing contradictions continued to plague his defense in *Weighed in an Even Balance*'s short chapter on the probate records. In it he did not dispute the specific corrections of his critics but he did for the first time introduce the startling new claim, "Because of the many conversations I had with scholars over the years about probate records I decided to make little use of them in *Arming America*." He continued that he had reduced his use of the probate records in the book to "four paragraphs and a sentence (pp. 74, 109–110, 266–67, and 386)."[48]

Not once in the course of the long controversy over the probate records, running from 1997 through 2001, had he ever made a concession of this sort to his critics. What is more, his comment in *Weighed in an Even Balance* about the appearance of probate records in the book is wrong. The probate records are not only mentioned on the pages he gave, but also on pages 148–49, 262, and, most important, in Table 1, on page 445. Bellesiles doesn't mention this table or its many problems in his pamphlet, and the table's absence from the pamphlet's chapter on the probate records speaks volumes.

Inquiry

B esieged by Bellesiles's critics, in the spring of 2002 Emory's history department arranged for a formal inquiry into his research methods by a panel of expert historians: Stanley Katz of Princeton and Laurel Thatcher Ulrich of Harvard, both specialists in early American history, and Hanna Gray, an emerita at the University of Chicago who had served as the president of the university. Emory wished to know whether the committee felt that Bellesiles had violated the official guidelines set forth in "Policies and Procedures" and had committed "misconduct in research," including "the intentional fabrication or falsification of research data."[49]

In the meantime, the NEH stepped in—very publicly—to demand that its name be taken off the fellowship Bellesiles then held at the Newberry Library, in Chicago, and Emory gave Bellesiles paid leave for the fall semester. In March 2002, the critics whose comments had been published in the WMQ forum went on NPR's Morning Edition to repeat, in even stronger terms, their concerns about the research. Roth declared, "It really appears to be far beyond—it's way beyond the normal level of error in a scholarly work." Ronald Hoffman, director of the Omohundro Institute, would later agree that Arming America was "marred by unusually careless and disorganized scholarship."[50]

On July 10, after three months of investigation that included a series of conversations and one full-dress interview with Bellesiles, the Emory committee of inquiry reported that it could not determine whether Bellesiles had engaged in intentional fraud because of "the absence or unavailability of Professor Bellesiles' critical and apparently lost research records and . . . the failures of memory and careful record keeping." They went on, "Given his conflicting statements and accounts, it has been difficult to establish where and how Professor Bellesiles conducted his research into the probate records he cites." But his "subsequent failure to be fully forthcoming, and the implausibility of some of his defenses," led the committee to conclude that Bellesiles "did engage in 'serious deviations from accepted practices in carrying out [and] reporting results from research.'" In particular, "dealing with the construction of the vital Table One, we find evidence of falsification." According to the committee, he had violated Emory's regulations on research and the integrity code of the AHA, "the standard of professional historical scholarship." These were the judgments of Bellesiles's peers, not partisan amateurs. His reputation in tatters (though he refused to admit wrongdoing), he resigned on October 25, 2002. Emory accepted his resignation, effective December 31, 2002.[51]

There was a swift denouement to the story. Classical tragedies revolve around hubris—reaching too high, refusing to see the consequences of overreaching, and crashing down hard. The tragedy of

Arming America was no different. In April 2001, Columbia University had awarded Bellesiles one of the coveted Bancroft Prizes in History. In December 2002, the university withdrew the award, an unprecedented act. The three-member prize committee would not comment when later asked why they had made the decision to award the prize to the book when it was already under fire, but one member has told me that the committee had no objection to rescinding the award.

To top it all off, on January 8, 2003, Jane Garrett, Bellesiles's editor at Knopf, told the Associated Press, "We are in the process of ending our contractual arrangement with Michael." Knopf would not go ahead with the revised edition it had previously announced and would not keep the book in print. When interrogated by the book's critics, both Knopf's spokesperson and Garrett's assistant replied that the press routinely "trusted" its authors to do their own cite checking. Despite the sneers and raised eyebrows of opponents of the book, trust always and inevitably lies at the heart of publication of scholarly works. At major trade publishing houses even as distinguished as Knopf, editors do not send books out to referees. Instead, when trade editors know, respect, and above all trust the authors or the agents who represent them, they feel comfortable in making a decision in-house about a manuscript. As another distinguished acquisitions editor has recently written, "The basis of the relationship between a historian and an editor, of necessity, must be trust . . . a good faith commitment by each party." As for checking "facts," it would be impossible for editorial staffs to check authors' facts—these publishers do hundreds of books a year and they do not have squads of graduate students to check citations. No one at PublicAffairs checked my reference notes. In the end, the relationship between trade editor and author must and will continue to rest upon trust.[32]

This was especially true of Jane Garrett, a Knopf senior editor. She has acquired and nurtured history manuscripts at Knopf since the early 1970s. In her stable of authors are Pulitzer Prize winners such as Bernard Bailyn, Gordon Wood, Jack Rakove, Laurel Ulrich, and Alan Taylor. No editor of history has ever had a more deserved reputation for helping authors and keeping faith with projects than Garrett. She reads all the manuscripts closely and follows their development, mix-

ing patience and prodding. I've known Jane Garrett since the fall of
1965, when I was starting graduate school and she was helping
Bernard Bailyn put out the first volume of *Perspectives in History*. I have
never published with Knopf, nor has Jane ever been my editor, but I
can say with absolute conviction that if one needed a person to model
for the integrity code, it would be Jane Garrett.[53]

"Weighed in
an Even Balance"

If Columbia University and Knopf agreed that the errors were significant enough to take action, Bellesiles still thought that the
errors could be remedied. He closed his posting on H-Law of November 3, 2003, with "'Oh, Lord, Forgive the Errata' [;] Philadelphia editor Andrew Bradford's last words, 1742," which sounds like a
concession that he had made mistakes. He admitted some of them in
Weighed in an Even Balance. Consequently, when I found a copy of the
new Soft Skull Press edition of *Arming America* in late December 2003,
I looked for Table 1 expecting to find corrections based on new
research in the original "38 counties."

I found the table in its familiar position in appendix 1, page 445—
but the table itself was entirely different from its predecessors in the
1996 article and the Knopf editions. The 38 (later 40) counties had
been replaced by 12, though the precise location of the probate
records and the citation of the court documents was still missing, and
fewer than half of the counties had entries in the first (1765–90) column. None of the new counties were from Massachusetts or Rhode
Island, supposedly the source of much of the probate data in the
2000 book, and the two California counties from the 2001 edition
were missing. To deepen the mystery, the Westchester County data
from Bellesiles's 1994 OAH talk had reappeared as eerily as it had dis-
appeared from the article and the previous editions of the book.

In the new version of Table 1 there were no percentages, only raw
numbers. That was fine; exact numbers are what should be reported

in tables. The total number of probate records examined for the entire table was now 2,353 instead of 11,170, as reported in the 2001 edition of *Arming America.* I noted also that the first column of the new table had 1185 records, but none of the other columns had more than 409, the error in sampling design that concerned me when I first looked at Table 1 in the article.[54]

The real problem was that these new figures, county records, and research were obviously not the same as in the article or the Knopf versions of the book. To be sure—and to be fair—Bellesiles had done what he should have done in the first place, gone to the courthouses or gotten the microfilms and kept careful records of his tallies. But what had happened to the data and records of the other counties he said he consulted? If for his article and the Knopf book he had actually consulted probate records at the archives, libraries, courthouses, or repositories where the records were stored, he could have gone back and redone the count. But he did not, and if Lindgren and Heather are right about what they found when they did consult probate records for these counties, he could not. Indeed, the new Table 1 was the strongest possible admission he could have made without a full and honest confession that he did not consult all those other records in the first place.

I calculated percentages myself, and found, for the first column (1765–1790), 256 probate records with guns out of 1,185 probate cases, or 21.6 percent. Even if one regards his new 21.6 percent figure as trustworthy and truly representative of the unexamined data, with it he has demonstrated that all his explanations of his earlier research—research he could not duplicate even when he set about reconstructing Table 1 for the 2003 edition—must be false. In his relentless drive to prove his thesis of a paucity of guns he had convicted himself of the charge of professional misconduct in his earlier presentations of his research.

By this time the profession was taking almost as much of a beating from the affair as Bellesiles himself. It seemed to one observer that "historians have ceased to read carefully and critically, even in awarding book prizes." Had the gullible professors been dazzled by trade reviews and media blitz? Consensus history grew out of an unstated trust between author and reader based on common values and prejudices. The new history replaced that inchoate and often narrow-minded trust with the integrity code, an explicit canon of trustworthiness based on training, peer review, and professional criticism. But the new history, in its eagerness to prove that consensus history represented the worst kind of politicization, neglected its own inclination to one-sided, moralistic preaching. New history is not by definition political in a partisan sense; in fact it complicates the stories it tells by adding social, cultural, and economic movements and motives to the political narrative. But new historians are often partisans in their classrooms and their opinion pieces. These new historians see history as a hammer to dent racism, poverty, and tyranny. As historian Elliott J. Gorn pointed out, "The irony is that, far more than most of us, Bellesiles was doing something very worthy: engaging an important public issue and bringing a historian's perspective to bear on it." But noble goals are not necessarily scholarly or historically minded. Bellesiles is a good man and often a fine historian, but motivated by the potential impact of his thesis, he apparently assumed that the ends justified the means.[55]

Bellesiles's condemnation by Emory University, the trustees of the Bancroft Prizes, and Knopf provided the gun lobby with information to blast the entire history profession. The NRA gloated and demanded that all copies of the book be removed from libraries. Gun control scholars became experts in damage control. Some among Bellesiles's early supporters, such as Jack Rakove, admitted error: "It's clear now that his scholarship is less than acceptable." Roger Lane, whose *JAH* review of Bellesiles's work had been supportive, saw the matter in more personal terms, according to Joyce Malcolm, who reported that he said, "I'm mad at the guy. He suckered me. It's entirely clear to me that he's made up a lot of these records. He's betrayed us. He's betrayed the cause."[56]

In a time when historians have become sensitive about the loss of public faith in their profession, and when the public has become wary of what historians promise they can deliver, trust within the profession becomes paramount. Whether or not Bellesiles's use of evidence was a misdemeanor grounded in occasional negligence and excusable zeal to prove a thesis or intentional falsification meant to deceive; whether or not the initial assaults on him were motivated by the politics of the gun lobby; he used the new history and its professional agencies against themselves. Even though H-Law, the Omohundro Institute, the OAH, and the AHA rushed to his side and stated principled objections to the politicization of history, they hesitated to ask the equally important question of whether he had manipulated them and betrayed their trust.

CHAPTER 6

Plagiarism:
The Cases of
Stephen Ambrose and
Doris Kearns Goodwin

M ICHAEL BELLESILES SOUGHT FAME AND FOUND
infamy; Stephen Ambrose and Doris Kearns Goodwin
were household names among readers when the stories of their misconduct broke in the media. Bellesiles was a new historian who fell
like Icarus into the gulf between popular and professional history;
Ambrose and Goodwin had advanced degrees and had taught college
students, but crossed over to the popular genre and stayed there.
Bellesiles's work never gained a popular following; Ambrose's and
Goodwin's popular followings were large and loyal. Bellesiles scoffed
at the myths of keen-eyed hunters and brave militiamen; Ambrose
and Goodwin burnished the reputations of heroes. But the three stories overlapped in one vital respect: Ambrose and Goodwin too had
violated a clause of the integrity code. They stole others' words.

While I was doing the research for this book, the media were pounc-
ing on one alleged plagiarism case after another. The late labor histo-

rian Philip Foner was denounced as a serial plagiarist for stealing from graduate students' unpublished papers; a book on the A-bomb scientists by a history professor at the Naval Academy, Brian VanDeMark, was withdrawn by the publisher, Little, Brown, and he was demoted in rank because it contained over 50 passages copied from other historians' work but not fully credited to them; and the *New York Times* reporter Jayson Blair resigned after other reporters and an internal investigation revealed that he had plagiarized others' reportage. On top of everything else, student plagiarism had grown to epidemic proportions. As one reporter graphically described the rash of cases: "the bills are paid, the recycling taken out; time to leaf through this month's crop of plagiarism accusations."[1]

Plagiarism is nothing new. Benjamin Franklin, writing as "Poor Richard," borrowed word for word from English books of homilies. In his doctoral dissertation, Martin Luther King, Jr., lifted entire passages from other theologians' work without giving them credit, much less using quotation marks. Years ago the satirist Tom Lehrer set plagiarism to verse in the "Lobachevsky Song," whose chorus included the line "Plagiarize, let no one's work evade your eyes . . . but please to call it 'research.'" Periodically there would be reports in the press that there had been a "rash of cases" involving journalists: a reporter would be fired, an editor would be reassigned, and commentators would scratch their heads trying to define plagiarism precisely.[2]

Most of the complaints that came to the Professional Division of the American Historical Association during my tenure on it involved plagiarism. As the most recent and authoritative essay on plagiarism among historians reminds scholars,

Whatever the cause and the actual number of cases, writers, readers, and teachers of history found plagiarism both infuriating and perplexing. It is infuriating because it is a species of crime—the theft of another person's contribution to knowledge—that educated, respectable people should not commit. It is perplexing because, despite the public shame that invariably accompanies revelations of plagiarism, it continues to occur at every level of the profession, from prize-winning historians to students just beginning their careers.[3]

It may seem that professional historians have become too sensitive to accusations of plagiarism, and, as Judge Richard Posner insisted at an AHA forum on plagiarism in 2002, "there is a danger of overkill" in what appears to be a crusade against plagiarism. As I can now reveal that I was the one who recommended that he be added to the AHA panel, I feel some responsibility for explaining his comment. In legal writing, particularly the crafting of opinions on the bench, reliance on earlier writings, including the adoption of unique phrases in their entirety, is not only a stylistic tradition but also the very marrow of the common law. Prior case law—the opinions of judges in earlier cases—sets precedent, and in our system of judging, precedent can be compelling. Thus we use without any citation to the author or quotation marks famous phrases such as Chief Justice Earl Warren's "all deliberate speed," written in his opinion for the U.S. Supreme Court's second, implementation, decision in *Brown v. Board of Education* (1955). In fact scholars still debate where he got the phrase (the usual suspect is Justice Felix Frankfurter, himself quoting his idol, Justice Oliver Wendell Holmes, Jr.).[4]

Historians do not allow one another such latitude when the author claims originality. Other disciplines' definitions of plagiarism involve the offender's seeking an advantage of some kind from the use of another's work, or include an "intent to deceive." For professional historians, however, plagiarism is a strict liability offense, like going through a stoplight. Plagiarism in historical writing has nothing to do with accuracy or inaccuracy. A book or article can be absolutely accurate and still be riven with plagiarism. Nor is plagiarism the same as copyright violation. The latter is a legal wrong that involves using material that is in copyright without permission from the copyright holder. For historians plagiarism is an ethical matter, not a legal one. It is plagiarism to take as one's own the words of other authors, even those no longer protected by copyright. As the AHA's *Statement on Standards of Professional Conduct* reminds us, plagiarism "takes many forms." These may include "the limited borrowing, without attribution, of another person's distinctive and significant research findings . . . or an extended borrowing even with attribution."[5]

In particular, in a historical work that is presented as one's own contribution to knowledge, not only must one acknowledge its sources, the writer must reveal the full extent of the work's indebtedness. No historical author may paraphrase so closely to the original that the change of a few words would result in a direct or exact quotation. As the legal scholar and historian Eugene Volokh recently reminded students: "Don't use close paraphrases as a way of avoiding direct quotations. Really close paraphrasing can also constitute plagiarism." It is not sufficient to thank the author of a secondary source, or to cite the source in the references or in the bibliography; one should either change the phrasing entirely or use a direct quotation. Changing a few words when lifting a passage to avoid having to quote is no better than failure to put the borrowing of exact words in quotation marks or failure to cite the source of the quotation in the reference notes.[6]

Occasional errors of citation or missing quotation marks may reflect no more than accidental sloppiness, unfortunate but hardly fatal. A consistent pattern of omitted quotation marks; the repeated appearance of combinations of uniquely worded phrases taken from a variety of other historians' works (sometimes called "mosaic plagiarism"); incorrect, misleading, or missing citations in a single work; or errors of similar types in a number of one author's works, suggest that the author is committing serial plagiarism, a mortal sin.

When an author employs research assistants, the helpers' work becomes the author's responsibility, including omission of quotation marks around a direct quotation, omission of appropriate references at the end of a paraphrase, or other forms of plagiarism. Research assistants are going to make mistakes, but the author bears the blame because the author's name is on the published work. The general rule that the supervisor is responsible for the acts of the employee applies here. What is more, the author has the chance to review the entire text before publication, and with that last clear chance goes the onus for all errors.[7]

Unlikely Plagiarists

What does a plagiarist look like? You will never find a poster of one on a post office wall. Try the mirror instead. We all have a little word larceny in us. But I could not have imagined, before the sensational revelations of their misdeeds, that Stephen Ambrose and Doris Kearns Goodwin were plagiarists on a large scale.

I have Stephen Ambrose's books on my shelves and enjoy reading them. In my opinion, and that of millions of other American readers, he was a superb storyteller. Advances for his later books from Simon & Schuster were reported to exceed a million dollars apiece (and the books sold in the millions). He incorporated himself as a business, and his son Hugh acted as his agent. On the eve of his untimely death, on October 13, 2002, he confessed that he loved telling stories, particularly stories of men who braved great dangers and overcame great odds to perform great deeds:

> I make my living by reading other people's mail, listening to their stories, reading their memoirs. My job is to pick out the best and most representative, the ones that illuminate common themes or illustrate typical actions. Long ago I learned . . . to let my characters speak for themselves. They were there. I wasn't. They saw with their own eyes, they put their own lives on the line. I didn't. They speak with an authenticity no one else can match. Their phrases, their word choices, their slang are unique, naturally enough, as their experiences were unique.

At the University of New Orleans, where he taught, he said of teaching and writing, "Teaching and writing are one to me—in each case I am telling a story." He was also a lecturer, tour guide to battle sites, and an adviser in the making of movies such as *Saving Private Ryan*, and cable television series such as *Band of Brothers*.[8]

And the rate of his publications increased throughout the 1990s. Over the course of the decade, relying upon his six grown children as research assistants, he had turned out the story of a company of paratroopers from D-Day to the end of the war, *Band of Brothers* (1992); the sprawling *D-Day* (1994); and his retelling of the Lewis and Clark story, *Undaunted Courage* (1996). *Citizen Soldiers* and *Americans at War* (1997); *The Victors* (1998); and *Comrades* (1999) all were about Americans in World War II. He also produced two new editions of his diplomatic history textbook, *Rise to Globalism* (1991 and 1997), and a number of edited works. In 2000, he brought out *Nothing Like it in the World*, on the transcontinental railroad, and in the next two years there followed *No End Save Victory* (2001); *The Wild Blue* (2001), the story of a B–24 crew in Europe; *The Mississippi and the Making of a Nation* (2002); and a personal memoir, *To America* (2002). As if something were chasing him, and perhaps gaining, Ambrose seemed to be writing for dear life.

Ambrose never had much use for the complex multiple perspectivism of the new history. He insisted, "Nothing is relative. What happened, happened. What didn't happen, didn't, and to assert it is a lie. Historians are obsessed with what is true. They have to prove what really happened. In quoting someone, they must demonstrate that person really did speak or write those exact words." There was no excuse for using primary sources improperly, failing to cite them, or ignoring the ones you didn't like.[9]

What about the secondary sources—the work of other scholars who had written about his subjects before he got there? Ambrose was generous in his acknowledgments, even effusive. He gave credit in notes, citing those on whom he relied. But the last year of his life was marked by accusations that he had plagiarized others' work to create much of what he written, stealing other writers' words and presenting them as his own. Had he so worshipped his subjects that he lost track of his own scholarly integrity? Was he in such a hurry to get and tell the stories of the veterans of World War II before they passed away that he failed to follow the rules against plagiarism? Or was he so seduced by the wealth his books were producing, estimated in the millions of dollars, and the celebrity that his tours and lectures brought him that he improperly borrowed from others' works, putting his name on what was not his?[10]

Ambrose shot back that the supposedly plagiarized words his critics discovered amounted to about 10 pages out of a total work of some 15,000 pages in print. "The investigative reporters found them by using my footnotes," he continued—how could he be accused of intentional misconduct when his reference notes were so scrupulous? His work stood, he said, whatever nits his critics, motivated by politics or envy or ignorance, might pick in his corpus of books. "It made me angry," he told one interviewer, "not only because of the negative damning remarks and innuendoes, but more so because none of it was true." In another interview with a reporter from the *Los Angeles Times*, Ambrose shot back at his critics: "Any book with more than five readers is automatically popularized and to be scorned. . . . I did my graduate work like anybody else, and I kind of had that attitude myself. The problem with my colleagues is they never grew out of it." Finally, "on the advice of his editor" at Simon & Schuster, Alice Mayhew, who had shepherded his book on Lewis and Clark to sales of 3 million, he kept silent and kept working on new projects.[11]

It was advice that any reasonable man would follow. In the words of J. Anthony Lukas, one of Mayhew's other authors, her "keen intellect, her shrewd judgment, and her infinite professionalism" had carried him along when his own strength flagged. She was capable of great toughness, according to other editors, and they regarded her as "legendary" in the field of popular history and historical narratives by journalists. She was an indefatigable advocate of her own authors, including Taylor Branch and Lukas, to name just two of her stable who had won Pulitzer Prizes for their historical writing. Another was Doris Kearns Goodwin.[12]

I had not read Goodwin's work before I began the research for this book, but I had heard and seen her on television and knew something of her remarkable career. I felt some instinctive kinship to her. Like my family, the Kearnses were from Brooklyn, New York, and had moved out "to the Island" in the 1950s. A go-getter, she graduated from Colby College with high honors; held summer internships at the State Department, the Department of Health, Education, and Welfare, and the House of Representatives; had won a Woodrow Wilson Fellowship; and got her Ph.D. in political science at Harvard. We must have overlapped there for a time, although she took a year off to serve as a White House Fellow in 1967 and then served as a special assistant to President Lyndon Johnson in his last year in office. From that experience sprang a remarkable friendship with Johnson. Seeing death approaching, he asked her to write his biography. She was awed: "He's still the most formidable, fascinating, frustrating, irritating individual I think I've ever known in my entire life," she said in a 1996 interview. "He had an enormous voice. He was a great storyteller. The problem was that half his stories, I discovered, weren't true." But his habit of embroidering the truth did not deter her from crafting a biography of him, *Lyndon Johnson and the American Dream,* published in 1977.[13]

I knew that her biographies had been much read and highly regarded. Her 1987 900-plus-page biography of the Fitzgerald and Kennedy women, *The Fitzgeralds and the Kennedys: An American Saga,* I had seen as a miniseries on television, and her 700-plus-page *Franklin and Eleanor Roosevelt: The Home Front in World War II* (1994) had won the Pulitzer Prize in 1995. Literary critics sometimes distinguish biography from historical writing. I do not see the reason for such distinctions, for all history's basic unit is the individual. Even those historians who write about great forces and material determinism have to concede that without individuals there are no masses. And biography is inherently more interesting to general readers than traditional history. The historian Alan Shelston has explained that biography is popular because "curiosity about human personality" is universal. Allan Nevins, a biographer himself, made the point even more pointedly: we want to know how the subject "lived, moved, spoke, and enjoyed a certain set of human attributes. We must not merely be shown what he did, but what he was, and why he was that kind of man." Biography "humanizes the past," bringing it closer to all of us. For Goodwin, biography was something more than dry scholarship. It gave her a chance to become intimate with people she truly admired and to share that admiration with her readers.[14]

At the close of the 1996 interview, the interviewer asked her, "What is the place of integrity in your line of work, as you see it?" Her answer is the one I think all professional historians would give, in part at least:

When I look at what a writer owes to the reader, it's critical to know

that everything you're writing about is not made up in your head. . . .
I feel that unless you can document and be certain about what it is
that you're writing about, the reader is going to lose faith in your own
integrity. So I try to make it come alive as much as possible by endless
research. . . . I think my integrity depends upon not stretching over
that line that separates nonfiction from fiction, as too many nonfiction writers are doing nowadays.[15]

Plainly, she was no more a new historian than Ambrose. Instead,
she celebrated her subjects, critically but with love and admiration.
Like Ambrose, she strove for accuracy and abhorred falsehood. But as
readers discovered, two of her books had insidious flaws—missing
quotation marks, missing citations, and paraphrases so close to the
originals that they should have been treated as direct quotations.
Goodwin's initial denials, followed by halting admissions, only fueled
the fire. She tried to go on the offensive, apologizing for errors, setting her research assistants to look for additional mistakes, giving
talks and interviews on the subject, and explaining how the purloined
sentences might have slipped into her drafts. But coupled by
reporters with the revelations about Ambrose, the Goodwin story
refused to die. Indeed, the two stories became intertwined, a dual
indictment of historical celebration and celebrity historians.[16]

Denying Plagiarism: The
Case of Stephen Ambrose

In the course of his public travail, Ambrose offered his own definition of plagiarism. "I always thought plagiarism meant using other
people's words and ideas, pretending they were your own and profit-
ing from it. I do not do that, have never done that and never will."
Some errors might creep in because, "I do my writing at a computer,
surrounded by my research . . . documents of all kinds, books. I mix
them to describe an incident. Usually I have five or more transcripts,
plus copies of documents and books on the table. I take material

from them all." In the course of writing, he put quotation marks around the primary sources, and "when I'm using information from books by scholars, I always cite the source." He did not regard a close paraphrase as plagiarism, even when he borrowed entire phrases.[17]

Ambrose's collaborator, Douglas Brinkley, a University of New Orleans historian and the head of the Eisenhower Center, dismissed Ambrose's critics' efforts as "looking for Waldo" in Ambrose's books. (The problem with this allusion as a defense is that in the Waldo books, Waldo is always lurking somewhere.) CNBC's Tyler Mathisen and Dorothy Rabinowitz agreed with Brinkley's take on Ambrose's critics in a program that aired after his death: Mathisen said, "Sometimes academic historians look down their noses at people like Ambrose, maybe enviously." Rabinowitz responded, "It really doesn't matter. He was a popularizer. He was enough of a scholar and his works were so successful. . . . He infused all of those books with his enormous love of being an American."[18]

Was Ambrose guilty of plagiarism? From the publication of his first book in 1962 until his death at the end of 2002, Ambrose was a remarkably productive scholar. Sometimes a writer of history can spin off a book from another, or use the same collection of documents to write a number of books, or revise an existing publication periodically to bring it up to date. Ambrose did all three of these. This kind of piggybacking is not plagiarism. We cannot plagiarize our own work.

In fact, Ambrose was a master of piggybacking his books. He started early, with two books on Civil War generals, continued with a series of books on Eisenhower, then moved on to books on D-Day. His methods shifted from archival research to oral history, but he continued to include published and unpublished archival materials in his writing. If he copied from himself, none of this involved plagiarism, except insofar as he might have failed to indicate occasions when he took primary materials from other historians' writing and quoted the primary source as though he had gone to the original.[19]

There is no way to answer the questions about Ambrose's supposed plagiarism without doing our homework. We have to find his books, check the notes, find the books cited in the notes, and then lay his writing alongside theirs. This is called parallel text comparison, and it is the only way to uncover plagiarism of the sort alleged against him. *The Wild Blue: The Men and Boys who Flew the B–24s over Germany*, published in 2001 by Simon & Schuster, was the book whose questionable research and writing methods started the assault on Ambrose. In it, his techniques were fully developed, and, unlike his first books, he could not claim for it the innocence of youth and inexperience. We start with it.

The Wild Blue is a swiftly flowing story about the training and performance of a group of servicemen, George McGovern's B–24 crew in World War II. Ambrose relied primarily on interviews with McGovern himself, his surviving crew, and the oral history of veterans collected by the World War II Oral History Project at the Eisenhower Center for American Studies, at the University of New Orleans, founded by Ambrose himself. He also "did a lot of reading, of both books and memoirs." The book has 305 endnotes, but relatively few secondary sources are cited. Indeed, except for a few pages, the book is highly personalized, a reflection of the recollected experiences and emotions of a relative handful of the over 100,000 airmen who flew bombers over Germany and its satellites during the war. But there is nothing untoward in that—there are official histories of the Eighth and Fifteenth Air Forces and Ambrose did not set out to duplicate their comprehensive authority.[20]

Ambrose claimed meticulous accuracy in quoting what his primary sources said. We will take him at his word, because as we saw in the Bellesiles case, it is hard to go back and recheck the primary source record, in this case much of it based on interviews with McGovern and others deposited at the Eisenhower Center. We have to trust the author. In fact, some of Ambrose's problems with secondary sources —the works of other scholars—derived from the way that he conflated them with his primary sources. Whenever he quoted from a primary source, including those that he found in a secondary source, he used quotation marks. To set off these first-hand accounts, he almost never put quotation marks around quotations or closely paraphrased language he took directly from the secondary works' authors. Thus the reader got the impression that Ambrose, not the secondary source author, had found the primary source. Nor did his end notes ever say "A—the primary source" as quoted in "B—the secondary source," the proper way to cite a primary source found in a secondary source. Almost every secondary source he used in *The Wild Blue*—all the books in print by other authors he cited—were pillaged in this way. Worse, although he did cite the secondary sources, many of the citations in the notes either give no page number or offer a long enclosed run of pages. This made it difficult for a casual reader to see how much of Ambrose's writing really belonged to others.

On January 4, 2002, the *Weekly Standard* published an article whose author, Fred Barnes, claimed that in writing *The Wild Blue*, Ambrose had plagiarized Thomas Childers's *Wings of Morning* (1995), a moving account of one B–24 crew that did not return from a mission near the end of the war in Europe. Howard Goodner, Childers's uncle, was lost in that mission, and the book was an attempt to reconstruct what life was like in those B–24 squadrons, using as sources Goodner's surviving correspondence, the recollections of two of his crewmates who survived, and other evidence. Childers is a professor of German history at the University of Pennsylvania; no one can mistake him for an amateur historian or a memorialist or misread his work as one long primary source. Ambrose certainly could see that *Wings of Morning* was not merely a primary source in print, as would have been the case if Childers had merely edited his uncle's letters. It was a work of scholarship.

There are three references to *Wings of Morning* in the endnotes of *The Wild Blue*. In each case, Ambrose compressed a block of pages of Childers's description, including primary source quotations, into a few paragraphs in *The Wild Blue*. On page 65 of *The Wild Blue* Ambrose devoted portions of four paragraphs to Howard Goodner that are based on *Wings of Morning*'s pages 8–14 (according to Ambrose's note 26 on page 265): "Like all radiomen, Goodner went to gunnery school, in his case to Panama City, Florida. There he shot skeet with a shotgun, then progressed to firing from moving platforms, first with small arms, then with automatic weapons and finally heavy machine guns. He learned how to operate the power-driven turrets, how to sight and swing them and their twin .50 calibers." On page 13 of *Wings of Morning* one finds strikingly similar prose: "They began shooting skeet, then progressed to firing from moving platforms, from small arms to automatic weapons and finally to the heavy machine guns. They learned how to operate the power-driven turrets, how to sight and swing them and their twin fifties." Note how Ambrose had altered a word or two and left out some words from Childers's text, for example, changing "twin fifties" to "twin .50 calibers." The borrowing was not exact, hence it did not have to be placed in quotation marks, unlike the language of Goodner's own letters home.[21]

In his defense, Ambrose admitted that *The Wild Blue* contained lines taken from secondary sources that were not in quotation marks. "For the past four months," he wrote in May 2002, "diligent reporters have found some phrases, a few sentences and at least six times two entire sentences copied by me and footnotes to the source, but without putting quotations marks around the material." Was this defense credible? The second passage from the paragraphs on Goodner in *The Wild Blue*, on page 64, cited pages 8–14 of Childers's *Wings of Morning*. The text of *The Wild Blue:*

[Goodner] went to school in Illinois, where he learned electronics, mechanics, code, and the working of a radio. He mastered the internal electronics of the radio, built generators, studied vacuum tubes and amplifiers, transformers and transmitters. He learned to disassemble a set, then reassemble it blindfolded. Morse code was hard for him, as it was for most people. "The sounds come through ear phones," he wrote his parents, "and they sound like a swarm of bees."

Ambrose put the material from the primary source, Goodner's letter home, in quotation marks. But compare the rest of Ambrose's passage with page 11 of *Wings of Morning*, in which Childers described his uncle's electronics training:

The demanding course included electronics, mechanics, code, and a comprehensive study of the radio set itself. Sitting in the labs during the long, hot afternoons or in the still, sultry hours of the night shift, Howard struggled to master the internal electronics of the radio, building generators, studying vacuum tubes and amplifiers, transformers and transmitters. He disassembled the sets, examined the intricate ganglia of tubes and wires, and reassembled them blindfolded. . . . Electronics was a challenge, but the Morse code, bombarding his ears night and day with its relentless metallic chirping, was maddening. . . . "The sounds come through earphones," he wrote to his parents, "and they sound like a swarm of bees."

If Ambrose was simply being sloppy and had forgotten to use quotation marks to set off Childers's prose, the sin would be venial only. But Ambrose's technique was to remove a few terms, move around others, and copy the rest from Childers, then put quotation marks only around the primary source taken from Childers. The changed words and phrases are the telltale marks of an intent to borrow illicitly, proof of a pattern of unethical conduct.[22]

Ambrose studiously avoided exact duplication of all of Childers's uniquely picturesque phrases. For example, *The Wild Blue*, page 94: "Eighteen-year-old Albert Seraydarian, an Armenian-American, was from Brooklyn. His 'dem's' and 'dose's' and other Brooklynese were so thick the southern born Goodner could hardly understand him." *Wings of Morning*, page 17: "When he spoke, casually swearing at the cards, the words sauntered out in a string of 'dem's' and 'dose's,' a Brooklynese so thick and melodious it sounded to Howard's southern ear like something straight out of the Dead End Kids." Ambrose omitted the reference to the movie and the card playing, but the "dem's" and the "dose's" were too good to leave behind. Nor could Ambrose forego copying Childers's striking phrase that the aluminum wings of the B–24, "glittering like mica, were popping up out of the clouds all over the sky." In *The Wild Blue* this became "glittering like mica, were popping up out of the clouds over here, over there, everywhere."

Sometimes Ambrose's need to blur the extent of his reliance on the original prose led to factual error. *The Wild Blue*, page 164: "The lead squadron of the B–24s penetrated the flak. 'Mary, Mother of God,' one crew member mumbled into the intercom. 'Mary, Mother of God get me out of this.' [The pilot, Richard] Farrington[,] took them right into it." Compare *Wings of Morning*, page 88: "It was everywhere, flak so thick, he had heard the veterans say, you could get out and walk on it. Nobody could get through this. It was impossible. 'Mary, Mother of God,' he heard himself mumbling, 'Mary, Mother of God get me out of this.'" Ambrose garbled the story, turning Farrington's own prayer into that of an anonymous crewman. Sloppiness alright, but the cause of the sloppiness was not all right.[23]

Journalists for the *Weekly Standard* and the *New York Times* confined the problem with *The Wild Blue* to the failure to put quotation marks around copied text. In a January 11, 2002, interview printed in the *New York Times*, Ambrose said, "I am sure going to put quotes around anything that comes out of a secondary work, always." But even that admission was sly, for as we have seen, by "anything that comes out of a secondary work" Ambrose could mean the primary sources that he took out of the other book. Ambrose's publisher, David Rosenthal of Simon & Schuster, agreed that the error was one of omission rather than commission. "I think again that the material has been appropriately footnoted, and if there have been omissions it appears to be in the methods of citing as opposed to the citation itself. . . . We will act to rectify them," Rosenthal told the *Times* reporter. Again, the comment missed the point—Ambrose's citations were not the issue; his theft of entire sentences (with slight alterations) from another author without quotation marks was.[24]

Some leading academic historians, like Eric Foner, at first read Ambrose's admission of sloppiness in a broad way, as though Ambrose and his publisher were conceding that they should have put quotes around material taken from secondary sources. Foner said, "Nobody can write as many books as he has—many of them were well-written books—without the sloppiness that comes with speed and the constant pressure to produce. It is the unfortunate downside of doing too much too fast." Thomas Mallon, a journalist who published a much-admired work on plagiarism, *Stolen Words,* in 1989, also read more into the confessions than was there. Mallon told a reporter for National Public Radio,

> When you're writing a work of history, you have a great deal of paraphernalia around you. You have printed sources, archival sources, handwritten notes that you've made. You've got xeroxes that you've

made. You've got things that you've, perhaps, stored on your computer. . . . And it is certainly possible that honest mistakes occur. People get tired. People get sloppy. . . . And then what also happens is that sometimes that is made as the excuse for something more serious, which is a more deliberate lifting of material and passing it off as the writer's own.

Ambrose had said as much when he described his writing technique—the desk covered with a variety of primary and secondary sources.[25]

But Ambrose—who had a much clearer idea of what he had conceded and what he did not intend to concede—did not agree that his method was prone to error. "I tell stories, I don't discuss my documents, I discuss the story. It almost gets to the point where, how much is the reader going to take? I am not writing a Ph.D. dissertation." No one read the published version of his dissertation, he added. And after all, said Jeff Guinn, a Fort Worth reporter, the whole thing amounted to a few "bits and pieces" that Ambrose had "transposed" from others' work. That was the fallback position of the popular historian. It derived from the canon of consensus history. Facts were facts; how they were phrased, or how one author's phrasing was repeated by another, was not an important matter.[26]

But as the story unfolded, professional historians belatedly recognized the peril in which Ambrose's technique placed the entire enterprise of history. Eric Foner took another look at Ambrose's work:

I actually found Professor Ambrose's response rather more damaging in a way. . . . Professor Ambrose's explanation that when he finds a good story he just plugs it into his own writing, that's not what most of us consider writing to be. Even if you put quotations around it or put a footnote, writing is putting these things into your own words, creating your own argument, not just sort of scavenging other people's books and taking their good writing and putting it out as your own words.

If readers bought Ambrose's defense, then academic historical research would lose its special quality and academic historical works their authority.[27]

When the revelations of close paraphrasing were published, Childers was upset, but not enough to "be the scholarly guy rapping the famous guy on the knuckles in a schoolmarmish way." He admitted that he was surprised and angered, but he did not speak out at first. He recognized that Ambrose had gone from an academic to a popular writer. "His later books are less and less critical. There's a lot more boosterism. He's been writing more to his market." And Childers was moving in a parallel course, saying, "I've become more broad-minded. I want to make the past come alive, to put a reader back so thoroughly that they can understand the events." Thus he had put aside a scholarly treatment of Germany in the last year of World War I to write *Wings of Morning*, a narrative about "real people and real stories whose lives were profoundly changed by the war." His colleagues at Pennsylvania might be dismissive: "If you do a narrative, they think you're just telling a story, but writing these books is just as challenging. I'm bound by the facts as I know them." Ambrose could not have agreed more.[28]

So what was Ambrose doing that was so wrong? His technique, polished and almost seamless, was to mine Childers's book for quotations from Goodner or others, reuse them in *The Wild Blue* (careful to put them in quotation marks), and frame them with close paraphrases from Childers's own descriptions of events and people (never using quotation marks and intentionally changing a few words so that they were not exact quotations). The issue was not inaccuracy but of giving credit. Ambrose repeated the pattern throughout the book: take the good primary-source quotation from a secondary source and put it in quotation marks, but avoid putting quotation marks around the words of the author of the secondary source even when he substantially copied them. In the case of passages lifted from *Wings of Morning*, the borrowing was mentioned in the notes, but the citation was just a block of pages (pages 8–14, 15–20, and 82–91 respectively) rather than the exact page from which Ambrose had stolen the wording.

In a fashion remarkably similar to Parkman's, Ambrose reduced the other scholars from whom he appropriated exact language virtually to the status of research assistants, incorporating into his own documents and passing off as his own their findings and their unique way of looking at those findings. The tip-off is a fact that none of his critics noted: Only once in *The Wild Blue* did Ambrose quote the authors of a secondary source. This one exception offers a telling clue. He mentioned by name the two editors of the official history of the Air Force, followed by a long quotation from their work. Ambrose or his assistant must have recognized that this was a secondary source that had to be treated differently from all the other secondary sources they used, although other passages from it were paraphrased closely throughout the book. The chapter in which it appears, on the Fifteenth Air Force, is the driest and least personal in the book, and the chapter most like conventional scholarship. In this chapter Ambrose most closely adheres to the rules for quotation, citation, and use of others' scholarship. It proves beyond any doubt that Ambrose still remembered what he had learned in graduate school at the University of Wisconsin about citing secondary sources.[29]

Though Ambrose conceded the charge that he should have put the exact language he took from Childers in quotation marks, neither he nor his assistant offered to look for additional errors of the same sort. This may be read as evidence that they did not seem to understand the extent of their impermissible practice of compilation, or that they did not wish to admit to the extent of plagiarism I have described. In fact, the portions of *The Wild Blue* that rested heavily on other scholars' work constituted a veritable anthology. Far too much was taken directly from secondary sources without adequate recognition of the contribution of the secondary sources' authors. He compiled rather than composed. And he knew it, which is why, in one of his final interviews, he said, "Screw it, I don't know that I'm all that good at academics. I am a writer." Ambrose's bitter rejoinder recalls Boorstin's depiction of himself as an "amateur," for both thrusts had the same sharp point: How dare the academics question my ethics or my writing style? I am not an academic.[30]

But once upon a time Ambrose was an academic, and that time lasted until the last decade of his life. He was a professor of history, trained in historical methods, with its highest educational credentials, teaching history to students. He carried these credentials when he set

up the Eisenhower Center at the University of New Orleans, when he
interviewed veterans, when he gave lectures to audiences all over the
country. He was a professional historian before he was a popular writer.

One may thus ask when in his career he developed into a plagiarist.
If the serial malfeasance of *The Wild Blue* were a product of the haste
of his final years or the overzealousness of poorly trained assistants, it
might be forgiven if not forgotten. As the Bancroft Prize–winning
Brown University historian James Patterson put it, "The publishers
are complicit in this." Certainly one could understand how modern
financial burdens on trade presses, demanding two-figure percentage
profits from every division of every commercial publisher, could end
up placing terrible burdens on a best-selling historian's shoulders.
But if the malfeasance was deeply ingrained in his work long before
his last years, the verdict would be more certain.[31]

The first two books Ambrose published, *Halleck: Lincoln's Chief of
Staff* and *Upton and the Army* (both with the Louisiana State University
Press), on two Union officers in the Civil War, Henry Halleck and
Emory Upton, were based on his graduate studies. Published immedi-
ately before and soon after he was awarded his degree, they give us a
better idea of how he used sources at the start of his career.

Indeed, Ambrose was a prodigy when it came to publication. His
first book, *Halleck: Lincoln's Chief of Staff*, appeared in 1962, a year
before he finished his Ph.D. dissertation, on Upton. *Halleck*, clearly a
work of considerable polish and energy, was based on primary sources
and official records, and drew on archives as well as published collections. It is, like so many of the thousands of books on Civil War generals and campaigns, nicely paced and full of incidents, and its footnotes
indicate where in the official records these stories first appeared. It
was a fine start to what promised to be both a productive and a reputable career.[32]

But the volume that Ambrose published hard upon *Halleck: Lincoln's Chief of Staff* was of a very different order. *Upton and the Army*,
published in 1964, the year after he finished his dissertation, relied
greatly upon Peter S. Michie's 1885 *The Life and Letters of Emory Upton*.
But Ambrose concealed his excessive and improper dependence on
the earlier work.

In the Bibliographical Note to *Upton and the Army* one finds: "Without the help of Peter S. Michie's *The Life and Letters of Emory Upton* (New York, 1885), this study could not have been undertaken." But Ambrose did not mention the fact that Peter Smith Michie was Upton's classmate and close friend, or that Michie was a professor at West Point, and thus that Michie's account was not just another nineteenth-century amateur life-and-letters book but was the work of a solid historian who knew his subject intimately. These are facts that Ambrose had at hand, if for no other reason than that they appear at the outset of a chapter devoted to Upton in Russell Weigley's *Towards an American Army: Military Thought From Washington to Marshall* (1962), a work that Ambrose repeatedly cited. And they are certainly material facts the reader should be told if Ambrose is going to say anything at all about Michie's book.

Instead, Ambrose merely said of Michie: "He made no attempt to analyze the man or his influence, but he did include the pertinent events of his career and printed letters not available elsewhere." In what looks like the beginning of a fairly complex scheme to make his own work appear more original, Ambrose neglected to inform the reader of the importance of Michie's work. In the citation of pages 100 to 127 of Weigley's book (Ambrose's note 31, page 170), Ambrose similarly neglected to tell his reader that Weigley's pages constituted a chapter entirely devoted to Upton. Instead, Ambrose characterized the Weigley material as a "further discussion" of the material in Ambrose's own text on the influence of German military thinking on Upton. Again, Ambrose intentionally diminished the importance of another, rival, secondary source.[33]

Ambrose was right—he could not have done without Michie—but despite the fulsomeness of his credit to the man, he did not properly credit what he took from the book. It is certainly permissible—indeed often necessary—to quote from letters published in a collection or edition of papers and documents, but this must then be stated. Yet none of the 43 notes of Ambrose's that cite Michie's *Life and Letters of Emory Upton* indicate what Ambrose took from the letters that Michie included (the primary source) and what from Michie's own commentary (the secondary source). As with *The Wild Blue*, the citations of

Michie are often to page ranges. Ambrose treated Michie's biography of Upton and the letters within it as a primary document, and made no distinction between Upton's writings and Michie's.

Mark Lewis, an investigative journalist working for *Forbes* magazine, deserves the credit for being the first to go back to the thesis "Upton and the Army" and compare its language with Michie's. He found outright theft. Michie, page 5: "If he ever had to speak, it would be to his men in the face of the enemy, and on such occasions an orations must be necessarily short, and he thought he would be able for that." Ambrose, page 7: "If they ever had to make a speech, it would be in the face of the enemy, when orations necessarily are short, and he thought he could handle that." The slight alterations turn an exact quotation into a paraphrase. Michie, page 5: "Always in a hurry . . . he often cut a person off in the middle of a remark with his own reply, which was always to the point." Ambrose, page 7: ". . . and that he was always in a hurry, often cutting a person off in the middle of a remark to make his own observation." Lewis found five more examples of Ambrose's brazen robbery of Michie's passages.[34]

Ambrose plagiarized other secondary sources in the writing of his *Upton and the Army*. He lifted entire paragraphs from more recent and better known secondary sources than Michie, hiding the extent of the borrowing by changing a few words, then citing a block of pages rather than the exact page from which he copied the language. Commenting upon the unpreparedness of the regular army for the coming of the Spanish-American War, Ambrose wrote,

No general staff, or any other agency, existed to plan for mobilization, organization, and training. No provision had been made for assembling or transporting an overseas expedition, or for the handling of large bodies of troops. Except for some aged Civil War veterans, no officer in the army had even seen a force larger than a regiment, and few had seen even that much.

The citation at the end of the paragraph was to Walter Millis's popular book on the Spanish-American War, *The Martial Spirit* (1931). The citation gave a block of pages, 152–57, but did not indicate that on page 152, Millis had written:

> There was no plan of mobilization, no higher organization, no train-
> ing in combined operations, no provision for the assembly or trans-
> portation of an overseas expedition, or for the handling of any large
> body of troops whatever. . . . Except for the ageing veterans of the
> Civil War, there were no officers in the Army who had ever even seen
> a force larger than a regiment together in one place, and there were
> few who had even seen that much.[35]

Along with blockbusters like his plagiarism of Millis, Ambrose
lifted shorter passages from a wide variety of secondary sources and
jumbled them together, an example of the mosaic plagiarism common in undergraduate papers today. For example, Ambrose wrote,
"The Continental Army was to be a federal rather than a state force,
secured through volunteering," and cited Weigley's pages 218–220.
On page 218 of Weigley, one finds: "The Continental Army was to be
a federal rather than a state force, but secured through volunteering." Ambrose had merely omitted one "but." His endnote—as one by
now might guess—cited a block of pages in Weigley, so that Ambrose
concealed the copying by blurring the exact place from which Weigley's words came.[36]

Ambrose was also practicing his skills at taking primary-source quotations from secondary sources without indicating in the notes what
he was doing. For example, at the very end of *Upton and the Army*,
Ambrose included a long quote from Elihu Root's view of Upton's
proposed reforms. The reader who read the text but not the note
might assume that the quotation came from Root's papers, but the
endnote cites Frederick Palmer and Newton D. Baker's *America at War*
(1931). And the citation does not say, "Root, as quoted in Palmer and
Baker," thus does not indicate that Ambrose had used Palmer and
Baker as a source of Root's words. On page 157, Ambrose has one
Colonel Pettit saying of Upton's *Military Policy*, "A careful reading of
its pages will give a complete answer to the title of our [prize] essay."
One would expect the endnote to cite Pettit. Instead, it cites Weigley's
Towards An American Army, page 156, with no further information. It

does not say "Pettit, quoted in Weigley." In his book on Upton, Ambrose had already perfected the technique he would use in *The Wild Blue*.[37]

Ambrose's motives can only be surmised. Perhaps he was already in a hurry when he wrote his dissertation. Perhaps he had a job offer that was contingent on a completed Ph.D. Halleck was not Ambrose's approved dissertation topic, so he had to write a dissertation on another topic quickly. Dissertations must feature original work based on primary sources. By not quoting where he should have quoted in his dissertation on Upton, Ambrose concealed the extent of his dependence on others, particularly Michie, and made his work look more original than it was. He fooled his dissertation adviser and his reading committee, for rarely does an adviser or a member of a dissertation committee look for plagiarism. Just in case, Ambrose covered his tracks by citing the works from which he took the material. If caught out, he could then (as he did in 2002) say with perfect honesty that he had cited his sources and the untoward copying must have been a mechanical error, for example, simply forgetting to put quotation marks around the sources he had copied into his own notes.

Then Ambrose's ambition entered the scene like Macbeth's hunger for the crown: he could not forgo the opportunity to publish the dissertation with the Louisiana State University Press, the publisher of *Halleck: Lincoln's Chief of Staff*. The book *Upton and the Army* came out in 1964, a scant year after his dissertation had been completed. There was no time to go back and correct all the plagiarism. In any case, how would it look to his editor at LSU, or to his teachers at Wisconsin if they were informed of the changes? Better to go on ahead, like Macbeth, through the gore, than to go back.

A pattern was set in Ambrose's writing: heavily and energetically researched works, such as *Halleck*, alternated with fastbacks filled with shortcuts and sometimes outright theft, such as *Upton and the Army*. Shortly after publishing a number of highly regarded works on Eisenhower based heavily on primary sources and official records, Ambrose whipped off *Crazy Horse and Custer: The Parallel Lives of Two American Warriors* (1975) for the trade press Doubleday. Ambrose told readers that he had "started in June 1971 at Wounded Knee, South Dakota; finished in July 1974 at Camp Robinson, Nebraska." That's fast work for a book of 486 pages.

Ambrose acknowledged a lot of help from his family, colleagues at the University of New Orleans, archivists and librarians, and his publisher in the course of writing *Crazy Horse and Custer*. Most of all, help came from his secondary sources. His very first end note is a tribute to "Walter P. Webb, *The Great Plains* (Boston, 1931), 10–47. Readers who know this classic will realize how dependent I am on Webb's great work." The huge block of pages cited, rather than specific page references for specific information, is telling. Ambrose was just as liberal in his thanks to Jay Monaghan, a biographer of Custer. "There is no need to go into the details here, fortunately," Ambrose reported of Custer's service in the Civil War, "because Custer's biography has been written, accurately and wisely, by Jay Monaghan. Indeed, Monaghan's *Custer* is a model biography—scholarly, detailed, and lively. It cannot be surpassed and hardly needs to be summarized." Indeed, it was so lively and detailed that Ambrose could not help but copy from it as liberally as he had praised its author.[38]

Take Monaghan on Custer at West Point: "He enjoyed athletic stunts, like twisting his legs behind his head or bounding to his feet from a prone position. Easygoing and friendly, he got in no fights of record at the Academy." Compare Ambrose on Custer at West Point, on page 96: "He was a natural athlete and much admired for it. He loved to show off, twisting his legs behind his head or bounding to his feet from a prone position. . . . He was easygoing, slow to take offense, and neither violent nor vicious. There is no record of his engaging in any fist fights as a cadet." No quotation marks, just a general citation of Monaghan in the notes. Monaghan: "On August 28, 1859, Custer returned to West Point. Cadet James Barroll Washington, a great-great-grandnephew of George Washington, entered that year. He remembered hearing the crowd shout, 'Here comes Custer!' The name meant nothing to him, but he turned, and saw a slim, immature lad with unmilitary figure, slightly rounded shoulders, and gangling walk." Ambrose, page 97: "When he returned to West Point, Cadet James B. Washington, a relative of George Washington, remembered hearing the crowd shout, 'Here comes Custer!' The name meant nothing to Washington, who was just entering the academy, but he turned and saw a slim, immature lad with unmilitary figure, slightly rounded shoulders, and gangling walk, surrounded by back-slapping, laughing friends."[39]

Like Michie's book on Upton, Monaghan's account is in the genre of popular rather than academic history. Monaghan did not copiously cite sources. Throughout the book there are many pages of dialogue without any citation at all, almost as if Monaghan were writing a historical novel rather than a biography. Thus, if Monaghan seemed to be a "model" to Ambrose, it was not for his research notes, but for his prose. Here Ambrose wrote in the tradition of the nineteenth-century consensus historian, borrowing freely because there was no rule against it. Childers's *Wings of Morning*, though a remarkable work of scholarship, exhibits the same imaginative characteristics as Monaghan, thus exposing itself to the same sort of word pilfering.[40]

Fame had come to Ambrose in the 1990s, but it did not slake his thirst for others' words. His *Undaunted Courage* (1996), a *New York Times* best-seller, was described on the back of the paperback cover by a *Washington Post* book reviewer as "a fine and important book, intelligently conceived and splendidly written." But by whom?

Ambrose's subject was the Lewis and Clark expedition, and he relied in part on the work of other scholars to fill in the gaps in the primary sources and his own yearly travels along the two explorers' route. Donald Jackson, on whose monograph on the Lewis and Clark trek, *Thomas Jefferson and the Stony Mountains* (1981), Ambrose relies, was his first victim. Ambrose's first citation of Jackson's book comes on page 68 of *Undaunted Courage*. Ambrose writes, "Thomas Walker was once again chosen to lead the expedition [to the Missouri River], but the French and Indian War intervened before he could get started. Nothing came of the plan after the war." Ambrose's note 1 cites page 8 of *Thomas Jefferson and the Stony Mountains* as the source of the material but does not reveal how close Ambrose's prose is to Jackson's. On page 8 of Jackson's book one finds: "These plans were laid in 1753, with Dr. Walker chosen to lead the expedition. The French and Indian War intervened and nothing came of the scheme."

Ambrose changes a few of Jackson's words and repeats the rest. No quotation marks. The close paraphrase of Jackson's own words is plagiarism.[41]

Ambrose did it again and again. Ambrose, page 74: "Mackenzie's account was not published until 1801, in London. It was probably ghostwritten, for Mackenzie was not learned enough to have written the book in its published form." The citation is to Jackson, page 94. Go there and find, "*Voyages* was published late in 1801 in London, probably ghostwritten for Mackenzie by a professional writer named William Combe. The explorer was hardly learned enough to have written the book in its published form." Jackson had done the research; Ambrose not only copied it, he copied Jackson's language without telling the reader he had done so. One supposes that too many quotation marks would alert the reader to the unoriginality of Ambrose's account. It is not hard to find these examples; any diligent undergraduate could do as well as I—and at least one did.[42]

Once the *Weekly Standard* story appeared, a flood of accusations poured down on Ambrose's work. Journalists, historians, railroad buffs, military experts, and even undergraduates came forward with evidence of plagiarism in a large portion of Ambrose's later works. For example, in the preface to the much-ballyhooed *Citizen Soldiers* (1997), Ambrose admitted that he "stole material, shamelessly if profitably" from Joseph Balkowski's *Beyond the Beachhead*. But, as Balkowski explained to a reporter in March 2002, that was not the half of it. Ambrose not only recounted the stories that Balkowski's research had uncovered about the drive inland from the D-Day beaches, a perfectly acceptable use of earlier studies, but he also used Balkowski's own words without benefit of quotation. He did the same with secondary sources in his *Nothing Like It in the World* (2000), a narrative on the building of the transcontinental railroad.[43]

Admitting Plagiarism—
The Case of
Doris Kearns Goodwin

As if in eerie echo of the charges against Ambrose, two weeks after the *Weekly Standard*'s disclosures on Ambrose, the conservative journal published an accusation against Doris Kearns Goodwin. Together, the two denunciations shook the history profession to its core. The delight that conservative critics seemed to take in the exposé suggested that it had a political side, but politics or not, the evidence against Goodwin seemed convincing to many observers. One case of plagiarism by a star historian might be exceptional; two cases suggested a deeper problem. Reporters and pundits kept asking what was behind it all. Consequently, each new revelation about one of the cases fed interest in the other.

On January 18, 2002, a *Weekly Standard* editorial assistant, Bo Crader, wrote an on-line piece, subsequently printed, purporting to show how Goodwin had appropriated whole sentences from other scholars' work in her *The Fitzgeralds and the Kennedys*, published in 1987. The revelations of direct quotations from three sources—primarily Lynne McTaggart's 1983 *Kathleen Kennedy: Her Life and Times*—were undeniable, and Goodwin admitted that errors had been made. Indeed, Goodwin's initial response was the same as Ambrose's—a few errors, all unintentional, hence not plagiarism, the result of using yellow legal pads to take notes from secondary sources in the course of which someone had forgotten to put quotation marks around some direct quotations. (McTaggart's book, pure journalism published by Dial Press, had no notes whatsoever and was another example of the Childers-Monaghan style that had made Ambrose's plagiarism so easy.) There were 3,500 notes in Goodwin's 900-plus-page book on the Fitzgerald and Kennedy women. Some error crept in. After all, it was her first major research effort, she said (apparently exempting her biography of Lyndon Johnson).[44]

Goodwin did not initially admit what reporters soon uncovered:

Simon & Schuster had made a payment to McTaggart to silence the matter in 1989, and in subsequent editions, Goodwin added citations to over 40 passages and a strong acknowledgment to McTaggart in the introduction. The settlement (made, presumably, to avoid a lawsuit for copyright infringement) did not resolve the ethical and professional question that unattributed borrowing raises. McTaggart's acceptance of the settlement put the legal issue to rest, but not the ethical ones.

Plagiarism is an event, a set of actions that happened at a particular time. No legal settlement with a person or persons from whom Goodwin plagiarized materials—that is, no form of monetary reparations, apology, or acknowledgment—can change the fact that she plagiarized, so no legal settlement can obviate the need for a moral judgment on Goodwin's conduct. There is no real financial remedy for the ethical offense of plagiarism, because the ultimate victim is the reader. Readers are angry, bewildered, and "heartsick" when they discover that an author has stolen another's words. The appropriate moral response is public acknowledgment of the error, apology, contrition, and a promise to reform. But a private settlement like the one Simon & Schuster made with McTaggart is the exact opposite of a public acknowledgment and apology. It protects the reputation of the alleged perpetrator and hides the delict from readers.[45]

When she learned of the *Weekly Standard* story on Goodwin's response, McTaggart grew uneasy. She was even less pleased with Goodwin's statement that she had only taken a few passages. Though quiet at first, like Childers, McTaggart soon began to give interviews, and her account of the amount of supposedly illicit borrowing began to grow, from a few sentences to over 50 cases, to "173 instances," to 30 pages of photocopied side by side comparisons, to "thousands of my exact or nearly exact words" taken from "the heart and guts" of 91 of 248 of her pages.[46]

Part of the widening dispute between the two authors was Goodwin's decision not to add quotation marks to the purloined passages when she revised the work in 1989. In the midst of the later controversy, she explained that too many quotation marks would have broken the narrative flow. That explanation is not convincing. Goodwin had over 3,500 notes, and found no problem adding 40 or so more to give credit to McTaggart; why not add the quotation marks too. Biographies and works of fiction featuring dialogue among characters have quotation marks running down every page like rabbit tracks in the snow. Those quotation marks do not break the narrative flow.

Goodwin's response to the query about quotations was not so much evasive as irrelevant. She insisted that plagiarism had to be intentional, and that she might have copied sentences inadvertently, but had no intent to steal from McTaggart. In fact, she and her defenders made the same argument as Ambrose: If she had intended to steal, why would she have had citations at all in the 1987 edition? One answer is that citations make the work look scholarly; whereas putting too much of the narrative in quotation marks makes the book appear a cut-and-paste job, derivative rather than original.[47]

For a time, the reporters on the two stories quoted one another in a feeding frenzy, but by the end of spring 2002, the matter seemed destined to become a footnote itself. Then the *Los Angeles Times* gave the Goodwin story new legs by reporting its finding of uncredited borrowing in Goodwin's hitherto above-reproach and Pulitzer Prize–winning *No Ordinary Time* (1994). Goodwin had been explicit about the latter work in her first responses to the accusations about the earlier book, telling a reporter, Thomas Palmer, in January 2002, "By the time I did *No Ordinary Time* I was very careful to understand what happened in that [the McTaggart] situation." She did not make the same mistake twice, she was suggesting. But "an outside reader" asked to review the book for an article on Goodwin in the *Los Angeles Times* found more than one instance of copying directly from another secondary source, Joseph P. Lash's *Eleanor and Franklin* (1971). Confronted with this evidence, Goodwin replied, "As long as a [secondary source] person is credited . . . [the author has] some leeway to use some of the words. Just using individual words now and then, and when it is clear where it is coming from, that is what paraphrasing is." Again, "The most important thing I keep coming back to, and what most people would agree with, is that the standard to be met in every instance is providing appropriate credit to the source."[48]

Goodwin's defense was very close to Ambrose's for good reason, for her instances of misappropriation raise familiar questions about what is permissible in paraphrasing. The *Los Angeles Times* article included this passage from Goodwin's *No Ordinary Time*:

> Eleanor quickly composed herself, walked back into the living room, and said in her most disarming manner, 'It was kind of Mr. Aldrich to offer to be chairman, but is it not better from the point of view of geography to have someone from the Middle West?' At that, she turned immediately to Chicago philanthropist and New Deal loyalist Marshall Field; she knew it would be a bother for him, but could he accept? Though caught somewhat off guard, Field gave his assent.

Her source was Joseph Lash's *Eleanor and Franklin*, and in it, on page 635, we read:

> So Eleanor composed herself, returned to the living room, and said in her most disarming manner: 'It is kind of Mr. Aldrich to offer to be chairman, but is it not better from the point of view of geography to have someone from the Middle West?' At that, she turned to Marshall Field; she knew it was a bothersome responsibility, she said, but could he accept the Chairmanship? Somewhat startled, the Chicago philanthropist and stalwart New Dealer did.

This is not a "few words" here and there, but so close a paraphrase as to be a direct quotation. And it should have been handled as such and placed within quotation marks. The only differences are the transposition of the phrase "stalwart New Dealer" and the replacement of "returned" with "walked back."[49]

Was the close paraphrase an example of simple sloppiness—leaving out the quotation marks? A closer look reveals that Lash's documentation (his note 6) for the entire paragraph, including the direct quotation, is "Lash Diaries, 1940." Nothing in Goodwin's references suggests that she was quoting the exact words Lash had used in 1971 to describe the incident, only that she was reusing primary sources that he had quoted in his book. The absence of quotation marks in Goodwin's book around Lash's words—"So Eleanor composed herself . . ." effectively transformed his entire book into a primary source no different from the diaries he had kept in 1940. He ceased to be a scholar and became a living document, and his book simply a continuation of his earlier diary. That was exactly Ambrose's technique with his secondary sources, beginning with his treatment of Michie.

Ambrose stood like a colossus above politics by the time he died. Goodwin was and is very much a political figure. Was there a political spin to the accusations against Goodwin? Certainly. If one believes that there is a liberal intellectual establishment, she must be considered part of it. From the floor of the U.S. House of Representatives, Congressman John J. Duncan of Tennessee, a Republican, denounced her: "It is well-known that Ms. Goodwin colors her history with a very strong liberal bias." An amazing discovery to him, apparently. Within academe, where one would expect a little less shock at such discoveries, David Horowitz, a leading conservative sociologist, found her name all over his list of commencement speakers "on the left." There, according to Horowitz, she kept company with other notorious liberals like Jim Lehrer of PBS, Peter Jennings of "NBC" (sic) and Daniel Schorr, of PBS. Long before a whiff of her plagiarism had reached their nostrils, conservative columnists were wheezing at her defense of President Clinton during his impeachment trial.[50]

Even if such an institution as a liberal intellectual establishment is a chimera of the conservative imagination, Goodwin was certainly a Democratic insider in the Johnson and Clinton administrations. Taking as a whole the glee with which some of observers attacked her and the hesitation of others to blame her, knowing what we know about these individuals, one would have to say that the right wanted to knock her down a peg—which may be why most of her defenders were liberal academics themselves. On October 25, 2003, a group of historians protested a *New York Times* article entitled "Are More People Cheating?"; the point of the protest was the inclusion of Goodwin on the list. This group decided to send a letter in defense of Goodwin to the *Times,* insisting: "She did not, she does not, cheat or plagiarize. In fact, her character and work symbolize the highest standards of moral integrity." Their contention was that plagiarism has to be intentional, an incorrect statement according to the integrity code of the

AHA. The signers to the *Times* letter, including Arthur Schlesinger, Jr., Douglas Brinkley, Robert Dallek, and David Halberstam, were all estimable scholars and liberals. The names of some signers, including Sean Wilentz's, did not appear in print but were on the letter when it was posted at the History News Network website.[51]

In the end, I am convinced, Goodwin did plagiarize, but only because the definition of plagiarism in the AHA's *Statement on Standards of Professional Conduct* makes no allowances for motive or intent. She made mistakes, inadvertently and infrequently, and when confronted with them tried to repair the damage, though she was not as forthcoming as she might have been. She hoped that her reputation would shield her from revelations about the McTaggart affair, and then that *No Ordinary Time* would be safe from scrutiny, but when there was no place to hide, she admitted those errors. "I took the notes. And they were in my longhand. And then, when they got into the text, that was the mistake." Goodwin had a researcher, and the researcher, Goodwin explained, did not "cross check. . . . It was [the researcher's] responsibility to cross-check it, but she didn't." In the end, however, "That doesn't matter. It's mine. I'm the one. . . . So simple. It would have taken, you know, an hour." Unlike Ambrose, who would only change errors if someone else documented them, when the *Weekly Standard* aired its charges Goodwin instructed her assistants to go back over all her work and find any additional places where she did not cite another author, or did not put a quotation in quotation marks. Goodwin amended her work where error was found, though as Mark Lewis put it in another of his Forbes.com exposés, she only brought *The Fitzgeralds and the Kennedys* up to "Ambrose code [standard]: footnotes but no quotation marks around the borrowed passages."[52]

Who Is Really at Fault in Plagiarism Cases?

A perplexing question lingers after the verdicts are in and the judgments rendered in the Ambrose and Goodwin cases. Why did so esteemed scholars sink to plagiarism? At first, both Ambrose and Goodwin insisted that they did not think that they were in any way culpable for what they were doing, because they had not intended to deceive anyone. That is why they were so scrupulous, most of the time, with crediting secondary sources. Laurel Thatcher Ulrich, a prize-winning historian of exquisite personal integrity, was sympathetic to this explanation. As she commented when asked about the Goodwin case, "I find it plausible that someone could be careless and mess up their footnotes. . . . If you are doing an immense project with multiple sources, you have to be systematic and careful." Other historians were a little less sympathetic than Ulrich. Jack Rakove, fresh from the Bellesiles affair and himself a master crafts-man, rejected Ulrich's thesis (and by implication Ambrose's and Goodwin's denial of intent): "It's hard to understand how one could merge note-taking and composition, which are fundamentally differ-ent processes."[53]

The second line of defense to which Ambrose and Goodwin retreated was that the extent of the alleged plagiarism was minuscule compared to the vast number of words that were their own or were properly quoted and cited. Although this is surely true, it is not a defense. Thomas Mallon, in *Stolen Words,* demolishes that argument: "If the police enter the house of a suspected thief and find fifty-three stolen objects [the number of documented plagiarized passages in a novel Mallon was discussing] amid say two thousand legitimately pur-chased by the occupant, should they proceed not to arrest him?" In short, plagiarism is plagiarism.[54]

Motive need not reduce to intent, however. Might celebrity status itself have made Ambrose and Goodwin indifferent to the care that professional historians must always exercise in the use of sources? As one of their books' vendors commented, "What is new is you've made stars out of these nonfiction history writers, which didn't happen before, and now there's a lot of pressure on them to keep on produc-ing books. So, mostly all use secondary sources. And if you use sec-ondary sources, you are going to run into copying other people's work." This explanation has much truth to it, echoing as it does Pat-terson's comment on the trade presses, save that both Ambrose and

Goodwin's public demeanor was not as stars, but as modest and hard-working writers and intellectuals.[55]

If celebrity is at fault in Ambrose's and Goodwin's fall, it played a more subtle role than simply making them too busy to cite-check their books. The historian Elliot J. Gorn, writing in the *Chronicle of Higher Education,* went further down this road, seeing Ambrose and Goodwin as a "fable for our times. . . . The rot of greed spread, finally reaching into the historian's study." For Gorn, a willingness to pilfer others' work was merely symptomatic of a larger malaise. If harping on dollars and cents sounds like sour grapes of the variety that Ambrose's defenders thought his professional detractors harvested, think again about the money to be made in popular histories, and the dependence of those histories on other scholars' academic mono-graphs.[56]

To sell, popular history has to be written in a particular style. Ambrose and Goodwin were superb storytellers who catered to the general audience. For general readers (and the editors who know what general readers want), well written means a balance of lively pace and telling anecdote. Deep analysis, including references to earlier scholarship, can clutter and fatally slow a narrative. A (very unscien-tific) sampling of over a thousand readers' reviews of popular histories at Amazon.com shows that most of the time, reader-reviewers com-plained when a history bogged down for any reason, including too much reliance on prior scholarship or too much analysis by the author. Instead, readers wanted a page turner, with fascinating detail, first-hand accounts, revelations, heroes, villains, and the triumph of good over evil. With a few exceptions, readers did not demand intel-lectual originality or analytical acuity. I found no accusations that someone else's work had been unethically incorporated into the book under review. In fact, the reverse was true; the existence of earlier books on the same subject was a reason for praise for the newcomer in print, even when the new book covered the very same ground as all its predecessors. "It will go on my shelves next to all the other books on the same subject" was the refrain. In sum, the Amazon.com readers' reviews were endorsing the old consensus canon, the very canon that the new history has discarded.[57]

This not-so-surprising result returns us to the advice that Alice Mayhew gave to Stephen Ambrose when accusations of his plagiarism appeared. She had told him, he said, to keep on writing. He did. Ambrose's and Goodwin's plagiarism gained momentum from the way that popular history is produced and consumed. With sales and topicality as the prime determinants of publication and commercial success, the canons of scholarship must take a backseat. Consider what it would require to reverse this order of march. Timothy Noah, writing in *Slate* magazine, tried. "Mayhew has a matchless reputation as an editor of journalist and pop-historical trade nonfiction," he wrote, so she should take "moral leadership" in plagiarism cases. But did Noah want Mayhew to check her author's thousands of notes? Paste labels in the frontispieces of all her books certifying them free of plagiarism? Hire a small army of researchers to read every passage for illicit borrowings?[58]

As high in quality as the books it publishes may be, a publishing house like Simon & Schuster is not in the scholarship business. It is in the merchandising business, and history books (even history books with thousands of reference notes) are commodities for them. The trade press market and the trade press editorial process gave both Ambrose and Goodwin the means and the opportunity to borrow from others without looking back, because there are no controls on what a trade press author does with his or her sources save the editorial process. In other words, trade houses carry on the tradition of the old consensus history. Originality is nice, but not paramount. Another readable biography of a Civil War or World War II leader will always find a home in a trade house because readers will buy it.

So long as Ambrose's and Goodwin's misconduct did not affect their sales, they were protected by the entire system of trade publishing. That they were denounced at all was thus surprising, and was only possible because—just as they said—they included citations of their secondary sources. Indeed, one would have had a hard time discovering plagiarism in the trade books of leading historians in bygone days even if one had looked as hard for it as critics of Ambrose and Goodwin did. Trade books such as Daniel Boorstin's trilogy *The Americans* and Oscar Handlin's *The Uprooted* had no reference apparatus whatsoever, save the quotation marks around primary source quotations and an annotated bibliography at the end. No numbered citations, no notes at all.

By making such clear distinctions between popular history and academic history, and then abjuring any supervisory role over popular history (popular histories are not reviewed in the *Journal of American History* or the *American Historical Review* or the *William and Mary Quarterly*, for example), were not professional historians just a little to blame for Ambrose's and Goodwin's offenses? Walling off popular history from scholarly pieces allowed professional historians to dismiss Ambrose's and Goodwin's (and any other popular historian's) plagiarism, and enabled the profession to shirk responsibility for investigating claims of plagiarism. Had not their media critics insisted on an auto-da-fé, complete with stake and faggots, Ambrose and Goodwin would not have had to make their confessions and atone for their sins at all.

CHAPTER 7

Fabrication: The Case of Joseph Ellis

I AM A LATE-NIGHT WATCHER OF *Booknotes* AND OTHER programs on C-Span; Ambrose and Goodwin were familiar faces there, and that is where, in 2001, I first saw Joseph Ellis. For nearly twenty years I'd owned a paperback copy of his *After the Revolution: Profiles of Early American Culture,* and I had recently read *American Sphinx* (1997), his quirky, delightful biographical essay on Jefferson, and *Founding Brothers: The Revolutionary Generation* (2000), an episodic musing on the leaders of the new republic, but the first time I laid eyes on the man was when he participated in a panel on biography in 2000.

I was immediately impressed. I knew that I would have liked to take a course from him, any course, because he seemed totally at ease with himself and his material. Whether talking about Adams and Jefferson or about the craft of writing, he was wry, full of anecdotes, and thoroughly at home. He seemed, in fact, to be a perfect blend of academic and popular historian. I would never have suspected him of telling untruths about himself in front of a class of history students.

Everyone lies sometimes. I do not mean telling half-truths; in Dilbert's cartoon "weasel-zone" where everyone "is aware that you're a manipulative, scheming, misleading sociopath." I mean telling bald-faced lies, intentionally fabricating. The highest elected officials in our government sometimes fib with such routine insouciance that they seem to forget which lies they have already told and which they have reserved for later use. Business leaders mislead, sometimes in court under oath when they are on trial for lying to their shareholders, customers, or colleagues. Generals in the field make up body counts and deny knowledge of the atrocities their troops commit. Lawyers' prevarications seem so commonplace that it has become a joke to ask, "How do you know when lawyers are lying?" (Answer: when their lips are moving.) Reporters who are supposed to be ferreting out the truth prevaricate, sometimes inventing sources to help make the falsities more believable.[1]

Lying on résumés has reached epidemic proportions. "Résumé fraud" has entered the lexicon of employers: coaches add degrees and varsity playing time; judges add military service; public officials add a wide variety of whoppers. One on-line résumé service finds that the most common misstatement is embellishment of official titles, while others have estimated that between one quarter and one half of all résumés have intentional material errors. The American Historical Association's *Statement on Standards of Professional Conduct* recently added a warning against padding one's accomplishments: "Historians are obligated to present their credentials accurately and honestly in all contexts." But who doesn't airbrush his or her résumé? Isn't it an advertisement for ourselves? No one expects their lies to be uncovered, though many are. Some observers find this unrealistic expectation of immunity proof that lying is the norm, and catching the liar uncommon.[2]

It is human to lie. We lie because the truth is harsh or hurtful; because we see an advantage in the lie; because lying is easier than explanation. We lie to save ourselves from extra work or the consequences of the truth. We lie to make ourselves look smarter, bolder, richer, or more worthy of another's admiration or friendship. We lie to save souls teetering on the edge of the abyss of damnation. We lie to bring low those whose guilt is clear to us but may not be as clear to others. We lie because we are paid to lie. Some of us have a compulsion to lie.

Lying in public would make no sense—certainly it would have little use—unless the people who heard the tales wanted to be lied to. Consensus history was a lie, a reassuring lie, one that fabricated a false history through selection, omission, mischaracterization, and carefully chosen emphasis. Its lies were effective for the same reason that we believed politicians when they told us it was morning in America; businesspeople who insisted that the economy was on the rebound; and generals who swore that they could see the light at the end of the tunnel of war. Lying works because of consumer demand for lies.

As a group of human beings, historians are not especially prone to lie. In fact, historians set high moral standards for themselves, their colleagues, and their students. They stress the importance of truth, of the quest for objectivity even when they know they cannot be truly objective. But historians are realists, and as Arthur Schlesinger, Jr., told a subcommittee of the House Committee on Judicial Affairs when it was investigating President Clinton, "Most people have lied about their sex lives at one time or another. We lie to protect ourselves, our spouses, our children, our lovers."[3]

What Schlesinger did not reveal was that historians have a professional interest in one kind of fantasy. Imagination enhances our professional abilities. Who is the historian who does not want to climb aboard Mr. Peabody's "way-back machine" and see the past as it actually was? Indeed, historians must be fabricators of a sort. They tell stories about things they could not possibly know of their own experience and ask their listeners and readers to believe them without blinking an eye. They are not allowed to invent scenes, dialogue, and events, but the historical imagination is a clever dodger of the brute realities of perception. Historians cannot see, hear, taste, or touch the past but they act as if they could. Though the past is ever receding from all of us, historians make believe they could travel back in time and even take their readers with them. As my good friend and colleague Michael Winship has told me, in utter seriousness, "I think like a seventeenth-century Puritan." Impossible—except that his belief gives his writings on early-modern Puritan life a verisimilitude they would not otherwise have.

Not only do historians believe they can travel through time, they try to take their readers and students with them. Readers suspend disbelief and journey with the historian James Merrell, "Trailing along behind [the negotiators], crowding in with them as they crossed the threshold [of the meeting places], peering over their shoulders, picking up the snatches of their conversations. . . . We can make our way back to where Indian met colonist face to face." We join Christine Heyrman, a historian of religion, to "read over the shoulder of Edward Dromgoole a letter. . . . Eavesdrop as James Finley urges a younger itinerant to preach. . . . Listen as John Brooks sulks." As the biographer Edmund Morris has suggested,

All human communication, outside of the driest exchanges of statistical and other scientific data, involves a certain amount of storytelling—which is to say, creative license. Information has to be arranged in some sort of sequence, tiny touches of humanity or drama or pathos added, unnecessary details subtracted, hidden patterns emphasized. Such arts are applied instinctively, and quite justifiably, even by those of us who have no creative gifts.[4]

To travel back in time, historians usually follow the track of documentary sources. But sometimes they step off the trail to recreate the past as it "might have been." Simon Schama, a historian of early modern Europe and the British Isles, urges his colleagues to indulge in "pure inventions, based, however, on what documents suggest." This may be too far from the beaten path for most of us, but perhaps, with the historian John Demos, we can reimagine what scenes and dialogue must have been, learning a lesson from the best historical novelists? In *The Unredeemed Captive*, his exquisite tale of a girl the Indians captured during a raid on a colonial New England town, he imagined how, many years later, the little girl, Eunice, now grown and married to an Indian, viewed her rescuers: "Perhaps it went something like this," Demos starts.

Cuyler gives the traditional greeting (in Mohawk), and they are admitted inside. Smoke from the firepit stings their eyes. Voices float indistinctly toward them from the far walls. Human forms, a dozen or more, loom in the murk:

squatting, lounging, bent to one or another little task. Slowly, one of the forms — no two — move forward: a woman slightly ahead, then a man. . . . [T]urning back, Stephen makes a little bow: "I am your brother. I rejoice to see you. Thanks be to God." Eunice returns the bow, and looks warily, almost beseechingly, into his eyes . . . This, of course, is no more than conjecture. What Stephen [that is, the documentary evidence] actually tells us is something of the emotional impact. It was, he says, "a joyfull, sorrowfull meeting."

Demos uses italics to set off the invented scene and its dialogue. One of the foremost modern exponents of the study of texts has told us that even our treatment of the documents is about "the interplay between 'the book of nature' and its human decipherer." We need to be able to see something we cannot; hear words long lost; touch a world that is gone.[5]

Turn from writing about history to teaching history. There the temptation to manipulate truth grows more enticing. In front of an audience of students, historians may embellish their importance in the academy, or tell stories about themselves that are not strictly true. They exaggerate and posture to keep students' interest and their own. In recreations and reenactments, they practice a kind of mass pedagogic hypnosis that sometimes involves role playing—acting the part of a living tour guide to the past. At one time or another, all teachers of history become one with the people whose lives the class is studying. But lying to students is another matter entirely.

An Imagined Past

At the start of 2001, Joseph Ellis held a distinguished chair at elite Mount Holyoke, in South Hadley, Massachusetts, had won the Pulitzer Prize for *Founding Brothers* (2000); the National Book Award for *American Sphinx* (1997), on Thomas Jefferson; and public acclaim for *Passionate Sage* (1993), on John Adams. It was a remarkable achievement—three major works on the Founding Fathers, perhaps the most important figures in our history, and all within a decade. He told stories about the Founders with such insight that one could almost imagine he was there, a fly on the wall.

His career at Mount Holyoke began in 1972. Fresh from teaching at West Point (from 1969 to 1972) and earning a Ph.D. in near-record time at Yale (1965 to 1969), he moved up the ladder quickly: head of the history department by 1978 and dean of the college from 1980 to 1990. His teaching seemed exemplary. His students loved the "Viet Nam and American Culture" course he introduced, according to students interviewed in 2001 for a story in the *Boston Globe*. "When he is teaching," one of them told the *Globe*'s reporter, "he uses different anecdotes from his own personal experience in Vietnam . . . to help us understand it better." Another recalled, "The course was something so central to him because he did serve there." Indeed, his experience as he related it to his students, "changed the dimension of the course. His having that personal experience gave the course more gravity." Students at Amherst College, where he also taught a course on the Viet Nam era, agreed.[6]

His scholarship seemed impeccable as well, if by his own admission a little old-fashioned. As he told Mark Feeney, a reporter with the *Boston Globe*, on November 1, 2000, "I'm on a bit of a crusade to do something so old-fashioned some people might regard it as fresh and novel . . . [to turn the Founding Fathers] into human beings with foibles." It was much the same language he had used in the preface to *Founding Brothers*. A few years before, he had been a center of controversy when he first denied Thomas Jefferson's relations with his slave Sally Hemings, then reversed himself on the issue, but that controversy was behind him, and the praise for his new book was swelling. Carried along by that tide, he told the *Globe* interviewer how he "spent the summer of 1964 as a civil-rights worker in Mississippi" and found himself the next year as a platoon leader in Viet Nam "with the 101st Airborne." Feeney was impressed, remarking that "in Ellis's bluff manner and vigorous bearing, one can see his military background." In private settings, among friends and colleagues, he also "reminisced" about "the war."[7]

It was not the first time he had divulged to others, including students in his courses on Viet Nam, that he was a combat veteran or that he had played a role in the civil rights movement. In 1997, in the course of promoting *American Sphinx,* he revealed to the *Globe* his service with the paratroopers in Viet Nam, and how he had been assigned for a time to General William C. Westmoreland's headquarters. In a piece that he wrote for the *Chicago Tribune* book review, he hinted that he regularly visited the Viet Nam Memorial on the Mall, presumably to grieve for lost comrades, though he did not say so, and in a second newspaper piece, he mentioned "my military experience in the Viet Nam War."[8]

But these were untruths, and their unraveling started, as in the Ambrose and Goodwin affairs, with a tipster. The *Globe* reporter Walter V. Robinson (himself a Viet Nam veteran) broke the story on June 18, 2001. Ellis, according to Robinson a "beloved mentor to many students" and "literary icon," had spent "his three years in the army teaching history at the U.S. Military Academy" in West Point. Asked by Robinson face to face about the revelations, Ellis replied, "I'll have to suffer the consequences of this." There was more: He never played on the high school football team for which he had said he scored the winning touchdown in his senior year; the year he claimed to have spent in combat he was in residence in New Haven, in graduate school at Yale; his Yale contemporaries did not remember any occasions of his joining, much less leading, antiwar protests, and though he went south to recruit for Yale's program for minority students, he did not participate in civil rights activities, as he had intimated to earlier interviewers, according to their notes.[9]

Ellis immediately apologized, saying, the *Globe's* Robinson reported, "Even in the best of lives, mistakes are made." He was sorry for any "distortions" he may have promulgated in his account of his past. At first his friends rallied around him, and the president of Mount Holyoke, Joanne V. Creighton, was quoted as stating that his "great integrity, honesty, and honor" were hallmarks in his long career at the college. Indeed, she did not see "what public interest the *Globe* is trying to serve through a story of this nature." But other academic leaders had a somewhat different view of the matter. Arnita Jones, executive director of the AHA, was quoted in the Globe's coverage as commenting that truth in the classroom was an "obligation" of teachers, and

Robert Kreisler, at the American Association of University Professors, agreed that "scholars have an additional responsibility" not to falsify personal credentials.[10]

Although Ellis was best known to the public as an author, his duties at Mount Holyoke lay primarily in the classroom, something that he and administrators there understood. As the college website explains, "While devoted to furthering knowledge in their respective fields, faculty make teaching and advising students their first priority. Small classes and a 10:1 student-to-teacher ratio help ensure a high degree of interaction." For the vast majority of academic historians, teaching is the most important duty. That is why the OAH executive board, some months after the Ellis story broke, reminded all history instructors of the importance of "honesty and integrity in the classroom, and specifically condemn[ed] lying by teachers and professors."[11]

On June 21, Mount Holyoke announced that Ellis had decided he would no longer teach the course "Viet Nam and American Culture." By the end of the week, the college administration fully changed its official stance on his case: it would begin an investigation. Faculty members had expressed their dismay at being "betrayed," and President Creighton wrote a letter to the *Globe* in which she stated that "Misleading students in the classroom is a serious academic matter." She added a retraction of sorts of her earlier pique: "I do not question the right of the press to pursue the truth."[12]

The matter might have rested there, but through his literary success Ellis had achieved a measure of national fame, and the story was soon on the wire services. The historian James M. Banner Jr. explained in a newspaper op-ed, "Ellis's dishonesty is now known to one and all because of the superiority and justified popularity of his historical works. . . . When respected men and women make mistakes, society re-measures itself." David Oshinsky, then a Rutgers University historian, suggested in an op-ed in the *New York Times* that the temptation to lie about taking part in the momentous events of one's time, particularly the turbulent days of the 1960s, when he (and Ellis) were young, was almost irresistible:

It is not surprising that so many of us, even the spectators, look back

longingly to these years. To stay connected to the 60s is to bear witness—sometimes false witness—to an era of turbulent action and
unfulfilled dreams. The brave soldier doing a thankless job, the
young protester confronting an unjust war, the civil rights activist facing daily terror—these are the roles we remember most fondly today,
the roles that some people played for real in the 60's and that others
now play in their heads.

Other historians were less philosophical and more accusatory. David
Garrow, the author of a Pulitzer prize–winning biography of Martin
Luther King Jr., called it "a horrible scandal." David Hackworth, an
author and much decorated veteran of the 101st division, put it more
simply: he thought Ellis a "phony."[13]

There was a pattern in Ellis's fabrications. He was not just a grunt
in Viet Nam, he was a platoon leader in an elite airborne division. He
was not just any high school football player, he scored the winning
touchdown in the last game. He was not just a civil rights worker—he
trained other activists and then went south into the belly of the beast.
He did not simply object to the war while at Yale, he led protests
against it. His accounts were all exaggerations, highly dramatic, even
heroic, fictions. They made him bigger than his life. Instead of trudg-
ing from William and Mary to graduate school at Yale to teaching at
West Point and then earning tenure at Mount Holyoke as one of the
many young scholars who cursed the war and stayed well away from it,
he projected himself into the center of the decade's most important
events: the Viet Nam War, the civil rights movement, and student
protest. He even developed the bluff, gruff, affectionate mannerisms
(like Ellis's John Adams, "colorful and tart") that matched the lies.[14]

But there was also a prudent strain of reticence in his inventions.
In his courses on Viet Nam, he never enlarged on his supposed experiences in combat. He simply hinted that he knew first-hand what the
books he assigned his students talked about. He begged interviewers
not to stress his combat experiences. It was in the combination of
exaggeration of his role and reluctance to elaborate on it that the real
Ellis held together the stories of the fabricated Ellis.

The denouement was predictable, if not particularly swift. The college cobbled together a committee of investigation, which after a two-month-long inquiry recommended, and Mount Holyoke enforced, suspending Ellis for a year without pay (the academic year 2001–2) and withdrawing his Ford Foundation–funded chair. The far right was delighted. Ellis was a liberal. Ann Coulter snarled that Ellis deserved whatever he got, for "whil[ing] away the Vietnam War in his college dorm room, presumably, like most academics, smoking pot and listening to the Beatles' *White Album.*" Ellis was reinstated in September 2002. To his class in American history to 1865 he apologized once again. They accepted his apology.[15]

Of Books and the Man

When the facts are so incontrovertible, the judgment of the Professional Division should have been easy, right? But judgments of motive and merit, as anyone who appreciates Ellis's work would readily agree, are not so swiftly rendered. In particular, one can ask whether there might be some complex and deeply human relationship between a man's ability to invent himself and his ability to reinvent the past in his books. Artistic genius may be a legitimate excuse for personality flaws; can it also excuse professional misconduct? Can we at least conceive of the possibility that he could not have written the three books on which his reputation depends if he had not possessed the ability to imagine himself in another life?

Ellis had surveyed "the imaginative leeway provided by fiction for people to leap across those interior gaps of silence" but joked that he did not fill out the forms to "apply for a poetic license." But had he not termed his comrades at Mount Holyoke "my fellow conjurers"? Only magicians, who fool the eye, can conjure. If we move back and forth through these books, can we see Ellis's own shadow, a conjurer at his work?[16]

Let's begin with the book published a year before he was brought low. Like all of his recent work, *Founding Brothers* is a work of biography, but in addition it is a series of riddles, key moments in early American history when the Founders came together and changed the course of our nation. The first chapter is an attempt to resolve what happened at the Aaron Burr–Alexander Hamilton duel, in 1804. The second concerns a dinner party that Jefferson threw for Madison and Hamilton in 1790 at which Madison and Hamilton agreed to put aside their party differences—at least for a time. Other puzzles concern the first congressional debate over slavery, the origins of Washington's Farewell Address, and perplexing moments in the often turbulent collaboration of Jefferson and John Adams. Each riddle has important precedents and consequences; each allows Ellis to review the achievements of the Founders while making their human foibles and fears clear. All are written with a detachment and clarity that is remarkable. But at the center of each episode there is a mystery, because the historical record, so full for what happened before and after the event, is spare on the event itself.

And that, I think, is what attracted Ellis to the particular stories he tells. What really interests him is what we cannot know and must therefore surmise—thus his fascination with Aaron Burr, of whom he said, "Given Burr's matchless skill at concealing his motives, covering his tracks, and destroying much of his private correspondence, unambiguous answers are not a realistic prospect," and his admiration for "the labyrinthine corridors of Jefferson's famously elusive mind."[17]

At the heart of the allure of the mysteries and hidden meanings of these encounters is a kind of make-believe. Hamilton, born in mean surroundings, reinvents himself as a gentleman and an officer through his own dash and intellect. Jefferson, at heart a passionate man, acts the cool and unruffled host. George Washington, whose presence always made a difference and gave everyone a boost of confidence, was "a virtuoso of exits." A man of studied courtesy, he was also a master of the "melodramatic" gesture. What attracts Ellis to these encounters among the Founders are the tantalizing hints of what lay behind the facade, the real man, whom only the imagination of the historian can recapture.[18]

The significance of these meetings expands as Ellis narrates their course. He repeatedly exaggerates what was at stake and what followed from them. The duel at Weehawken at which Burr fatally wounded his longtime rival and reviler Hamilton had a "rightful place of primacy" among the fabled face-offs of American history. A "succinct summary" could not do it justice. The Jefferson-Madison-Hamilton dinner party, "if true . . . deserves to rank alongside the Missouri Compromise and the Compromise of 1850 as one of the landmark accommodations in American politics . . . [and] top the list as the most meaningful dinner party in American history." Washington's Farewell Address of 1796 was "a classic . . . a perennial candidate for historical commentary." The Jefferson-Adams relationship was "the greatest collaboration of them all. Choosing between them seemed like choosing between the head and the heart of the American Revolution."[19]

Founding Brothers is a tour de force because Ellis's powers of imagination supply all that the vagaries of missing documentation and the many false faces of the participants conceal. Behind the "constructed or posed version" of events, Ellis finds truth; in the "irresistibly dramatic spell" of the events, Ellis can read the meanings of "memorable exchanges." In short, it is his power to invent truth—on its face an oxymoron—that allows him to tell us the story. We enter the mysterious closed space where the document does not go because we are following Ellis where only he can go.[20]

Ellis was, like Ambrose, a master of the piggyback book. The format of *Founding Brothers,* a series of vignettes expanded into broader stories, was borrowed from his 1997 National Book Award–winning intellectual biography of Jefferson, *American Sphinx.* In the latter he broke Jefferson's long life into a sequence of episodes, each a few years long, each finding Jefferson in a different place: in Philadelphia in 1775–76; in Paris from 1784 to 1789; at Monticello, Jefferson's home near Charlottesville, Virginia, from 1794 to 1797; in Washington, D.C., from 1801 to 1804, during Jefferson's first term as president; and finally, Jefferson in the last decade of his life, in retirement at Monticello, from 1816 to 1826. Portions of the material and the treatment of Jefferson would reappear in *Founding Brothers,* for example the "dinner table bargain" that Jefferson hosted in 1790. Earlier, in *Passionate Sage,* Ellis had devoted a chapter to the correspondence of Adams and Jefferson that reappeared in *Founding Brothers.* In all of these books, Ellis's eye for details of character was sharp, particularly when the details lay at the edges of the documentary evidence, places where only a conjurer might safely peer. Indeed, Ellis revealed that he conceived the study of Jefferson in 1993, after attending a reenactor's "elegantly disguised lecture" that "drew deftly on modern Jefferson scholarship." Seeing and hearing an actor's "bravura performance" as Jefferson, and watching even more carefully the attentive delight of the overflow audience, had convinced Ellis to probe the "mystery" of our "unconditional love for Jefferson."[21]

But this Jefferson who transcended all parties was the myth, not the man. Ellis would find the man wrapped in enigma, a puzzle that could only be solved by decoding Jefferson's gift for rhetorical flourish and his deep love of language. The ups and down of Jefferson's reputation, his relationship to his slave Sally Hemings, and his refusal to free any but her and her children in his will, these Ellis regarded as beside the point. What was inside the man mattered.[22]

The first chapter of *American Sphinx* begins like the first chapter of *Founding Brothers*—with a magnificent historical recreation of a moment that demonstrated Jefferson's capacity for performance. Jefferson "arrived in Philadelphia in an ornate carriage, called a phaeton, along with four horses and three slaves." He had "dawdled" along the way "to purchase extra equipage for his entourage." So he would dally all his life, buying what he could not quite afford, enjoying life, acting the provincial gentleman, polite to everyone, suppressing his emotions until they exploded. Jefferson the *American Sphinx* is a consummate master at hiding his feelings, and Ellis demonstrates an empathy for this strategy that goes to the edge, and perhaps beyond, of historical-mindedness. Ellis's Jefferson is a romantic in an age of reason, well ahead of his time. He had an "impulse to invent and then embrace such seductive fictions"; his almost compulsive need for privacy, to withdraw from the public light, showed a kind of childlike desire to invent a world safe from adversity and confrontation; he had a "sentimentality" that bordered on the adolescent.[23]

Like Ambrose and Goodwin, Ellis was an indefatigable writer—but that was not all there was to his days. Mount Holyoke College is an undergraduate institution, not a research university. As a dean and then a chaired professor Ellis was a busy man, with a significant teaching load, advising duties, and responsibility for faculty governance. From the notes to his books one can see that he made extensive use of published primary sources. Given his topics—the lives of Adams, Jefferson, Madison, Hamilton, Burr, and Washington among others, for all of whom there are extensive published collections of correspondence and public papers—there was no need to race about to archives and libraries to find manuscripts. Ellis did not need to go to courthouses and count inventories. There were no living participants from whom to obtain oral histories. Instead, he shared an imagined world with Adams, Jefferson, and a crew of founders. What was more, everything he wrote was in longhand—no modern conveniences (he admitted that he could not type). Even the act of writing about them brought him closer to his subjects.[24]

The ready availability of the primary sources in published form and the fame of his subjects had a drawback. There were thousands of books on these men already in print. Ellis handled that problem as well. From his notes one can see that he did relatively little with the secondary literature. He was familiar with the classic biographies and sometimes offered asides on recent scholarly literature, but he did not rely on others' scholarship to tell his story and did not pile up references to the most recent articles and conference papers. The context for his account—the embellishments of detail and place—came from the primary sources themselves, through the filter of his own reading of the words of his subjects. His assessments of the merit of other works is similarly confident—he admits their value, and credits those that had "a decided impact on my thinking." But he is beholden to no other scholar, trusting his own reading of the primary sources over others'. No "conspicuous erudition" for him, only a "commonsensical approach."[25]

Such confidence in his own ability to fabricate the historical scene fed his tendency to exaggerate the importance of the events. He could say of the drafting of the Declaration of Independence, "But whether they knew it or not—and there was no earthly way they could have known—the members of the Continental Congress had placed the ideal instrument in the perfect position at precisely the right moment. Throughout the remainder of his long career Jefferson never again experienced a challenge better suited to call forth his best creative energies." How did Ellis know all this—how could he say "perfect" and "ideal" and "better suited" with such aplomb? Or, say, "indeed, it is possible to argue, without much fear of contradiction, that during the nine months Adams, Franklin, and Jefferson represented American interests in France the United States enjoyed the greatest assemblage of sheer intellectual talent in the whole subsequent history of American diplomacy." Exuberance, hyperbole, perhaps extravagance bordering on cliché? But certainly a confident statement that needed no archival evidence (in fact, a judgment that was susceptible to neither proof nor disproof). Familiarity with the subject matter over a course of three decades helped, but the real source of his confidence, and his power as a writer, was his gift for putting into words what only he could see. It was the same kind of exuberant exaggeration as marked his description of "The Duel" and "the dinner party" in *Founding Brothers.*[26]

But always accompanying the confident hyperbole was a reticence to go too far into the minds and motives of the Founders. "It is, on the other hand, by no means safe to estimate Jefferson's thoughts and feelings" and "in the end, then, it is impossible to know with any clinching certainty what the stout, balding, toothless, ever proud John Adams was thinking." Ellis had been similarly reticent about his own accomplishments, never allowing himself to expand on them. Ellis must have seen something of himself in Adams. Perhaps at some point Ellis—a dean in midcareer whose days were filled with meetings and whose desk was covered with forms, a professor who wished he had more time to write—perhaps, like Adams, his "Passionate Sage," he started to wonder "where he stood in this procession of aspiring" men in his profession. For Adams, the "aspiring men" were statesmen. For Ellis, they were historians.[27]

Such thoughts come to every historian sometime in midcareer. The first one or two books, probably based on the dissertation research, are done. Tenure and perhaps promotion to full professorial rank are the rewards. There's some recognition, mostly from peers, but little chance to move up to the elite research university. History professors may or may not have graduate students, but in any event the exciting days of being a graduate student at Yale are fast-fading memories. For Ellis, fame must have seemed beyond his reach, as it is for almost all working historians. The lure of fame was a strong motive for the Founders, however. If he could see a little of their ambition in himself, or more elusive still, a little of himself in them, it might raise his work to a higher level.

A comparison of the books Ellis wrote before he reinvented himself as a sixties hero with those he wrote afterward reveals remarkable differences. The telling asides of the later books, the lightning-like brilliance of the insights into character (for the later books are all about character) do not appear in the earlier work. In 1971, while still teaching at West Point, he began a project on four leading cultural figures of the post-Revolutionary generation: the artist Charles Willson Peale; the Scotland-born writer Hugh Henry Brackenridge; William Dunlap, an American dramatist and theater manager; and Noah Webster, the lexicographer and grammarian. He was not able to finish it until 1978, and it was published a year later, as *After the Revolution: Profiles of Early American Culture*. It shares with his later work a biographical approach to history, in which the themes of the Revolutionary generation are "clothed in the flesh and blood of real human beings." He admitted to "feeling a special kinship" with those times, and with men caught between older ideals of art and newer commercial demands of markets. Ellis identified with his subjects—he too was an artist caught between a love of the art and a need to publish. The four men, he said, exhibited "polarities . . . to me familiar."[28]

It is clear that Ellis was never afraid to inject himself into his work and was quite comfortable with comparisons between past and present. But the earlier work itself was profoundly different from his 1990s books. In *After the Revolution*, the moving forces were external, not internal; the "impact of these social changes" made the four men products and reflections of their times. Ellis called the events they lived through "a great divide in history," but unlike the Founders of Ellis's later works, the four subjects of *After the Revolution* were corks in a frothing sea: "Successes or failures are surely influenced by individual intelligence and energy, the kind of personal powers that Webster possessed in abundance," Ellis noted, "but long-range developments and personal forces of which the individual is usually unaware invariably shape lives and attitudes and frequently define what constitutes success or failure in particular historical situations." Did Ellis see himself trapped in this fashion? Was "eclecticism . . . an economic necessity" in his life, as it was in Peale's? Ellis looked closely at them; they might despair, but showed no inclination to fabricate other than in their artistic work. Was Ellis also aware of these limitations on his life and work? Peale insisted that "truth is better than a high finish," and Dunlap "retained the conviction that all practitioners of the arts in America had social responsibilities." Was Ellis feeling similarly constrained by events?[29]

In the end, I think we can conclude that the same bravado that Ellis injected into his fabrications went into his later books and made them different, and better, than his earlier efforts. In the later works, the reinvented Ellis and the reformatted Founders match one another in style and content. Following his imagination's lead gave his voice greater confidence and led his eye to places it could not go before—to the dark side of the Founders, where lies and self-deception multiplied.

I believe that the lies he told about himself and the way he told them changed the way he wrote history. They turned able craftsmanship into high art. But one cannot say that he needed to reinvent himself in order to explore the mysteries of the founding era, and because one cannot so conclude, one cannot redefine his fabrications concerning his own life as artistic license.

Judgments

Is the judgment of his culpability then clear? He admitted guilt and apologized—does that mean he was guilty? Guilty of what? Ellis lied about himself in class to stimulate his students; by appropriating and personalizing what were in fact others' experiences of war, he encouraged his students to look more deeply into themselves. The lies were effective tools—the students valued the course-work more highly than they would have if he had not told them he had participated in the sixties' great events. Ellis, who had opposed the Viet Nam War, had found a way to pass on that opposition to a generation that did not experience the war as his had. It was moral instruction if not a moral method. Or perhaps that is what he told himself.

The mystery, the silences, the combination of exaggeration and reticence that made his writing about the Founding Fathers in the 1990s so much more compelling than his writing in the 1970s, before he started telling stories about himself, all of these were a refracted vision of his invented life. He wished to appear larger than life, like them, and wishing made it so. All this is speculation of course, which is what Ellis was wont to do when the documentation ran out. But one fact is indisputable—when Ellis was writing *American Sphinx* and *Founding Brothers* he knew that he had left behind him a trail of lies.

If the potential damage to his reputation from revelations of lying was so great, why did he repeat the lies to reporters for the *Boston Globe*? The answer, again, may lie in the books. It was in an interview promoting *American Sphinx* that Ellis could not stop himself from making the Viet Nam stories public, and in another interview, during the promotional campaign for *Founding Brothers*, Ellis expanded on his fabrications. It was as if Ellis was competing with the subjects of his books, vying for attention with them, his life against theirs. Adams, too, had in play such a competition with "Washington's shadow," the memory of the great hero, said Ellis. For an ink-stained scribbler, a mere scholar and professor at Mount Holyoke, an isolated girls' college in the middle of Massachusetts, it was harder to compete with his heroes, but he tried. Certainly Ellis began each of the biographies with himself—Ellis explaining "my motives" in feeling that Adams in retirement merited another look; Ellis going to hear a Jefferson reenactor and relating how "the germ of the idea made its first appearance in my mind"; Ellis reading Lytton Strachey's *Eminent Victorians* and revealing how "the idea that gave this book [*Founding Brothers*] its shape first came to mind."[30]

But even in the most mundane recitals of the origins of his interest in the topic, he sometimes let his imagination run away with him. Take for example *American Sphinx*'s two-page-long, highly dramatic depiction of a week's meeting in 1992 at the University of Virginia devoted to the subject of Jefferson and slavery. Reading it, one gets the strong impression that Ellis was there, taking down the "argument for the prosecution" made by Paul Finkelman, a leading student of slavery and law, who, Ellis wrote, accused Jefferson of "failing the test" of his own ideology. The "spirited exchange" Finkelman's comments incited that Ellis describes did take place, but Ellis was not there; in fact, relying on a newspaper report, Ellis misquoted what Finkelman said at the time, according to Finkelman. Moreover, if one looks at the notes to the passage, one finds in note 16 no reference to Finkelman's talk, but to an article by Finkelman in the proceedings of the meeting that Peter Onuf, another leading Jefferson scholar and the convener of the meeting, later edited. (There is no mention at all of the newspaper report in the note 16—shades of Ambrose.) Was Ellis fabricating? He never actually says that he was there. *Caveat lector*—Let the reader beware! Had he simply quoted the Finkelman piece, or even quoted the newspaper report (citing it properly in the notes), the passages would not be nearly so powerful. By imagining that he was there, he could recreate the scene for the reader. But hinting that he was there is awfully close to his fabrications about other, personal, matters.[31]

At one point in *Passionate Sage* and at two points in *American Sphinx* Ellis hinted that fabrication or at least untruth was an important part of the Founders' lives, and, perhaps, his own. Of Adams's recollections in retirement, Ellis opined, "The accuracies and inaccuracies of Adams's account cannot easily be sorted out. In a historical episode as complex as Adams's handling of the French question, . . . the very notion that there is a single true or objective version of the story probably requires scrutiny." And Adams would be "the last person to set the record straight." Ellis could not bring himself to admit to his own fabrications until someone else revealed them. When Jefferson found himself trying to refute charges of having had sexual intercourse with Sally Hemings, he repeated a long-standing pattern: "Jefferson denying to himself and then to the world his complicity . . . then being genuinely surprised when the truth came out." Of Jefferson's self-deception, Ellis wrote, "His position as a mature man invites skepticism for its self-serving paralysis and questionable integrity. But latter-day moral judgments are notoriously easy to render from the comfortable perch that hindsight always provides." Ellis, like Jefferson when confronted with evidence of his lies, insisted, "I believe I am an honorable man." And like his plea for Jefferson, Ellis insisted that "such judgments ought not become a substitute for recovering Jefferson's own understanding, no matter how flawed, of what he was doing." Jefferson was flawed; I am flawed, hints Ellis—don't be so eager to rush to judgment. The comparison of himself with Jefferson, if not in his mind then in ours, bespeaks the same self-inflation as the tall tales of combat in Viet Nam and at the protests.[32]

In Ellis's defense, there was no time lapse between the accusations of fabrication and Ellis's apology. He never tried to tough it out with more lies. He accepted with good grace his demotion at Mount Holyoke. Perhaps, like Adams, Ellis hoped that posterity, "uncontaminated by the prejudices of historians," would vindicate him. Maybe it will. The historian Bruce Schulman makes a further point: the sixties generation (Schulman's—Ellis's—mine) required personal testimony as part of one's teaching credentials; "authenticity" was prized: "The current premium on personal experience grew out of the social and cultural experiments of the 1950s and 1960s." At that time,

Activists and intellectuals unleashed a withering assault against the alienation and phoniness of national life. . . . In this heady atmosphere, historians and scholars joined the wider cultural rebellion against impersonal precision. . . . The racial revolutions of the 1960s and 70s intensified this desire to personalize to achieve authenticity. . . . While few universities openly asserted that a professor needed a Spanish surname, a Jewish mother, or an Indian ancestor to assess a group's history, art, or literature, no one doubted that the right bloodlines strengthened a scholar's claim to the ethnic past.

The cultural commentator Michael Eric Dyson agrees with this view: "We expect our artists and intellectuals to live the experience about which they speak." Perhaps Ellis simply slipped under the burden of too heavy a forged authenticity.[33]

What judgment, then, do we reach on Ellis's missteps? We could take a poll to render a final verdict. That is just what the History News

Network did—in September 2001 it conducted a survey of its users, posing the question "What should be Ellis's fate?" Larry Tise, a historian of the antebellum South, voted to "turn him out to pasture." James Brewer Stewart, a former dean at Macalester College in St. Paul, was equally severe, reasoning that Ellis "served for several years as Dean of the Mount Holyoke Faculty. This position gave him both the primary responsibility and the power to uphold and enhance the academic standards, accomplishments and aspirations of his faculty colleagues." Charlotte Borst, a historian and dean at Union College, in Schenectady, New York, expressed similar concerns: "An endowed chair [which Ellis held] is a privileged position—a position of intellectual leadership within not only a department, but also the wider college and university and the national community. This leadership position, in turn, means that the endowed chair has responsibilities for intellectual probity." Ann Lane of the University of Virginia took a different, gendered, view: "The academy in many ways defines excellent teaching as mesmerizing lectures that students adore hearing. I think I can fairly say that those who excel in this show-biz version of education are in general men." Karl Brooks, a law professor at the University of Kansas, offered another perspective: "I take a very dim view of lying. A former trial lawyer, I know how prone people are to exaggerate and how likely they are to forget the past and invent something to fill in the gaps." Richard Jensen had the most striking point of view on the Ellis case, one that was at variance with those of all the other historians polled: "It makes every historian—every professor in his own class—fair game for any disgruntled student who can try to show that Prof. X gave out 'false' information in class. . . . There is something curiously postmodern about the Ellis case: what caused the trouble was irrelevant colorful claims and background details ('I was nearby') rather than core historical questions about the Vietnam War itself."[34]

———————

When the Professional Division was still adjudicating cases of alleged misconduct, its members would confine their discussion to answering a simple question: Did the individual violate a material condition of the AHA's *Statement on Standards of Professional Conduct?* In Ellis's case the answer would surely have been yes: he had falsified his credentials before his students. He did not do it to gain employment or advancement. The value of his prizes and his scholarly reputation did not gain from his falsification (although I am personally convinced that the fabrication of his own life and his rising powers of historical imagination were linked). Lying on an official dossier or application would have led to his firing from Mount Holyoke, and I am sure that the committee of inquiry that was set up to look into his case there examined his vita, his official biography, the very first day they met. In point of fact, nothing of the combat service appeared in his dossier. All he had done was falsify his life experiences to his students and to the media. But that is more than enough to earn our censure, and he has admitted as much.

I can sympathize with the way little lies can become big ones and retraction becomes harder than repetition. I understand that Ellis did not mean the lies to hurt anyone (however much the veterans of combat in Viet Nam may feel aggrieved), and the fictions seemed to work wonders for Ellis's powers of historical description and insight into the character of his subjects. He walked a narrow path in fabricating these stories, and it seemed to lead to fame. It was the path he chose and with it came the risk of exposure and censure. If one applied no other test than asking whether his conduct should be a model for all of us, however, the answer would be obvious.

CHAPTER 8

History as "Fair Game"

BELLESILES, AMBROSE, GOODWIN, and Ellis should have known better than to do what they did, and one would suppose that their sad but instructive example would deter others from committing the same offenses. But as I have suggested, in all fairness, they had been tempted by the demons of the marketplace. These demons hawk their wares in more than one kiosk. They offer cut rates on the services of research assistants. They sell to the historical novelist who conveniently forgets where he got the information. They bargain with researchers for movies and television miniseries for damaged goods of uncertain provenance. What we do and what we write are fair game, ripe for the free ride and the rip-off.

Is There an Author in the House?

Charles Ogletree, Laurence Tribe, and Alan Dershowitz are arguably among the most important legal pedagogues and public advocates in America. All had written histories that purported to be scholarly. Yet from 2003 to 2005, these three Harvard Law School professors were accused of plagiarism. The accusations against them stung, as their public responses made plain, but hidden in those accusations of uncredited borrowing was an even more sinister offense: they had made their students a party to their misconduct.

On September 3, 2004, Harvard's Ogletree conceded that in his *All Deliberate Speed,* an account of the impact of the *Brown v. Board of Education* decision, he had inadvertently included six paragraphs, word for word, from Yale law professor Jack M. Balkin's introduction to an earlier book, *What Brown v. Board of Education Should Have Said* (2001). Like Ambrose and Goodwin, Ogletree insisted that because he had not meant to copy, he could not be charged with plagiarism. It is not plagiarism that concerns us here, though. It is instead how Ogletree explained the lapse. It seemed that, in the wee hours before the page proofs were due back at the publisher, one of his research assistants had added the paragraphs, in quotation marks, and a second assistant, helping with the rewriting and the proofing, took out the quotation marks. Ogletree then missed the mistake. Why assistants would be adding text is unclear, unless they were coauthors. What is clear, then, is that, in effect, Ogletree at the very least collaborated with these students on the work, rather than writing it entirely and solely from research materials they provided. He apologized for the copying and said that he should have been supervising the students more closely, but never acknowledged that anything was wrong in authorship by committee of professor and research assistants.[1]

His colleague Laurence Tribe defended Ogletree, telling a reporter that Ogletree had erred simply because he was so busy helping people "who ask for his help on all kinds of things." Yet earlier in the year, a tipster called *The Weekly Standard* to reveal that Tribe himself had copied a number of passages into his *God Save this Honorable Court* (1985) from Henry Abraham's *Justices and Presidents,* published in 1974. Tribe's breezy history of the relationship between presidents and their nominees for the U.S. Supreme Court was rushed into print to aid in the campaign against President Ronald Reagan's nomination of Robert Bork to the United States Supreme Court, and in the rush, the extensive verbatim and closely paraphrased material from Abraham was overlooked.

Tribe owned up to the error, admitting that he had "failed to attribute" the borrowing and that he "personally took full responsibility," as he had to do, for he was the sole author of the book. "My well-meaning effort to write a book accessible to a lay audience through the omission of any footnotes or endnotes . . . came at an unacceptable cost." Again, the issue here is not the question of plagiarism (on that issue the thing spoke for itself), but what had actually happened. Quite possibly one of the student research assistants he routinely employed on his scholarly projects had made a mistake, failing to keep control of the material from Abraham. Quotations became paraphrases that were incorporated as is. Tribe was not concerned that his use of research assistants compels coauthorship, however, for they only reported back to him ideas that he had already discussed with them. Still, the issue would not go away.[2]

Ogletree's and Tribe's colleague Alan Dershowitz defended both of them. According to him, questions about their culpability were nothing more than a right-wing partisan attack. But Dershowitz had already found himself under assault for plagiarism from a left-wing maverick. In a book on Israel's alleged mistreatment of the Palestinians, political scientist Norman G. Finkelstein claimed that Dershowitz's defense of Israel, *The Case for Israel* (2003), had plagiarized an earlier work. Finkelstein even devoted a chapter of his *Beyond Chutzpah* to the allegation. Dershowitz went public with his denial of wrongdoing, even sending a "lawyer letter" to the University of California Press board of editors, the regents, and the governor of the state, threatening legal action (or merely expressing his disapproval, depending on whose reading of the letter one credits) to suppress publication. The press then submitted the book to an unprecedented number of outside readers, or "referees", none of whom saw significant problems with it. Despite Dershowitz's protests, the press went ahead with publication.

Finkelstein had agreed to emend certain portions of his manuscript and reword certain claims (removing the word "plagiarism," for example), but for our purposes, the key problem lies not in the matter of uncredited copying, but in the question of who did the copying. It appears that Dershowitz's research assistant was at least in part guilty of the errors, at least according to Finkelstein. What was she doing that so exposed her mentor to such harsh words? The answer may be that she, like Tribe's and Ogletree's bright young law students, was more than a research assistant doing her master's bidding. If she was writing up her findings, including her words, in her compilation of quotations (the latter of course was "source mining," looking for support for Dershowitz's views in the primary and secondary sources), then she was an author as well as a researcher, and deserved appropriate credit—or blame as the case may be.[3]

One may lay aside the law professors' history with the sneer that all "law office history" is intended to persuade rather than objectively explore the evidence, but leading academic historians have more than once noted the phenomenon of uncredited authorship. Pulitzer Prize winner David Hackett Fischer commented, "It's a problem that is very old in historical writing—the atelier problem, the work that is a product not only of the author or artist but also his students and assistants . . . That sort of problem is growing, with more pressure on historians and others to be more entrepreneurial. Teams are becoming more important in every field." Wisconsin's William Cronon recognized the danger, and told a reporter: "I can't imagine turning over my text to a research assistant. It's a different relationship to a work product when you have a team of people working on the output."[1]

But historians at elite universities, with squads of eager and able graduate students at their beck and call, much like the law students serving the Harvard Law faculty, cannot claim they are above using others to do their research. Alan Brinkley of Columbia University admitted, "Most people use research assistants to gather information for them, or sometimes to read and summarize material." Brinkley continued that "it is inconceivable to me that I would ever allow a research assistant to alter a manuscript," but who was the author of any manuscript if the research and its reporting was done by the assistants?[5]

Some authors, such as celebrity authors who are sometimes little more than "platforms" for books, may have an arguable case for needing research assistance that goes beyond fetching and carrying. In the case of student research assistants laboring for their professors, though, reliance of this excessive sort can be hidden under the many-colored umbrella of "mentoring." This kinder, gentler version of the older concept of master-apprentice, in which the senior advisor takes a younger scholar under his or her wing, supports, guides, and promotes the mentoree, and repays hard work with glowing letters of recommendation, lends itself to certain abuses. These were accepted, or at least common, in the heyday of mentorship some years ago. This form of tit-for-tat—service for help in finding a job—is still common in top-tier graduate and law school circles. Before the scandals at Harvard Law School came to light, Rochelle Cooper Dreyfuss, a law professor at New York University, wrote: "While there has always been something of a tradition to ignore student input into faculty research, that tradition was once accompanied by the equally strong custom of advisers placing their graduate students in jobs. When job markets in academia shrank, that sense of responsibility for students' careers declined. But, unfortunately, the tradition of failing to acknowledge student input survived."[6]

Graduate students are reluctant to speak openly of professors who have failed to credit them fully, or, in some cases, used their seminars to gather information for their own work. One such story reported to me by a colleague involved his own experience at Stanford, almost twenty-five years ago. The first day in a Latin American history seminar, the professor announced that he was working on a book on the professions in Brazil, and would be passing out a list of topics relating to his work. The students' research papers might or might not have found a way into his text, but the entire seminar was framed to further his labors.[7]

We know that assistants are used, for they are often thanked in fulsome terms. A wonderful case of credit given where credit is due is the Valley of the Shadow project at the University of Virginia. There, Edward Ayers led three generations of graduate students in a magnificent effort to put all the records of two counties, one on the Pennsylvania side of the Shenandoah, and the other on the Virginia side, from 1859 through Reconstruction, online and on CD-ROM. The website, valley.vcdh.virginia.edu, is open to the public, and reveals the tensions that led to the war in telling detail and striking visuals. The website names all contributions of every collector and transcriber and all technical support personnel. Without their work, the primary sources for Ayers's book, *In the Presence of Mine Enemies: The Civil War in the Heart of America, 1859–1863*, would not have been accessible to the rest of us. The book and the archive raise local history to the plane of high art. But only Ayers wrote the book, just as he directed every stage of the information gathering, and supervised the creation of the online archive.[8]

In inverse fashion, effusive thanks to researchers may conceal an undue dependence on them. Scholarly authorship is not just writing up someone else's research—it is doing the research and writing both. In her Pulitzer Prize winner, *No Ordinary Time*, Goodwin gushed, "this book would not have been possible without the research help of Linda Vandergrift. . . . Her diligence in digging through the archives, her love of detail, and her passion accompanied me every step along the way." While it is not clear if Goodwin was referring to Vandergrift's errors when Goodwin said that she should have double-checked the references in the book to avoid plagiarism, the team reassembled for Goodwin's *Team of Rivals: The Political Genius of Abraham Lincoln* (2005): "I owe an immense debt once again to my great friend and indefatigable assistant Linda Vandergrift." Should not the debt have included coauthorship?

Similarly, in the acknowledgments for her *Founding Mothers: The Women Who Raised Our Nation* (2004), political pundit Cokie Roberts reported "I couldn't do it without the help of my old friend Ann Charnley." Charnley did the research, aided by Roberts' niece Abigail, with footnotes by Annie Whitworth. Lest anyone find error (and with Goodwin's travail possibly in mind), Roberts continued, "if there are mistakes, blame me, not Annie." The classic admission of this sort was Esther Forbes's. At the outset of her Pulitzer Prize—winning biography of Paul Revere, she thanked her mother for doing all the research.[9]

Law school professors like Tribe are especially generous in their praise for their many nonauthorial collaborators. In the acknowledgments to his *Abortion: The Clash of Absolutes*, Tribe wrote, "This book could not have been written without the tireless and meticulous collaboration and assistance of Peter Rubin in every phase of the project, from the initial research to the preparation of successive drafts." That sounds like coauthorship, but Tribe's was the only name that appeared on the title page. Tribe was equally gracious to his fifteen Harvard Law School research assistants, whose "energetic and thorough research, their intelligent editing suggestions, and their careful proofreading all made a great difference."[10]

Of course, it could all be no more than what I call "acknowledgment inflation." Consider the following acknowledgment of a graduate student's contribution from prize-winning historian Lawrence W. Levine, in *The Opening of the American Mind* (2001): the student "worked closely with me on every part of this book. She located sources, aided me in resolving any number of dilemmas, and, with her remarkable critical skills, she commented on and improved the style and content of each chapter. Her discernment, enthusiasm, and humor helped me maintain my perspective and my good spirits. She was, in short, indispensable and I am deeply grateful to her." It may be that Berkeley graduate students are light years more sophisticated and able these days than the graduate students I have known in my four decades of toil in these fields, but no matter whether the acknowledgment is accurate in its detail, there is a word for this extent of contribution to a book: coauthorship. But I suspect that the student's contributions, while enthusiastic and helpful, did not quite match Levine's encomia. There is a growing tendency to inflate the language of these acknowledgments, similar to that in letters of recommendation (everyone is among the best students I have ever had), as well as grades.[11]

If the assistance of so many talented and able assistants does not amount to coauthorship, might it then be plagiarism? Edward Tenner, trained as a Ph.D. in German history and writing in the *Chronicle of Higher Education*, quoted Dreyfuss with approval, and continued, "Although plagiarism is relatively straightforward to prove (and increasingly, thanks to the Web, to detect), the use and abuse of graduate student ideas by senior researchers are still ethically sensitive. In practice, credit in the form of position of coauthor names and other public acknowledgment can be self-policing, and a reputation for exploitive behavior will turn away students. But, apparently, not always." I have reviewed books in which I knew from anecdotal evidence given me in confidence or from inference from the acknowledgments in the book that the author, wearing the garb of advisor or teacher, had set students in a research seminar the task of researching and writing papers that found their way into the advisor/teacher's book—without citation of the student's work by name, either of the student or the title of paper. In such cases, the student researcher is not just a photocopier or secretary, cite checker or editor. Even if the author told the student what to look for, and the seminar paper was required for a grade, the student's work should be cited in the professor's book in the same way that the work of any other scholar should be cited. When a student researcher's work spills out over many years, entails research in a wide variety of places, and includes primary as well as secondary source reading and interpretation, one can say, with more than a little truth, that the researcher is contributing more to the work than the title page author. Put in other terms, the author who uses the research has become a compiler rather than a scholar.[12]

For that is the real problem for scholars who misrepresent their dependence on others' works and research assistants. A true scholar is not just a compiler of others' research. An original work of scholarship combines research and writing. One cannot accept Tribe's notion that the researchers' ideas are only those planted by the professor for whom they work, nor Brinkley's aside that everyone has research assistants (a statement as patently false as it is misleading when one leaves the precincts of giant graduate programs like Columbia University's and joins the thousands of historians working in smaller universities, colleges, and other environments).

One might argue that the research assistant loses all claim to joint authorship because his or hers is "work for hire." This was common when professors had money of their own to pay researchers or when families or companies underwrote research into their famous members. For example, when Columbia University's Allen Nevins wrote his massive two-volume biography of John D. Rockefeller, the family provided a $15,000 stipend to pay for research assistance. Nevins's acknowledgments recorded the gift obliquely and the research openly. "Mr. Rockefeller Jr., provided for further research, which was most ably executed by Mr. Frank E. Hill, Miss Helene Maxwell, and

Mr. David K. Rothstein, three expert and impartial workers." Nothing more was said about the precise nature of their contributions, just as the precise manner in which the Rockefeller family financed the research was left vague.[13]

While the concept of work for hire means that the actual author/researcher has signed away copyright in return for the sum agreed, it does not and should not take away credit for authorship as well. The rightful claim of the real joint or part author is not monetary, it is scholarly. Parenthetically, the same reasoning may not apply to the ghostwriter or the "written with" author. In both of these cases, the real author has agreed, for money, to allow another person (usually a celebrity of some kind) to claim authorship, even though this individual is more a source of information than an author.

All of us—scholars, writers, and researchers—need to reassess the meaning of "research assistant." If someone does all or most of our research in a nonfiction work, they should be credited as coauthors or in some other formal, visible way on the title page (and in the Library of Congress catalog). Mention in the acknowledgments, no matter how fulsome, is not enough. Even if the contract does not name them and they are paid from other funds than advances or royalties, their contribution goes beyond mere acknowledgment. If they only contribute a part of the research, but write up their findings and any part of those reports are included in the text, the authors of those research reports should be explicitly credited for that contribution. This multiple crediting system is standard in science, and should be standard in the humanities.

Do Not Reproduce, Cite or Quote Without Permission of the Author

One way that younger historians have attempted to protect their work from pirates is the boilerplate injunction at the top of the draft of a talk or seminar paper: "Do Not Reproduce, Cite or Quote

Without Permission of the Author." Historians often announce their latest findings at seminars, colloquiums, and conferences. The written material on which the talk or presentation is based may in the future be submitted to a scholarly journal or become part of a book. In the meantime, the talk or paper itself is publication, and its language is protected by the copyright acts.

The precise terminology of the copyright line reflects the growing impact of intellectual property lawyers on our scholarship. Our publishing contracts have gotten longer and more involved, including our promise to hold the publisher harmless and indemnify the publisher for any lawsuits lodged against the work. For a brief time, the American Historical Association asked its book reviewers to sign contracts turning over the copyright, and not incidentally holding the *American Historical Review* harmless if the author of the book reviewed sued the reviewer and the journal for libel. (For example, for accusing the author of plagiarism.) This had a chilling effect on potential book reviewers but demonstrated how the culture of litigiousness had infiltrated the highest precincts of the academy.[14]

But the boilerplate language that warns off pirates, no matter how legalistic it seems, does not protect anyone from theft. Indeed, it claims too much and too little. The warning is unnecessary because copyright attaches even without the explicit claim of copyright. True, if the author takes the further step of registering copyright of the draft or paper with the copyright office, he or she can impose court costs and reasonable lawyers' expenses on someone found to violate the copyright. But the statement itself does not create any property right not already present when the work is made public.

The findings themselves, the ideas the author presents, cannot be protected from unauthorized use even with the statement in place. Only the author's precise formulation is protected by copyright law. Say that a scholar has discovered, after prodigious research in original sources, that the British Army in the American colonies widely practiced biological warfare against the Indian allies of the French by giving them blankets taken from deceased smallpox patients. The scholar presents this finding at a conference or in a seminar. The paper has the copyright statement. What legally enforceable rights does the scholar have to the exclusive use of this finding? Can anyone repeat it in their own work without the scholar's permission? What remedy at law would the scholar have to obtain damages or to enjoin another's use of this finding? The answer is none. One cannot copyright ideas. Susan Douglas coauthored a scholarly work on the idealization of modern motherhood in February 2004, and found to her consternation that every one of her key arguments reappeared, in that order, in a journalist's book on the same subject a year later. There was no attribution—for the journalist believed, correctly, that in law the ideas were there for the taking.[15]

What if the historian offers conclusions as fact? Facts cannot be copyrighted either. Even if those facts are in fact the work of years and years of painstaking research, and were entirely unknown until the scholar unearthed them, they are still free for the taking. Historians know, of course, that the "fact" is not a brick lying around, waiting to be laid in the construction of a building. It is a product of many pieces of evidence, and they in turn of much labor of sorting, weighing, and discrimination. "For all practical purposes, it is this affirmation about the [past] event that constitutes for us the historical fact." In short, some "facts" are as argumentative and hypothetical as scientists' postulations like the big bang theory of the origins of the universe.[16]

Consider the case of Valerie Lawson, the biographer whose work on Pamela Travers, the creator of *Mary Poppins*, was the basis of the articles that Caitlin Flanagan wrote for the *New Yorker*. When Lawson suggested that there were certain facts in her biography only available there, and these appeared without attribution in the *New Yorker* pieces, *New Yorker* editor Pam McCarthy replied, "But it also reflects the reality that some biographical facts about Travers have escaped the orbit of their discoverer and entered the wider universe's body of knowledge. This may be difficult to realize. I know you devoted an immense amount of time to the making of your excellent book and perhaps feel a proprietary interest in some of the facts you uncovered."[17]

Thus the historian finds himself or herself in a nasty variation of

Joseph Heller's catch-22. Neither new ideas nor newly uncovered facts are protected from pilferage. One journalist for Slate.com slyly suggested that the historian had a way out of this paradox: "they could portray their work as fiction." Or, as the *New Yorker* told a biographer whose work had been ripped off by one of the magazine's reporters, the biographer should be delighted that the subject had appeared in such a prestigious venue. Perhaps the way out is to call all our work fictional, which would make our texts protected by copyright law! For the historian to have to follow this course is surely absurd, but only it would lead to some protection.[18]

Lifting a historian's findings without permission is not piracy. It is, to continue the metaphor, a species of privateering licensed by the law. To this permissive legal stance, the scholarly answer must be ethical. Users should acknowledge the source. Every historian risks being scooped when he or she publicizes new findings or facts, but our ethical canons require that we fully and fairly acknowledge in our publications where we obtained information from others. The boilerplate injunction to seek permission may have no weight in law, but it does remind us of our collegial obligation to give another scholar a chance to publish his or her own material first, or to give permission to the rest of us to use the findings and facts.

Indeed, we should ask permission and get it in writing (an e-mail and reply is sufficient). In my experience, that permission is almost always readily given, on condition of acknowledgment. The author usually wants credit for the finding and is happy to have it widely disseminated under those conditions, as long as the use of the author's findings falls within reasonable limits. One should not expropriate the entire work, or even a substantial part of it.

In effect, the original author and the borrower agree to strike a balance between early dissemination by the user and full distribution by the author. Such balancing is part and parcel of the idea of a community of scholars and lies at the heart of the concept of copyright itself. Copyright is there to reward and promote individual scholarly enterprise. And the limits on copyright—including no copyright of ideas or facts—are there to ensure that everyone in the intellectual community has access to the latest information.

Borrowing Privileges

One unauthorized borrower that scholars cannot defend them-selves against—at least not yet—is the historical novelist. On March, 15, 2006, Dan Brown, the author of the blockbuster *The Da Vinci Code,* made a telling admission in a London courtroom. Facing a copyright violation suit against his publisher by the two historians on whose work he had allegedly piggy-backed his novel, Brown con-ceded that he had "reworked" their material for his own publica-tion. Their speculations about Jesus marrying Mary Magdalene and having children with her, not quite historical facts but based upon their extensive and original research, became one of the major struts in the framework of his plot. Earlier, he had acknowledged that he read *The Holy Blood and The Holy Grail* by Michael Baigent and Richard Leigh (and Henry Lincoln, though he did not join in the suit). If he did not "copy," as he denied, whatever did he mean by "reworked"?[19]

To Brown's defense came a small a legion of journalist-turned-novelists, defenders of free enterprise, and publishers (including Random House—publisher of both books). They chorused that were he to lose, all of historical fiction might fall prey to rapacious histori-ans, bursting from their cluttered library cubicles to launch an armada of lawsuits. After all, according to one of these journalists, all the Browns had done was carry on "diligent background research." The historians did not weigh in, save for Leigh and Baigent. This despite the uncredited use of scholars' totally uncompensated research labors, by proxy, for the novelists.[20]

Another of Brown and Random House's lines of defense against the suit was that he used many sources, not just *Holy Blood,* to thicken his plot. Indeed, in his statement to the court, Brown conceded that there were a number of art histories and other scholarly sources (uncited as it happened) in "researching and writing the book." His student days' interest in art history had taught him how exciting these beautifully illustrated and informative tomes could be: "I studied art history at the University of Seville. The course covered the entire history of World Art, including, of course, Leonardo da Vinci. The course made a great impression on me . . . Examining religion, art, and architecture was exciting to me. I loved researching these subjects; as did my wife, Blythe." There is no prohibition on copying and reusing at a later date one's professors' lectures. Unfortunately, Brown did not remember the professor's name.

In detailed fashion, Brown testified to his research methods, or rather, to how he and his wife used others' research. For the court, Brown produced a list of sources—not a real bibliography, and certainly not page numbers, though presumably he knew which pages he was reading and copying from into his research notes. He acknowledged that he relied on a number of historical works in addition to *Holy Blood, Holy Grail:* "An important book for this early research was *The Hiram Key* by Christopher Knight and Robert Lomas. This book examines the role of the Masons and the Knights Templar in excavating and then hiding a cache of early Christian writings. . . . Looking back at my copy of *The Hiram Key*, I can see that either Blythe or myself has underlined passages that speculate as to the nature of what the Templars found and the subsequent impact on Christianity." If one were to look at these notes, one would find the kind of unorganized, poorly acknowledged, messy copying that we warn students against, lest they succumb to acts of plagiarism.

But the writer of fiction is apparently immune to this disease. Dan Brown had little use for scholarly apparatus—after all he was an artist (of sorts). Brown eventually conceded that he had used *Holy Blood* in his research, yet he did not concede that he took from it any more than bits and pieces, or that it had influenced major plot themes.

The court agreed. Brown owed nothing to any other writer—neither Baigent or Leigh or any of the other authors he did not cite but borrowed from. Though the debt was pervasive and obvious, as a matter of copyright law it was decided that "none of this amounts to copying of HBHG or substantial copying of it (whether textual or non textual) nor of the Central Themes and does not amount to an infringement of the claimants copyright in the book." No words were taken, but entire chunks of character and theme were purloined. Not plagiarism, not copyright infringement.[21]

Whether or not the burrower or the borrower is legally culpable, surely the scholar need not bring a lawsuit to determine the ethical obligation of historical novelists to the scholarly secondary sources on which they wholly depend. Historical novelists rarely do original research in primary sources—instead, they go to the historians and pour over their work.

Unfortunately for the scholar, the conventional argument against such uncredited borrowing revolves not around professional or moral standards, but around legal concepts. In law, one cannot litigate against plagiarism, so long as the material taken is paraphrased in language sufficiently different from the original. Sufficiency is a quality in the eye of the beholders, but legal action for plagiarism of theme or content is almost unknown. Instead, if the historian robbed by another wanted legal redress, it would have to come in the form of copyright violation suit. Here, however, there is much latitude for borrowing, so long as acknowledgment is duly made. According to the United States Copyright Office's "Circular 21: Reproduction of copyrighted Works by Educators and Librarians," the "fair use" exception to the copyright laws allows quotation of significant portions of another scholarly work.[22]

Historical novels invariably do and must depend for their verisimilitude on the validity of the historical works consulted. The fiction writer, in short, is absolutely dependent on the nonfiction scholar, and should acknowledge that reliance as a matter of simple reciprocity. A simple thanks to all whose works were consulted would do. Every work of historical fiction should have a good bibliography of the works consulted—and nothing on that list but the works actually used.

Some novelists of note are doing just this—Norman Mailer is one. I visited the local Barnes & Noble recently for some hands-on research into historical novelists' acknowledgment of their sources. To my delight I found Sarah Dunant's *The Birth of Venus, A Novel* from Random House in 2004, in which she tells the reader that her work is "built on the scaffold of history" and then lists the "eminent scholars" whose work she consulted. Her next work, *In the Company of the Courtesan*, also from Random House, in 2006, has an even fuller bibliography. James Morrow's *The Last Witchfinder, a Novel* (2006) graciously lists the works of history he used.

It is simple justice for novelists to list their secondary sources. A bibliography of historical works consulted takes up little space and gives credit where it is due. Acknowledging intellectual debt not only provides readers with relevant information, it fosters a kind of reciprocity where little exists now. Scholars rightly feel abused by historical novelists because the borrowing is one-way, and even more importantly, because without the scholarship, the novelist would have no historical subject. Finally, and hardly the least important, if novelists fairly admitted where they obtained their information, scholars would be shamed into a fuller and fairer accounting of their own borrowings.

Who is to enforce on novelists a due appreciation of scholars' work? Editors? As Tom Connor wrote for a recent issue of *Writer's Digest*, "The interesting thing about the current run of questionable texts is how little it seems to bother editors." When it comes to historical novels, no one need cite sources. Snide suggestions that editors remake themselves into reference cite checkers or take personal responsibility for their authors' use of other works are impractical. Academic press editors acquire books and arrange for outside readers. Rarely do they have subject matter expertise. Trade editors work more closely with the text, but they rely on their authors. Still, editors can demand that authors keep a record of the books and articles they consulted and provide bibliographies of the works they actually used for the end matter of the book.[23]

If not the editors, perhaps their publishers. In the Ambrose, Goodwin, and Bellesiles scandals, publishers rushed to defend their authors. At risk was the reputation of the publisher as well as sales of the works. It turned out that sales did not suffer, nor, in any long term way, did the reputation of the publishers. Yet publishers should still insist on bibliographies in the contract, in the same way that the publishing contract requires that the author stipulate that the work is his own, has no defamatory statements in it, and that the author will not write a competing work without the publisher's permission. Publishing contracts are already many pages long, with clauses that protect the publisher from lawsuits. It would not take much to add another clause, not to protect the publisher, but to protect the reader.[24]

Reviewers are unlikely to provide any protection to the uncredited work. Novelists reviewing other historical novelists warn not of uncredited borrowing, but too much fidelity to historical sources. As novelist Andrew Sean Greer wrote of Greg Hollingshead's *Bedlam,* "History stands naked, clothed only by our imagination. So a historical novel has a particularly difficult task: breathing life into a story without losing it in a mass of research." Hollingshead had fallen into the trap, "the author seems too in love with the past," by which Greer seems to mean the documentary, scholarly recreation of the past, "to be willing to take liberties with it." So long as the trade reviews of historical novels are written by other historical novelists, no one is going to fault historical novels' misuse of their historical sources. But if the trade review editors reach out to well-known professional historians to write the reviews, both the historical accuracy and the indebtedness of authors to their secondary sources will quickly improve.[25]

Professional associations can also make sure that novelists give credit where it is due. Associations like the Authors' Guild work assiduously to protect the property rights of writers. To protect the integrity of the work and the reputation of the author, the Author's Guild, to which many of the historical novelists belong, should urge all of its members to include bibliographies or the equivalent forms of acknowledgment in all of their works. The guild is zealous in defense of its members' rights—for example, in the battle against the Google project to optically scan all books into an accessible database, with or without consent from the authors and publishers—but not so zealous in its obligations to readers of historical fiction and popular history.

Giving the Customer
What He or She Wants

For the masses of its consumers, history is just another form of entertainment. In entertainment, fabrication and borrowing are not only commonplace, they are taken for granted. A survey of readers' responses to popular history on Amazon.com suggests that accusations of misconduct against popular historians makes little difference to ordinary readers because, for them, reading history for them is not a critical intellectual act, but amusement. And if reading historical fiction is akin to reading history itself, the case becomes more compelling for historical novelists to cite their sources.

Reviewers who should know better or at least care more asked for a whopping good story told with as few obtrusive footnote numbers and quotation marks on the page as possible. As a scholar reviewing a dual history of Pocahontas and John Smith for a major newspaper recently complained, "Only another historophile would love this book. Despite the dust jacket assertion that the book is 'gripping' . . . the narrative is terribly bogged down by endless citations from primary documents— the sort of scholarship that college history teachers and doctoral dissertation directors delight in." The novelist/reviewer for *Entertainment Weekly* felt confident reporting that Melvin Konner's history of the Jews "is that rarest of achievements—a scholarly study that is entirely accessible to the common reader." A prize-winning book reviewer in the *Baltimore Sun* simply used the code words "is not intended for specialists" to convey the same message of praise to potential readers of historian Richard J. Evans's *The Coming of the Third Reich.*[26]

Popular history will always sell, whether or not its authors cut corners, because commercial success does not correlate with scholarly ethics. Notwithstanding all the hoopla about his plagiarism, Ambrose's books still fill a shelf at Barnes & Noble, and the Smithsonian website still features him as one of the "Voices from the Smithsonian Associates." The welcome page for his talk touts his books on the Transcontinental Railroad and the Lewis and Clark expedition as though they were above reproach. Bellesiles is still publishing for the general public. The new edition of his *Arming America* was published in 2003. There was no warning label for unwary readers that some material in it might be unusable. He is once again a frequent contributor to the H-List and writes with authority on the uses of history, among other subjects. Ellis is back in harness, penance done, speaking for the founding fathers, applying the lessons of their words to subjects as controversial as same-sex marriage and gay rights, eager to put the past he invented behind him. He reviews for the prestigious *New York Times Book Review* and has written a major biography of George Washington. Goodwin has composed a love song nearly one thousand pages long to the "political genius of Abraham Lincoln." Like Ellis, she has found a secure haven in consensus history, and the liberal media seems eager to let bygones be bygones. Both their post-travail books shot up to the bestseller lists.[27]

Readers and viewers do not care about the provenance of what they are reading or looking at when it comes to history. Ken Hitchcock was the coach of the NHL's Philadelphia Flyers and a confessed "history buff." He told a reporter, "I love the historical side of everything. . . . I could watch the History Channel all day." Actor Keith Carradine is more than a familiar figure in westerns; he is another history buff, and in 2004 he was hosting a cable TV show entitled *Wild West Tech*. On it, he boasted that "research based on original documents and newspaper accounts, plus input from historians and reenactors, ensures accuracy." That's what history was all about to him, and to his viewers. "There's no excuse for getting it wrong," he told an interviewer, "and getting it right, is, in fact, more interesting." For his own role as Wild Bill Hickock in the series *Deadwood*, Carradine "read biographies and historical articles, 'basically everything I could get my hands on.'" In short, both Hitchcock and Carradine were happy to buy used products from unlicensed sellers.

Carradine had no way to determine if those biographies and articles were done by freelancers, popular historians, or university professors; whether they were original research or synthesis, or even plagiarized. Only the interesting facts mattered—as witness the over three thousand websites that offer "interesting historical facts" of one kind or another, ranging from facts about lightships to facts about Lexington, Massachusetts. None of these websites exhibited the least concern about who originally gathered the facts or whether the language in which they were expressed was borrowed.[28]

I Saw It at the Cinema

If attribution is a dying art in history books and a rare occurrence in historical novels, it never really existed in historical films. The credits rarely list the books or articles the scriptwriter consulted, and rarely is the scriptwriter a historian, much less an expert in the field. Costume and set design may be accurate to a fault, but look in vain for a credit to the historians of dress, architecture, and interior design that the set designer or costumer relied upon. Often, the writers mined historical novels rather than more technical academic works for plot and detail. Even when the consultants or writers used scholarly historical works, they gave no credit. Not trained as scholars, it is not surprising that these researchers, consultants, and writers do not feel the need to credit their sources.

True, many studios hire history consultants, and scriptwriters often read histories. One very able study of Hollywood studio history found that nearly a third of the pressbooks for studio releases trumpeted "authenticity." The film should look right, though historians familiar with film add that verisimilitude does not equate to veracity. The historical consultants and studio researchers are not scholars with academic credentials, but burrowers, ensuring that details are correct, the same way that the continuity editor ensures that light, costume, and other characteristics of a scene match retakes and subsequent scenes.[29]

One must concede that movies are an art form—like painting, music, and poetry—and homage to another director's work, like Brian De Palma's to Alfred Hitchcock, is not only customary, it is taken as a mark of honor rather than condemned as copying. But the power of the movie medium to offer a version of history demands that the histories relied upon be named. Even when basic and elementary facts are altered, a movie "based on" history or "taken from real life" has an ethical duty to inform the reader of its sources.

Sometimes the historical depiction may perpetuate racial and other stereotypes. The best example of that was D. W. Griffith's 1915 blockbuster *The Birth of a Nation*. Coming in the high tide of lynch law and Jim Crow, the movie's demeaning account of blacks and their allies, and the heroic efforts of the KKK to save the white South from venal and lascivious Northern aggression, entranced millions of viewers. Indeed, it taught an entire generation that Reconstruction was an infamous episode in American history. The images of freedmen as bestial or indolent came not from historical research, as it happened, but from a Southern racist novel, *The Clansman,* and from Griffith, an unreconstructed Virginia Civil War buff. The underlying message carried by the movie was that the white race was the ruling race, and must be kept safe from dark blood. The not-so-underlying message was that slavery was good and proper, insofar as it kept the black man in his place.

Martin Scorsese's *Gangs of New York* disregarded much historical scholarship on the topic, including classic works as well as recent books by leading authors. He did this not in the name of art, or even imagery, which would be excusable (after all, it is a movie), but in order to evoke another ur-history of violence, class tension, racism, and urban rot. Scorsese wanted a hellish city, so he turned a real place into an imaginary one—keeping only the scattered details that hid truth and showcased falsehood. The result was a visual version of "sensational journalism . . . pulp fiction." Even the larger-than-life characters act in ways that are atypical of the actual gang leaders of the period. Despite this blatant inaccuracy, Scorsese has said the movie depicts "a cauldron of conflict and violence out of which New York and this country were created." As one astute reviewer replies, like Griffith's *Birth of a Nation,* "Scorsese's absurd fantasy trivializes history."[30]

Some dramatic license with facts, handled with respect for history, can foreground essential themes. As Pulitzer Prize–winning Civil War historian James M. McPherson wrote in praise of the movie *Glory:* "Can movies teach history? For *Glory,* the answer is yes. . . . it is also one of the most powerful and historically accurate movies ever made about . . . the American Civil War." The climax, when the Massachusetts 54th Regiment of Infantry assaulted Fort Wagner in Charleston Harbor, "is the most realistic combat footage in any Civil War movie."[31]

But *Glory* is not realistic in one sense: it is driven by argument as much as by fact. Its purpose, as McPherson admits, is to demonstrate to the modern viewer what the commanders at Fort Wagner wanted to show the nation—that black troops could fight with courage and skill. Such an argument, as appealing as it may be today, must include more than our faith in the movie makers' historical sensibilities. What we are not permitted to see—the reality of Civil War battle— is just as important as what we are shown. In *Glory,* men die bloodless, limbs intact, quietly. There is no sobbing, no crying for mothers and fathers far away, no cursing, and none of the awful rattling of lungs that can no longer fill with air. Perhaps it is better that way, for watching war movies like *Saving Private Ryan,* where the depiction of gore and death is almost too realistic, leaves the viewer totally drained.[32]

Steven Spielberg, the director, and Robert Rodat, the screenwriter, of *Saving Private Ryan* relied on Stephen Ambrose's works as they wrote and shot the film, and listed him as historical consultant for the movie's accuracy. Ambrose's credentials as a student of the D-day invasion and its aftermath cannot be questioned. Even though the central event in the movie, the dispatch of a patrol to find and return the young paratrooper to the lines, was concocted, the scenes reflected a composite of actual events and were depicted realistically. More important, Spielberg gave full credit to Ambrose's work by naming him a consultant. How hard would it be for other historical movies to credit either the historical consultants or the major written sources used? The screen credits at the end of the movie list everything else, including the caterer.

Like cinema, television miniseries "based on an actual event" sometimes display open disregard for historical accuracy. When the historical subjects themselves, including Bill Clinton, Madeleine Albright, and former national security advisor Sandy Berger, complained that an ABC miniseries *The Path to 9/11* invented dialogue, scenes, and government actions that did not happen, the network responded that the miniseries was "not a documentary" and was based on many sources that the network would not document. The resignation in protest of experts hired to help the scriptwriters ensure accuracy, and doubts expressed by some of the actors about the veracity of the words they were saying, did not deter the network, though it did cut several of the most egregiously inaccurate scenes. The network also revised its initial claim that the script was based on the *9/11 Report.* Even so, later polls of viewers revealed that they were not concerned by the brouhaha, or the question of strict historical accuracy. What mattered to them, as to readers of historical fiction, was the dramatic value of the presentation.[33]

The argument over historical veracity in *The Path to 9/11* had a political spin—who did what in failing to prevent the disaster had consequences for the two major political parties, particularly in the months before a critical midterm election. But the carefree indifference to historical probity has long characterized the makers of historical movies and plays. To be sure, it is often difficult, if not impossible, to recreate the mise-en-scène of past events, even with the biggest studio budget. The accents and even the language of the historical subjects must be changed for modern audiences. Plot and character must be simplified to fit the screen. Events are compressed in time and space. All this conceded, the liberties that directors like Oliver Stone and Mel Gibson, to name two famous offenders, have taken with well known historical events are notorious. Whether these excesses are motivated by profits, political and religious viewpoints, or simple indifference to historical facts, the resulting product misleads viewers and scandalizes scholars.[34]

The exception would seem to be the documentary, with its talking heads and list of historical experts in the credits. ABC at first promoted *The Path to 9/11* as a semidocumentary miniseries, based on the 9/11 Commission report. Later, the network insisted it had never intended to make a documentary. Those of us who have had the pleasure of appearing on such telecasts have rarely been happy with our portion. Often, our attempts to capture the nuance and the incompleteness of the story are cut short or reshaped by directors and scriptwriters who want a clean, fast-paced narrative with one rather than multiple story lines. The talking head must be a platform for the visual presentation—so voice, appearance, and oral skills matter more than precise subject-matter expertise. And the talking heads contribute sound bites much like news commentators. They are there for the verisimilitude and authority they lend, rather than for scholarly depth and complexity.[35]

Even the visual component of the historical documentary is fabricated. The reenactments are fun but misleading. To avoid anachronisms like automobiles, power and telephone lines, and buildings, many of the shots are from the ground up—a worms-eye view of history. The alternative, a pan and scan of photographs, drawn art, or other panoramas (accompanied by voice-overs and contemporary music), and newsreels, is closer to reality, but there is no time for critical assessment of sources—that would further slow the action. The result is that what is presented on the screen becomes what was.

But to their credit, documentaries' acknowledgments conventionally thank the historians who took part, either as talking heads or as consultants. Some even list the principal historical works consulted in the course of writing the script. Every visualization of the past owes this obligation to its scholarly sources.

A Rip-Off Culture

Although the culprits in the foregoing gallery of missing acknowledgments, misused research findings, and misshapen presentations may seem different, historical scholars' uncredited reliance on research assistants, historical fiction's uncredited reliance on historical scholarship, the consumers of popular histories' undifferentiated taste for everything that purports to be history, and moviemakers' undocumented rummaging through written histories looking for facts, ideas, and plotlines are all of a piece: the rip-off culture. One characteristic of the rip-off culture is the brazenness with which the culprit denies the charges. On July 2, 2006, "*The New York Post* reported that John Barrie, whose company iParadigms provides a plagiarism tracking service, had found 'textbook plagiarism' in Ann Coulter's latest vehicle for personal enrichment and self-promotion, *Godless*. The passages in question, lifted from the *San Francisco Chronicle*, a Planned Parenthood publication, and a newspaper in Portland, Maine, ranged from 24 to 33 words each. Coulter's publisher Crown responded, 'The number of words used by our author in these snippets is so minimal that there is no requirement for attribution.' Similarly, Universal Press Syndicate, which syndicates her column, dismissed the charges, 'There are only so many ways you can rewrite a fact and minimal match text is not plagiarism.'"[36]

Because they do not cite or credit their sources, the rip-off artists are victims of their own rapacity. If one looks a little more carefully at the histories that Dan and Blythe Brown used, for example, one finds that they are not all up to snuff. In fact, some of them verge on the fictional. *Holy Blood* represents a good deal of research, but its conclusions could hardly be called conventional. The same is true of what researchers report in their forays through the library. Because most of them are not trained as scholars themselves, they can be taken in by a source that a trained scholar would read with a far more critical eye.

By contrast, genuine scholarship is cumulative, a gradual building up of knowledge resting on full faith and credit to others. The essence of fair play is acknowledgment. It builds goodwill and is the moral foundation for both borrowing and consumption of knowledge. We need to convince the general reader that skill, precision, and academic training do matter. Although one may agree with Harvard's Laurel Thatcher Ulrich (a consummate professional) that "We need to have a little a bit of humility to recognize people can do what they want to with the past. Historians do not own history," we do have first claim on our readers' attention because our accounts are more accurate than others, more thoughtful, up-to-date, and trustworthy. And to say that "people can do what they want with the past," is a far graver giveaway than to say that "historians do not own history." Surely we as professional historians want that past to be as accurately portrayed, and our work as fairly acknowledged, as possible.[37]

Conclusion: The
Future of the Past

O nce upon a time, history meant everything to Americans, and historians were revered and trusted. Everyone knew that history's lessons were immutable and inescapable, and those who did not know history were fated to suffer its harsh judgment for their ignorance. . . .

But not today, and perhaps not tomorrow. Cable television's fast-talking pundits and the Web's all-purpose bloggers have taken the scholar's place as spokespeople for our past and oracles of our future. The old scholarly forums, the conference panel and the refereed book and article, have given way to the sound bite and the blog entry. As a result, Americans do not know whom to believe, and thus have come to believe that every historical statement, from whatever source, is the equivalent of every other. They are free to choose the history that suits their fears, prejudices, and politics. History does not make them think; it comforts and reassures.

Professional historians have not stemmed this tide of undigested and often partisan faux chronicle. Indeed, we have opened the floodgates to it, with our indifference to public tastes, our self-absorption in obscure and fragmented subjects, and our petty bickering. Echoes of the scandals of the early part of the decade continue among us, and in the face of them our professional organizations have stepped back from policing themselves. The Organization of American Historians announced that "professional integrity" was our lodestar, for "historians seek truth." But its leadership decided not to hear or adjudicate cases of alleged violation of professional standards. Similarly, in its revised "Statement on Standards" in 2004, the American Historical Association announced its intention to "mount a more visible campaign of public education, explaining why the historical profession cares about plagiarism, falsification of evidence, and other violations of scholarly integrity." But the AHA council has instructed its Professional Division to cease hearing complaints from individuals about such misconduct.[1]

In this vein, state legislatures and trustees of private colleges are increasingly concerned with the "academic bill of rights," made famous by former academic David Horowitz. The "bill of rights" is a misleading euphemism for a mischievous ploy that commands colleges to promote diversity in hiring and teaching, but is in fact a thinly veiled attack on a supposedly left-wing professorate. The underlying battle is one over the power to teach critical inquiry, and it affects every college and university board of trustees, administration, and faculty. The most important front in that battle is history.[2]

One need only examine the mandated subjects in Florida high school history courses to understand what is at stake. Under the "A ++" omnibus education bill passed by the Florida legislature in the spring of 2006, teachers were cautioned not to wander into realms of revisionism; the legislation commanded that "American history shall be viewed as factual, not as constructed, shall be viewed as knowable, teachable, and testable, and shall be defined as the creation of a new nation based largely on the universal principles stated in the Declaration of Independence." A noble dream, but alas, not quite a factual possibility, for the nation's history did not always illustrate the sentiments of the Declaration. Indeed, for a slaveholder who never got around to freeing more than a handful of his hundreds of slaves and who believed that black people were morally, aesthetically, and emotionally inferior to white people to write that "all men are created equal" was a far better proof of the irony of American history than its egalitarian facts. The drafter of the Florida bill and the governor who signed it agreed that its purpose was celebratory and patriotic.[3]

Professional historians understand that our history must take us beyond celebrating our achievements and pledging loyalty to our country. Knowledge of history is as vital to us today as it was to the founders of the republic. For us as to them, it serves mighty and pressing public needs. To the first generations of historians, that need seemed best fulfilled by a heroic history. They excluded the victims of progress, ignored or dismissed the millions whose labor built the nation and upon whose lands it was built. The first historians tried to perform a kind of magic act, keeping the dangers of dissolution and decay—the fate of all previous republics—at bay by denying all evidence of oppression.

The magic spell failed. Reality intruded in the form of a civil war, racial violence, and the struggle between capital and labor. Manipulating historical accounts to maintain a facade of national unity and celebrate material gains did not change history, though it may have made it more popular among history's literate readership and the managers of public school education. Such history reified existing authority.

Consensus history, then, was the direct descendent of this self-serving account, and the subsequent "new history" challenged not only the content of mainstream textbooks and popular histories, but the academic infrastructure that produced and rewarded consensus. That battle still rages, and its trumpet calls can be heard in the debates over academic bills of rights. The historical academy and history in the college has moved to the left, if moving to the left means discovering and critically assessing the role and fate of minorities, reform movements, and gender in our past.

But the body count in this more inclusive and critical view of American history is mounting. Patriotic and heroic history fills the shelves at Barnes & Noble and Borders. Journalists and freelancers dominate the authorial lists of these popular histories. Critical scholarly accounts are relegated to dusty shelves in library stacks. In the end, history and historians become consumer items faced with a kind of Gresham's Law—the derivative, worthless popularization driving the innovative scholarship from the market.

In such a climate, how can we few academic historians uphold the canons of the craft while putting our findings in front of a wide readership? We cannot claim to "own" history, for that is both unrealistic and unwise. But just as we grade the students we teach in the classroom, we grade one another's work in the small circle of academic publishing all the time. We "referee" one another's submissions to scholarly journals and academic publishers by making comments on the work's contribution, its accuracy, and its importance. When a piece of work is published, we review it. This too is a form of grading.

These collegial, scholarly forms of grading can be applied to popular history, trade books, and work by nonacademics. But we need help. Book reviews of history in trade papers feature trade books. How often does the *New York Times* or the *Washington Post* or the *Boston Globe* review an academic press history by an academic? When the reviewers are journalists, the books are trade, and the authors are themselves freelancers or journalists, the grading of the history in them is not based on historical expertise. That is why plagiarism and falsification in trade publishers' history books has passed unchallenged for so long.

No plea on my part will convince book review editors at major newspapers to let historians write the reviews in their arts and entertainment sections, but if our scholarly journals would devote a little space (for they devote no space now) to reviews of popular histories published by trade houses and written by non-historians, professional historians who are experts in the subject matter would be able to review, and thus grade, the books. Then we would not have to watch as outlets like Forbes.com, Salon.com, and *The Weekly Standard* selectively and polemically denounce historians and histories. We would have gained possession of our own ideas and products.

What about abuses of professional ethics within the community of historical scholars? What can and should we do to police ourselves? I ask this not for the Pulitzer Prize-winners who teach at the major universities, but for the students and professors whose work is prey to other, more powerful figures. Take the case of the undergraduate history major whose professor suggests to him a senior thesis, and then uses the material in that thesis to fill out an entire chapter in one of her books, and does not cite the senior thesis at all in the notes or the text (instead merely including the student in an omnibus acknowledgment). What recourse does this student have to reclaim his rightful credit for the work? Who will help him, if he dares raise his voice, against such a powerful but misbehaving mentor?

The answer is plain that only an organization of scholars has the cachet to protect such a wronged junior member of our community. But do our organizations have the will to act in this principled and courageous fashion? The OAH and the AHA as institutions are obligated, and have confirmed the obligation, to uphold standards. Yet both have stepped away from hearing individual complaints. The result, if not outright hypocrisy, is a kind of prudence that exposes the most vulnerable of our community to the most predatory in it.

To provide the means for investigation and adjudication of such claims as the one above is not costly in time or money, though such objections to adjudication have been raised. Nor are there *prima facie* legal obstacles, as the counsel for AHA once told me, so long as the procedures used are fair to all parties, give all parties the chance to take part, and do not impose any penalties other than the reporting of the findings. Universities, presses, and other professional associations regularly undertake such case-by-case adjudications—why not the historians? From 1989 to 2003, the AHA's Professional Division engaged in this activity, and although the number of cases was not great, on more than one occasion the division was able to resolve a claim or provide a finding that helped the "little boats" caught in the storm. There is always the threat of a lawsuit (anyone can threaten to sue, and anyone's legal counsel can write a "lawyer letter"), but transactional insurance (to cover legal costs and potential damages) is available to any association or institution that wishes to immunize itself against attorney costs in defending such suits.

Not all the omens are dire. Every how-to-write-history guide or manual accompanying a history textbook now features at least a page or two on plagiarism and how to avoid it. Some of these even mention the Ambrose and Goodwin cases. History course syllabi routinely warn students against plagiarism, items that did not appear on syllabi before the scandals.[4]

More good news: the Internet, that source of temptation for student plagiarists, has become a formidable weapon to catch plagiarists. Take the case of Bryan F. LeBeau, a well-known American historian serving as dean at the University of Missouri, Kansas City. In 2005, a law school professor named Sally Greene was searching the Internet for references to a Hegel quotation in 2005 when she found two she did not expect. The first appeared in Cornel West's commencement address at Connecticut Wesleyan in 1993. The second, almost identical, showed up in LeBeau's 2003 commencement address. When Greene examined the two addresses more closely, she found abundant evidence that LeBeau had repeated more than the quotation. He had lifted significant portions of West's talk, including unique phrasings and misspellings of a name. When confronted by a *Chronicle of Higher Education* reporter about the similarities, LeBeau conceded, "I probably very clearly got this from somewhere." Although he could not recall how the copying occurred, the West talk was available in its entirety on the Humanity.org website.[5]

LeBeau argued that commencement addresses should not be weighed in the same scales as original scholarship, and there is truth in the argument that historians routinely borrow words and concepts from other scholars for public lectures, teaching, and similar exercises in which citation is impossible and references to sources would be offputting to the audience or the class. The point of this example is not to revive the charges against LeBeau, but to indicate that access to the Internet has made it harder for anyone to borrow and publish without some kind of attribution or acknowledgment. Everyone from college presidents and high church officials down to first-year college students has learned—or should have learned—that lesson.

Where are we going, then, in our profession? What are our lessons for the next generation of historians, our message to our readers and students? When the hardcover edition of *Past Imperfect* appeared, Alan Taylor, a truly professional historian in all senses of the word, worried that the book's warnings were overdrawn. "I think Hoffer overly dramatizes it. The sun rises and several thousand historians go to work and produce scholarship that shows integrity." I agree wholeheartedly (as I said in the preface to the first edition), but a little dramatizing may be necessary. There will be more scandals, as those arising after the Ambrose, Bellesiles, Ellis, and Goodwin cases demonstrate. No set of admonitions, however public or overly dramatic, will prevent scholarly misconduct. The real question is what the profession will do about such cases, and if I read the omens correctly, the answer is: "Nothing."[6]

NOTES

Introduction

1. If you can't make it to Philadelphia and visit the center, see "The National Constitution Center—Building on the Words," *Philadelphia Inquirer,* June 29, 2003, section Q (special section).
2. Richard Beeman, quoted in Julia M. Klein, "A Union of Word and Deed," *The Chronicle of Higher Education,* July 18, 2003, B15; Beeman, "National Constitution Center," *OAH Newsletter* 31, November 2003, 1, 8 (also available at http://www.oah.org/pubs/nl/2003nov; all OAH newsletters cited can be found at this URL, with the respective date).
3. Oscar Handlin, *Truth in History,* rev. ed. (New Brunswick, N.J.: Transaction, 1998), x, xi; Eric Foner, *Who Owns History? Rethinking the Past in a Changing World* (New York: Hill & Wang, 2002), xvii.
4. James Davison Hunter, *Culture Wars: The Struggle to Define America* (New York: Basic Books, 1991), 60, 61, 211–24; Norman Podhoretz, *My Love Affair with America: The Cautionary Tale of a Cheerful Conservative* (New York: Free Press, 2000), 177, 179; Thomas G. West, *Vindicating the Founders: Race, Sex, Class, and Justice in the Origins of America* (Lanham, Md.: Rowman, 1997), 179; Joseph E. Ellis, *Founding Brothers: The Revolutionary Generation* (New York: Knopf, 2000), 12.
5. Michael Kammen, *In the Past Lane: Historical Perspectives on American Culture* (New York: Oxford University Press, 1997), 214, 217.
6. Peter Charles Hoffer, *Sensory Worlds in Early America* (Baltimore: Johns Hopkins University Press, 2003), 10–11.
7. Jonathan Rees, "What did Bush Mean by 'Revisionist Historians'"? History Network Newsletter, June 30, 2003, hnn.us/articles/1532.html; National Endowment for the Humanities, "President Bush Announces NEH American History Initiative," press release, September 17, 2002, available at www.neh.gov/news/archive/20020917.html; James M. McPherson, "Revisionist Historians," AHA *Perspectives* 41 (September 2003), 5, 6.

8. Bruce Craig, "Controversy Stirs over Reconstruction Theme Study," *OAH Newsletter,* August 2003, available at www.oah.org/pubs/nl/2003aug/newsprof.html.

9. Daniel Boorstin, "Books and Beyond," speech given at conference at the Center for the Book, Washington, D.C., December 4, 2000, quoted in Yvonne French, "Boorstin and Beyond," *Library of Congress Information Bulletin,* January 2001.

10. McPherson, "Revisionist Historians," 5–6; American Historical Association, *Statement on Standards of Professional Conduct* (Washington, D.C.: AHA, 2002), 1; Lawrence Levine, *The Opening of the American Mind: Canons, Culture, and History* (Boston: Beacon Press, 1996), 43.

11. Secrest acknowledgments recounted in Sam Roberts, "On Acknowledgments, the Inquisition Was Easier," *New York Times,* November 27, 2003, E16; Levine, *Opening of the American Mind,* xxi, xxii, xxiii.

Part I

1. John Higham claimed pride of authorship of the term "consensus history" in "Changing Paradigms," *Journal of American History* 76 (September 1989): 464, citing as proof his own essay, "'The Cult of American Consensus': Homogenizing Our History," *Commentary* 27 (February 1959): 93–100.

2. Robert Fogel and Stanley Engerman, *Time on the Cross: The Economics of American Negro Slavery* (Boston: Little, Brown, 1974); Herbert Gutman, *Slavery and the Numbers Game: A Critique of "Time on the Cross"* (Urbana: University of Illinois Press, 1975); Paul David et al., eds., *Reckoning with Slavery: Critical Essays in the Quantitative History of American Negro Slavery* (New York: Oxford University Press, 1976); Robert Fogel, *Without Consent or Contract: The Rise and Fall of American Slavery* (New York: Norton, 1989).

Chapter 1: The Rise of Consensus History

1. Webster, *An Examination into . . . the Federal Constitution* (1787), quoted in Peter C. Hoffer, *Revolution and Regeneration: Life Cycle and the Historical Vision of the Generation of 1776* (Athens: University of Georgia Press, 1983), 57–58.

2. Jefferson to Madison, February 27, 1826, in Paul L. Ford, ed., *The Writings of Thomas Jefferson* (New York, 1892–1899), 10:327; Madison to Daniel Drake, January 12, 1835, in Gaillard Hunt, ed., *The Writings of James Madison* (New York, 1900–1910), 9:546.

3. Mason Weems, *History and the Life and Character of Washington* (Baltimore, 1805), 3; William Tudor, *The Life of James Otis, Jr.* (Boston, 1823), 447; Timothy Flint, *Recollections of the Last Ten Years . . . ,* ed. C. Hartley Grattan (New York, 1932), 66–67; Frank Burt Freidel, *The Golden Age of American History* (New York: Braziller, 1959).

4. Review of *Letters of Washington*, by Jared Sparks, volumes 6 and 7, *American Quarterly Review* 7 (June 1835): 534; George H. Callcott, "The Sacred Quotation Mark," *The Historian* 21 (August 1959): 409–10.

5. "Review of *Documents of the American Revolution*, ed. Peter Force," *American Quarterly Review* 8 (September 1835): 83.

6. Russell B. Nye, *George Bancroft* (New York: Washington Square, 1964).

7. George Bancroft, *History of the Colonization of the United States* (1834; reprint, Boston: Little, Brown, 1846), v, vi; Nye, *George Bancroft*, 193; Callcott, "Sacred Quotation Mark," 419.

8. George Bancroft, *Literary and Historical Miscellanies* (1855), quoted in Russell Nye, introduction to *George Bancroft: The History of the United States* (Chicago: University of Chicago Press, 1966), xiv; George Bancroft, *History of the United States of America, From the Discovery of the Continent*, author's last revision (1885; reprint, Port Washington, N.Y.: Kennikat Press, 1967), 1:1–2, 3.

9. Bancroft, *History of the United States of America*, 1:127, 605, 46.

10. John Fiske, "Introductory Essay," Francis Parkman, *Pioneers of France in the New World* (1885; reprint, Boston: Little, Brown, 1902), xvi.

11. Ibid., xvl; Parkman, *Montcalm and Wolfe* (1884; reprint, Boston: Little, Brown, 1909), 1:viii–ix, 3–22 (discussing England and France on eve of war), 27–38 (discussing colonies on eve of war).

12. Fiske, introduction to *Pioneers in France*, xxi, xxiii, xxxi, xvi; Callcott, "Sacred Quotation Mark," 418–19; R. Kent Newmyer, "A Nineteenth-Century View of the Historiography of the American Revolution: A Footnote on Plagiarism," *Papers of the Bibliographical Society of America* 58 (1964): 164–69; Anthony Grafton, *The Footnote: A Curious History* (Cambridge, Mass.: Harvard University Press, 1997), 190–91.

13. Francis Parkman, *The Jesuits in North America* (1867), in Samuel Eliot Morison, ed., *The Parkman Reader* (Boston: Little, Brown, 1955), 26, 30, 38, 52, 41.

14. Francis Parkman, *Pioneers of France* (1865), in Morison, *Parkman Reader*, 65, 66, 87; Parkman, *The Old Regime in Canada* (1874), in Morison, *Parkman Reader*, 268.

15. Henry Adams, *History of the United States During the Administrations of Jefferson and Madison* (1891), edited and abridged by George Dangerfield and Otey M. Scruggs (Englewood Cliffs, N.J.: Prentice-Hall, 1963), 171; Theodore Roosevelt, *The Winning of the West*, ed. Harvey Wish (New York: Capricorn, 1962), 242.

16. For the arguments on race, see N. E. H. Hull and Peter Charles Hoffer, *Roe v. Wade: The Abortion Rights Controversy in American History* (Lawrence: University Press of Kansas, 2001), 38–41.

17. Theodore Roosevelt, *The Winning of the West*, in *The Works of Theodore Roosevelt*, memorial edition (New York: Scribner's, 1924), 10:90, 91; Daniel J. Kevles, *In the Name of Eugenics: Genetics and the Uses of Human Heredity*, rev. ed. (Cambridge, Mass: Harvard University Press, 1995), 74–75.

Chapter 2: Professions of History

1. John Higham, *History: The Development of Historical Studies in the United States* (Princeton, N.J.: Princeton University Press, 1965), 51–68; Carol F. Baird, "Albert Bushnell Hart: The Rise of the Professional Historian," in Paul F. Buck, ed., *Social Sciences at Harvard, 1860–1920* (Cambridge, Mass.: Harvard University Press, 1965), 165; Thomas Bender, *New York Intellect* (Baltimore: Johns Hopkins University Press, 1987), 278; George H. Callcott, "The Sacred Quotation Mark," *The Historian* 21 (August 1959): 409 n. 1.

2. Albert Bushnell Hart, "Imagination in History," presidential address to the American Historical Association, in *American Historical Review* 15 (January 1910): 232–33.

3. Woodrow Wilson, *A History of the American People*, Documentary Edition (New York: Harper Bros., 1901), 1:13, 28, 64.

4. Ibid., 10:17–18.

5. William A. Dunning, *Reconstruction, Political and Economic, 1865–1877* (1907; reprint, New York: Harper Torch Books, 1962), 58, 11, 213; William A. Dunning, "Truth in History," presidential address to the American Historical Association, in *American Historical Review* 19 (January 1914): 228.

6. Albert Bushnell Hart, *The American Nation: A History*, vol. 16, *Slavery and Abolition, 1831–1841* (New York: Harper Bros., 1906), 50–51, 94.

7. Claude G. Bowers, *The Tragic Era: The Revolution After Lincoln* (New York: Literary Guild, 1929), 216; Higham, *History: The Development of Historical Studies*, 71; Paul H. Buck, *The Road to Reunion 1865–1900* (New York: Knopf, 1937), 25–26, 33, 35, 294, 295, 309; E. Merton Coulter, *The South During Reconstruction, 1865–1877* (Baton Rouge: Louisiana State University Press, 1947). I met Buck at Harvard, in the 1960s, and Coulter when I went to teach at the University of Georgia, in 1978. Both small gentlemen, bowed with age, they were courteous and showed no awareness that what they had written could be seen as racist or biased in any way.

8. Carl Becker, "Detachment in the Writing of History" (1910), in Phil. L. Snyder, ed., *Detachment and the Writing of History: Essays and Letters of Carl Becker* (Ithaca, N.Y.: Cornell University Press, 1958), 11, 12, 13; Carl Becker, *Everyman His Own Historian: Essays on History and Politics* (New York: F. S. Crofts, 1935); Higham, *History: The Development of Historical Studies*, 123. A clear and easy-to-understand account of the philosophical dispute appears in John Tosh, *The Pursuit of History* (London: Pearson, 2002), 164–203.

9. Charles Beard, "That Noble Dream" (1935), reprinted in Fritz Stern, ed., *The Varieties of History* (New York: Meridian, 1956), 315, 316, 320, 322, 323, 324. On the origins of progressive historiography, see Peter Novick, *That Noble Dream: The "Objectivity Question" and the American Historical Profession* (Cambridge: Cambridge University Press, 1988), 232–33; Allan Nevins, *The Gateway to History* (1938; Lexington, Mass.: D. C. Heath, 1963), 41; Higham, *History: The Development of Historical Studies*, 81.

10. Frederick Jackson Turner, "The Significance of the Frontier in American

History" (1893), in *The Frontier in American History* (New York: Henry Holt, 1920); Frederick Jackson Turner, "The Development of American Society" (1908), in Wilbur R. Jacobs, ed., *America's Great Frontiers and Sections: Frederick Jackson Turner's Unpublished Essays* (Lincoln: University of Nebraska Press, 1965), 183. On the influence of the economists, see Higham, *History: The Development of Historical Studies*, 178.

11. Charles Beard, *An Economic Interpretation of the Constitution of the United States* (New York: Macmillan, 1913), 290, 325. Charles Beard's and Mary Ritter Beard's major works comprise 77 titles and revised editions. Richard Hofstadter wrote sympathetically on Beard in *The Progressive Historians: Turner, Beard, and Parrington* (New York: Knopf, 1968), 167–346; Beard gets a less sympathetic treatment in Forrest MacDonald, *We the People: The Economic Origins of the Constitution* (Chicago: University of Chicago Press, 1958).

12. Charles A. and Mary Beard, *A Basic History of the United States* (New York: New Home Library, 1944), 5, 6, 11, 12, 19, 23, 25, 28, 288, 216.

13. Allan Nevins and Henry Steele Commager, *A Pocket History of the United States* (1942; reprint, New York: Washington Square Press, 1963), 4, 5, 24, 53, 94, 248, 249.

14. Sales figures for college history textbooks are closely guarded secrets, but adoption figures—the number of school systems or courses for which the texts are required—are widely publicized, and sometimes exaggerated, by publishers. The market in the 1950s was huge, and was not saturated with adoptable textbooks. In the early 1950s, there were slightly under 3,000,000 undergraduates in this country. By 1992, the number had grown to 14.2 million and now it is over 15 million. Almost all of these students either elect or are required to take a survey course in American history. The vast majority of these courses adopt a textbook that students are required to use.

15. The key case involving history textbooks was *Oxford Book Co. v. College Entrance Book Co.* (U.S. Court of Appeals, 2nd Cir.) 98 F.2d 688 (1938), in which the judge held that one could not be guilty of plagiarism or copyright violation for merely copying historical facts from a prior publication.

16. Ralph Gabriel, quoted in Stephen J. Whitfield, *The Culture of the Cold War* (Baltimore: Johns Hopkins University Press, 1991), 102; Frances FitzGerald tells the larger story fully in *America Revised* (Boston: Little Brown, 1979), 53–58.

17. Nevins quoted in Michael Kammen, *In the Past Lane: Historical Perspectives on American Culture* (New York: Oxford University Press, 1997), 68; Commager quoted in Neil Jumonville, *Henry Steele Commager: Midcentury Liberalism and the History of the Present* (Chapel Hill: University of North Carolina Press, 1999), 232 (citing 1938 Commager quote in the *New York Times*), 233, 234, 235.

18. Doris Kearns Goodwin, *Wait Till Next Year: A Memoir* (New York: Simon & Schuster, 1997), 157; Ellen W. Schrecker, *No Ivory Tower: McCarthyism and the Universities* (New York: Oxford University Press, 1986), 170–71.

19. Paul F. Lazarsfeld and Wagner Thielens, Jr., *The Academic Mind: Social Scientists in a Time of Crisis* (Glencoe, Ill.: Free Press, 1958), 37. The terms "left" or "left-wing" and "right" or "right-wing" often heard in American politics derive from the seating plan in the French National Assembly on the eve of the French Revolution. Now they are used as epithets, depending on who is doing the attacking and who is being attacked. A synonym for "leftist" is "radical," but the origins of this term are equally foreign to America, arising out of the Liberal Party demands for parliamentary reform in early nineteenth-century England.

20. Edward A. Purcell, Jr., *The Crisis of Democratic Theory* (Lexington: University Press of Kentucky, 1973), 256; Schrecker, *No Ivory Tower*, 339, 265; Richard Hofstadter, *Anti-Intellectualism in American Life* (New York: Knopf, 1963), 237.

21. Daniel Boorstin, *The Americans: The Colonial Experience* (New York: Knopf, 1958), 29, 142, 143, 335–36.

22. Ibid., 108–10, 111, 116, 348, 372.

23. Ibid., 186.

24. Daniel Boorstin, *The Americans: The National Experience* (New York: Knopf, 1965), 1, 7, 49, 65, 108, 113.

25. Ibid., 55, 183, 191.

26. Ibid., 373, 377; Daniel Boorstin, *The Image: Or What Happened to the American Dream* (New York: Atheneum, 1962), 264.

27. Novick, *That Noble Dream*, 327–28, 334; Daniel Boorstin, *The Americans: The Democratic Experience* (New York: Knopf, 1973), 523, 553.

28. Billington quoted in "Books and Beyond" conference of the Center for the Book, December 4, 2000, Yvonne French, "Boorstin and Beyond," *Library of Congress Information Bulletin*, January 2001.

29. Boorstin and Foner quoted in Bart Burns, "Daniel Boorstin dies at 89," *Washington Post*, February 29, 2004, C1.

30. Daniel Boorstin coauthored a very popular high school textbook, *History of the United States*, that my younger son used in high school in the 1990s. It was pure consensus history and would not have been out of place, thematically, in the 1950s.

31. Richard Hofstadter, *The American Political Tradition, and the Men Who Made It* (New York: Knopf, 1948), vii, ix; Novick, for example, still finds Hofstadter a consensus historian (*That Noble Dream*, 333). But others disagree: see Eric McKitrick and Stanley Elkins (Hofstadter's graduate students), "Richard Hofstadter, A Progress," in their *The Hofstadter Aegis: A Memorial* (New York: Knopf, 1978), 324; Arthur Schlesinger, Jr. (a contemporary), "Richard Hofstadter," in Marcus Cunliffe and Robin Winks, eds., *Pastmasters: Some Essays on American Historians* (New York: Harper Torch Books, 1975), 286–87; and Michael Kazin (a later student of Hofstadter's work), "Hofstadter Lives: Political Culture and Temperament in the Work of an American Historian," *Reviews in American History* 27 (April 1999): 334–48.

32. Elkins and McKitrick, "Richard Hofstadter, A Progress," 314, 316; Richard Hofstadter, *The Age of Reform: From Bryan to FDR* (New York: Knopf, 1955);

Eric Foner, "The Education of Richard Hofstadter," in *Who Owns History* (New York: Hill & Wang, 2002), 41.

33. Perry Miller, *The New England Mind: From Colony to Province* (Cambridge, Mass.: Harvard University Press, 1953), 482, 485. The first volume was *The New England Mind: The Seventeenth Century* (New York: Macmillan, 1939). For Miller, I rely on my recollection of stories I heard at Harvard, from 1965 to 1970, and David Levin, *Exemplary Elders* (Athens: University of Georgia Press, 1990).

34. Perry Miller, *The Life of the Mind in America: From the Revolution to the Civil War* (New York: Harcourt Brace, 1965), 95, 105, 325, 206, 205, 209, 211, 214, 228.

35. Oscar Handlin, *The Uprooted* (Boston: Little, Brown, 1951), 228, 229, 252, 253, 256.

36. On Bailyn's views of irony and the irony in his teaching methods, see the tributes to him by Jack Rakove and Stanley Katz in James A. Henretta, Michael Kammen, and Stanley N. Katz, eds., *The Transformation of Early American History: Society, Authority, and Ideology* (New York: Knopf, 1991).

37. Bernard Bailyn, *The Ideological Origins of the American Revolution* (Cambridge, Mass.: Harvard University Press, 1967), 94, 95; Bernard Bailyn, *Voyagers to the West: A Passage in the Peopling of America on the Eve of the Revolution* (New York: Knopf, 1986), 203.

38. Bailyn, *Ideological Origins*, 230; Bernard Bailyn, *To Begin the World Anew: The Genius and Ambiguities of the American Founders* (New York: Knopf, 2003), 6.

39. Frederick Jackson Turner to Joseph Jastrow, October 5, 1910, in Wilbur R. Jacobs, ed., *The Historical World of Frederick Jackson Turner* (New Haven, Conn.: Yale University Press, 1968), 48; *Frederick Jackson Turner: The Rise of the New West, 1819–1829*, ed. Ray Allen Billington (1906; reprint, New York: Collier, 1962), 30, 65, 66.

40. William Palmer, *Engagement with the Past: The Lives and Works of the World War II Generation of Historians* (Lexington: University Press of Kentucky, 2001), 9–11; Carl Bridenbaugh, "The Great Mutation," presidential address to the American Historical Association, in *American Historical Review* 68 (January 1963): 322–23.

41. Lawrence Levine and Joan Wallach Scott, among others, have revealed what almost everyone at the AHA conference room where Bridenbaugh gave his talk immediately grasped. See Lawrence Levine, "The Unpredictable Past," and Joan Wallach Scott, "History in Crisis? The Others' Side of the Story," both in *American Historical Review* 94 (June 1989): 674–75, 685. As it happens, Harvard lore has Bridenbaugh referring in his AHA presidential speech to my mentor, Bernard Bailyn, a Jew who got the post at Harvard that Bridenbaugh coveted. See Schlesinger to _____ (on Handlin), February 12, 1935, and Schlesinger to Master of Balliol College, Oxford (on Boorstin), January 12, 1934, cited in Novick, *That Noble Dream*, 172–73; Howard K. Beale, "The Professional Historian" (1953), cited in Scott, "History in Crisis?" 688. On the quota system in the Ivy League, see, for example, Dan

A. Oren, *Joining the Club: A History of Jews and Yale* (New Haven, Conn.: Yale University Press, 1988).

42. Warren I. Susman, "History and the American Intellectual: The Uses of a Usable Past" (1964), in *Culture as History: The Transformation of American Society in the Twentieth Century* (New York: Pantheon Books, 1984), 8.

Chapter 3: The New History and its Promoters

1. Elizabeth Fee, Linda Shopes, and Linda Zeidman, *The Baltimore Book* (Philadelphia: Temple University Press, 1991), vii.
2. Ibid., viii.
3. Richard Hofstadter, *The Progressive Historians: Turner, Beard, and Parrington* (New York: Knopf, 1968), 453, 455.
4. Maurice Isserman and Michael Kazin, *America Divided: The Civil War of the 1960s* (New York: Oxford University Press, 2000), 170, 182, 184.
5. Jon Wiener, "Radical Historians and the Crisis in American History," *Journal of American History* 76 (1989): 406–7; Eugene Genovese to Jesse Lemisch, October 20, 1969, letter in possession of author; Jesse Lemisch, personal communication, January 10, 2004; Jesse Lemisch, "Radicals, Marxists, and Gentlemen: A Memoir of Twenty Years Ago," *Radical Historians Newsletter* 59 (November 1989): 2, 7, 8; Eugene Genovese, "Self-Evident Truths," *New York Review of Books,* December 18, 1968; Staughton Lynd, "High Noon," *New York Review of Books,* February 27, 1969.
6. Irwin Unger, "The 'New Left' and American History: Some Recent Trends in American Historiography," *American Historical Review* 73 (1967): 1245, 1249, 1261, 1262, 1263.
7. Barton Bernstein, ed., *Towards a New Past: Dissenting Essays in American History* (New York: Pantheon Books, 1968), 4.
8. Aileen Kraditor, review note of *Towards a New Past: Dissenting Essays in American History,* by Barton Bernstein, *American Historical Review* 74 (December 1968): 529, 530, 531. Kraditor moved away from her radicalism, and its Communist underpinnings, in later years. See her *"Jimmy Higgins": The Mental World of the American Rank-and-File Communist, 1930–1958* (New York: Greenwood Press, 1988), and David Horowitz, "Marginalizing Conservative Ideas," www.FrontPageMagazine.com, accessed December 1, 1998.
9. David Donald, review note, *American Historical Review* 74 (December 1968): 532, 533.
10. The 1969 paper and a narrative of the contretemps was published in Jesse Lemisch, *On Active Service in War and Peace: Politics and Ideology in the American Historical Profession* (Toronto: New Hogtown, 1975), 45, 51.
11. Howard Zinn, *Declarations of Independence* (New York: HarperCollins, 1990), 48, 49, 51; Eugene Genovese, "On Being a Socialist and a Historian," *in Red and Black: Marxian Explorations in Southern and Afro-American History* (New York: Random House, 1971), 6, 4.

12. Zinn, *Declarations of Independence*, 51; Peter Kolchin, "Eugene Genovese: Historian of Slavery," *Radical History Review* no. 88 (Winter 2004): 53. Kolchin gives no source for Genovese's actions at the AHA, but Jesse Lemisch and I both recall the same fact.

13. "The Ohio State University," report of the Committee on Academic Freedom and Tenure, *Bulletin of the American Association of University Professors*, Autumn 1972: 306–20. A number of faculty members told me what happened; it was still fresh in their minds two years later.

14. Richard Minear resigned as an act of protest..

15. For the protests at Columbia, see "Fact-Finding Commission on Columbia Disturbances (Cox Commission), *Crisis at Columbia* (New York: Vintage Books, 1968). I was in Harvard Yard the evening that the state police forcibly removed the demonstrators from the administration building.

16. See Ian Christopher Fletcher, introduction to "The Subjects of Radical History," *Radical History Review* 88 (Winter 2004): 164.

17. Jesse Lemisch, "2.5 Cheers for Bridging the Gap Between Activism and the Academy; or, Stay and Fight," *Radical History Review* 85 (Winter 2003): 239–40, 241.

18. Isserman and Kazin, *America Divided*, 178; Todd Gitlin, *The Sixties: Years of Hope, Days of Rage*, rev. ed. (New York: Bantam Books, 1993), 396.

19. John Higham, "American Historiography in the 1960s," in *Writing American History* (Bloomington: Indiana University Press, 1970), 167; Christopher Lasch, "Consensus: An Academic Question?," *Journal of American History* 76 (September 1989): 458.

20. Higham, "American Historiography," 167; Eugene Genovese, *The Southern Tradition: The Achievement and Limitations of an American Conservatism* (Cambridge, Mass.: Harvard University Press, 1994), 97, 98. On Genovese's intellectual pilgrimage, see Alex Lichtenstein (whose radical credentials are above reproach), "Right Church, Wrong Pew: Eugene Genovese and Southern Conservatism," *New Politics* 6 (Summer 1997).

21. E. Merton Coulter, personal communication, September 1978; David Hamilton, "In Conversation . . . with Historian Thomas D. Clark," *Perspectives* (American Historical Association) 42 (February 2004): 25–30; Oscar Handlin, *Race and Nationality in American Life* (Boston: Little, Brown, 1957), 174, 175; Walter Johnson, "Historians Join the March on Montgomery," *South Atlantic Quarterly* 79 (1980): 158–74; picture of the umbrella and the historians: Wiener, "Radical Historians and the Crisis in American History," 415.

22. August Meier and Elliott Rudwick, *Black Historians and the Historical Profession* (Urbana: University of Illinois Press, 1986), 179–220; 290–92; Eric Foner, *Who Owns History? Rethinking the Past in a Changing World* (New York: Hill & Wang, 2002), 11–12.

23. Meier and Rudwick, *Black History*, 291; Robert Starobin, "The Negro: A Central Theme in American History," *Journal of Contemporary History* 3 (April 1968): 37, 38, 41, 42–43, 44, 50–51.

24. Lester, writing in 1971, quoted in Peter Novick, *That Noble Dream: The "Objectivity Question" and the American Historical Profession* (Cambridge: Cambridge University Press, 1988), 475–76, an account of the events; Vincent Harding, "Responsibilites of the Black Scholar to the Community," in Darlene Clark Hine, ed., *The State of Afro-American History: Past, Present, and Future* (Baton Rouge: Louisiana State University Press, 1986), 284.

25. Meier and Rudwick, *Black Historians*, 154–56, 227–29, 288–98; John Hope Franklin, "On the Evolution of Scholarship in Afro-American History," in Hine, *State of Afro-American History*, 19.

26. Nell Irvin Painter, *Southern History Across the Color Line* (Chapel Hill: University of North Carolina Press, 2002), 2; Darline Clark Hine, "The Making of Black Women in America: An Historical Encyclopedia," in Linda K. Kerber, Alice Kessler-Harris, and Kathryn Kish Sklar, eds., *U.S. History as Women's History: New Feminist Editors* (Chapel Hill: University of North Carolina Press, 1995), 335–48; Darline Clark Hine, *Hine Sight: Black Women and the Re-Construction of American History* (Brooklyn, N.Y.: Carlson Publications, 1994), 53.

27. Joan Wallach Scott, "Women's History" (1983), in *Gender and the Politics of History* (New York: Columbia University Press, 1988), 17.

28. Gerda Lerner, *Fireweed: A Political Autobiography* (Philadelphia: Temple University Press, 2002), 370, 371.

29. Kerber, Kessler-Harris, and Sklar, *U.S. History as Women's History*, 2.

30. Information on women in the profession from Robert B. Townsend, "New Data Reveals a Homogeneous but Changing History Profession," *Perspectives* (American Historical Association), January 2002; Robert B. Townsend, "The Status of Women and Minorities in the History Profession," *Perspectives* (American Historical Association), April 2002; Gerda Lerner, "A View from the Women's Side," *Journal of American History* 76 (September 1989): 446–56.

31. Linda K. Kerber and Jane Sherron DeHart, eds., *Women's America: Refocusing the Past*, 2nd ed. (New York: Oxford University Press, 1987), vii; Aileen S. Kraditor, *Up from the Pedestal: Selected Writings in the History of American Feminism* (Chicago: Quadrangle Books, 1968), 3; ABC-Clio, *Women in American History: A Bibliography* (Santa Barbara, Calif.: ABC-Clio), vii; Laurel Thatcher Ulrich, *A Midwife's Tale: The Life of Martha Ballard, Based on Her Diary, 1785–1812* (New York: Knopf, 1991).

32. Available at www.fas.harvard.edu/~history/faculty/profiles_by_field/united_states.html, accessed September 11, 2003.

33. Frances FitzGerald, *America Revised* (Boston: Little Brown, 1979), 84–85; James D. Anderson, "Secondary School History Textbooks and the Treatment of Black History," in Hine, *Afro-American History*, 260–70; John M. Blum et al., *A History of the United States to 1877*, vol. 1, *The National Experience*, 2nd ed. (New York: Harcourt Brace, 1968), 12, 15, 55, 386, 115, 214, 289, 259.

34. Herbert Gutman, Stephen Brier, Joshua Freeman, Nelson Lichtenstein, David

Bensman, Susan Porter Benson, David Brundage, Bret Eynon, Bruce Levine, Bryan Palmer, Joshua Brown, and Roy Rosenzweig, *Who Built America?*, (New York: Pantheon Books, 1992), 2:x–xi.

35. Meier and Rudwick, *Black History*, 198–99; Leon Litwak, preface to Gary Nash, *Red White, and Black: The Peoples of Early America* (Englewood Cliffs, N.J.: Prentice-Hall, 1974), xiv, xv.

36. Nash, *Red, White, and Black*, 2, 4–5, 6, 318, 319.

37. Mary Beth Norton, personal communication, September 15, 2003; Roger Adelson, "Interview with Mary Beth Norton," *The Historian* 60 (Fall 1997): 8, 9, 11, 12; Mary Beth Norton, "Rethinking American History Textbooks," in Lloyd Kramer, Donald Reid, and William L. Barney, eds., *Learning History in America: Schools, Cultures, and Politics* (Minneapolis: University of Minnesota, 1994), 26, 27, 29.

38. Mary Beth Norton, David M. Katzman, Howard P. Chudacoff, Thomas G. Paterson, William M. Tuttle, Jr., and Paul D. Escott, *A People and a Nation* (Boston: Houghton Mifflin, 1982), iii.

39. Gary Nash, Julie Roy Jeffrey, John R. Howe, Peter J. Frederick, Allen F. Davis, and Allan M. Winkler, *The American People. Creating a Nation and a Society*, 4th ed. (New York: Longman, 1998), xix.

40. Randall Woods, personal communication, January 4, 2003; James Henretta, personal communication, September 14, 2003. I have worked on three textbook projects with three different textbook publishers, D C Heath, Houghton Mifflin, and Longman, and what I write here is as true of my experiences as it was for Norton, Nash, and their comrades.

41. John M. Murrin, Paul E. Johnson, James M. McPherson, Gary Gerstle, Emily S. Rosenberg, and Norman L. Rosenberg, *Liberty, Equality, Power: A History of the American People*, 2nd ed., vol. 1 (Fort Worth, Tex.: Harcourt, 1999), xiii; James L. Roark, Michael P. Johnson, Patricia Cline Cohen, Sarah Stage, Alan Lawson, and Susan M. Hartmann, *The American Promise: A History of the United States from 1865*, vol. 2 (New York: Bedford, 1998), xxiii; "American Album": Murrin et al., *Liberty, Equality, Power;* "The American People Gather" and "Diagraphics": Nash et al., *The American People*, "The People Speak" and "American Mosaic": James Kirby Martin, Randy Roberts, Steven Mintz, Linda O. McMurry, and James H. Jones, *America and Its Peoples: A Mosaic in the Making*, 4th ed., vol. 1 (New York: Longman, 2001); "Counterpoint": James West Davidson, Mark H. Lytle, Christine Leigh Heyrman, William E. Gienapp, and Michael B. Stoff, *Nation of Nations: A Narrative History of the American Republic*, 3rd ed. (Boston: McGraw-Hill, 1998); "student toolkit" and "American Views": David Goldfield, Carl Abott, Virginia DeJohn Anderson, Jo Ann E. Argersinger, Peter H. Argersinger, William L. Barney, and Robert M. Weir, *The American Journal: A History of the United States* (Upper Saddle River, N.J.: Prentice-Hall, 1998); "A Place in Time": Paul S. Boyer, Clifford E. Clark, Jr., Sandra McNair Hawley, Joseph F. Kett, Neal Salisbury, Harvard Sitkoff, and Nancy Woloch, *The Enduring Vision: A History of the American People*, 4th ed. (Boston: Houghton Mifflin, 2001).

42. Figures from American Historical Association, *American Historical Association Guide to Departments of History, 1975–1976* (Washington, D.C.: AHA, 1976), and *Guide to Departments of History, 1981–1982* (Washington, D.C.: AHA, 1982).

43. Figures for this and the previous paragraph from American Historical Association, *American Historical Association Guide to Departments of History, 1981–1982* (Washington, D.C.: AHA, 1982) and *Guide to Departments of History, 1989–1990* (Washington D.C.: AHA, 1990). Tables and statistical data on employment from Robert B. Townsend, "The Job Crisis of the 1970s" and "Odds for Applicants Improving," http://www.theaha.org/info/jobs7ort.htm.

44. Jacquelyn Dowd Hall, "Part-Time Employment Hurts the Entire Profession," *OAH Newsletter,* August 2003, available at www.oah.org/pubs/nl/2003aug/hall.html.

45. Novick, *That Noble Dream,* 628.

Chapter 4: In the Eye of the Storm

1. Thomas Bender, Philip M. Katz, Colin Palmer, and the Committee on Graduate Education of the American Historical Association, *The Education of Historians for the Twenty-first Century* (Urbana: University of Illinois Press/AHA, 2004), 24.

2. Thomas Bender, "Wholes and Parts: The Need for Synthesis in American History," *Journal of American History* 73 (1986): 120–36; Thomas Bender, "Venturesome and Cautious: American History in the 1990s," *Journal of American History* 81 (1994): 992–1003.

3. George H. W. Bush, quoted in John Yewell, Chris Dodger, and Jan DeSirey, eds., *Confronting Columbus: An Anthology* (Jefferson, N.C.: McFarland, 1992), 200.

4. Member of group of Ulali singers, quoted in Richard Rath, *How Early America Sounded* (Ithaca, N.Y.: Cornell University Press, 2003), 145; John Mohawk, "Discovering Columbus, the Way Here," in Yewell, Dodger, and DeSirey, *Confronting Columbus,* 27. For a survey of the period of American exploration, including what Columbus brought with him, see Peter Charles Hoffer, *The Brave New World: A History of Early America* (Boston: Houghton Mifflin, 2000), 83–84.

5. American Library Association, resolution, in Yewell, Dodger, and DeSirey, *Confronting Columbus,* 196; *Newsday,* October 14, 1991, 44.

6. Howard Zinn, address at University of Minnesota, St. Paul, April 12, 1991, in Yewell, Dodger, and DeSirey, *Confronting Columbus,* 8; Lynne V. Cheney, *Telling the Truth: Why Our Culture and Our Country Have Stopped Making Sense — And What We Can Do About It* (New York: Touchstone, 1995), 16.

7. Francis Jennings, *Founders of America* (New York: Norton, 1993); James Axtell, *Beyond 1492: Encounters in Colonial North America* (New York: Oxford

University Press, 1992), 267, 269, 305, 314; Delno West, "Columbus and His Enterprise to the Indies: Scholarship of the Last Quarter Century," *William and Mary Quarterly*, 3rd ser., 49 (April 1992): 277.

8. Diane Ravitch, "The Plight of History in American Schools," in Paul Gagnon, ed., *Historical Literacy: The Case for History in American Education* (Boston: Houghton Mifflin, 1989), 51–68.

9. Lynda Symcox, *Whose History? The Struggle for National Standards in American Classrooms* (New York: Teachers College Press, 2002), 40–49.

10. The first Bradley Prizes were awarded on October 7, 2003, to Professor Mary Ann Glendon, a Harvard Law School professor; Leon R. Kass, a University of Chicago philosophy professor; the columnist Charles Krauthammer; and Thomas Sowell, a Stanford University economist. All are conservatives; all are closely associated with President George W. Bush's administration and have written or spoken approvingly of his policies.

11. Kenneth Jackson et al., "Building a History Curriculum: Report of the Bradley Commission," in Gagnon, *Historical Literacy*, 23, 25, 26, 27, 28, 29.

12. Gary B. Nash, quoted in Gagnon, *Historical Literacy*, 237, 239, 241, 248; Gary B. Nash, personal communication, December 4, 2003.

13. Symcox, *Whose History?* 69, 72, 76, 77.

14. Ibid., 86, 87.

15. Ibid., 89.

16. Gary B. Nash, Charlotte Crabtree, and Ross Dunn, *History on Trial: Culture Wars and the Teaching of the Past*, rev. ed. (New York: Vintage Books, 2000), 150, 152–53; Nash, personal communication, December 4, 2003; John Morrow, personal communication, March 21, 2004.

17. Nash, Crabtree, and Dunn, *History on Trial*, 158.

18. Ibid., 159–60.

19. Ibid., 161, 162, 163, 172, 173.

20. Gary Nash, Charlotte Crabtree, Paul Gagnon, and Scott Waugh, *Lessons from History: Essential Understandings and Historical Perspectives Students Should Acquire* (Los Angeles: NCHS and UCLA, 1992), preface, 8, 9, 10, 11, 16, 19, 20, 21, 29.

21. Ibid., 170, 172.

22. Nash, Crabtree, and Dunn, *History on Trial*, 172; Symcox, *Whose History?* 105, 106.

23. Nash, Crabtree, and Dunn, *History on Trial*, 174; Gary Nash, "Creating History Standards in United States and World History," *OAH Magazine of History* 9 (Spring 1995), available at www.oah.org/pubs/magazine/standards/nash.htm.

24. Symcox, *Whose History?* 108, 109.

25. Ibid., 110, 111.

26. Nash, Crabtree, and Dunn, *History on Trial*, 180, 181. See also, Chester A. Finn, Jr., quoted in Carol Innerst, "Ideological Censorship Grips Conservative Profs," *Washington Times*, June 11, 1990, A4 on Finn's views of the uses and abuses of history by liberals.

27. Nash, Crabtree, and Dunn, *History on Trial,* 185; Nash, Crabtree, Gagnon, and Waugh, *Lessons from History,* 77–84; National Council on History in the Schools, *National Standards for United States History* (Los Angeles: NCHS, 1994), 70–91.

28. NCHS, *National Standards for United States History,* 219; Nash, Crabtree, and Dunn, *History on Trial,* 183.

29. Cheney, *Telling the Truth,* 114; Cheney, "The End of History," *Wall Street Journal,* October 20, 1994, A26.

30. Kennedy quoted in Nash, Crabtree, and Dunn, *History on Trial,* 206.

31. Newt Gingrich, "History Standards Are Bunk," *Congressional Record,* 104th Cong., 1st sess., February 8, 1995, E301.

32. Rush Limbaugh, *Rush Limbaugh Show,* October 28, 1994 (text in Lexis, *s.v.* "Limbaugh, October 28, 1994").

33. John Leo, "The Hijacking of American History," *U.S. News and World Report,* November 14, 1994, 36; Nash, Crabtree, and Dunn, *History on Trial,* 214.

34. Nash, Crabtree, and Dunn, *History on Trial,* 223–58.

35. U.S. Senate, Gorton Amendment S70, *Congressional Record,* 104th Cong., 1st sess., January 18, 1995, S1107; U.S. Senate, Resolution 66, *Congressional Record,* 104th Cong., 1st sess., January 18, 1995, S1282; Slade Gorton, "History Standards Are Political Correctness Run Amok," editorial, *Seattle Post-Intelligencer,* February 28, 1995, A7.

36. Chester Finn, quoted in Nash, Crabtree, and Dunn, *History on Trial,* 264; Oklahoma lawgiver quoted in Edward J. Larson, *Trial and Error: The American Controversy over Creation and Evolution,* updated edition (New York: Oxford, 1989), 50; Limbaugh, *Rush Limbaugh Show,* October 28, 1994; Cheney, "End of History"; Daniel Schorr, *Weekend Edition,* NPR, February 5, 1995; Wendy Faulkner, James Fleck, and Robin Williams, "Exploring Expertise: Issues and Perspectives," in Wendy Faulkner, James Fleck, and Robin Williams, eds., *Exploring Expertise* (London: Macmillan, 1998), 3–5.

37. Council for Basic Education, "History in the Making: An Independent Review of the Voluntary National History Standards," report (Washington, D.C.: CBE, January 1996); NCHS, *National Standards for History,* basic edition (Los Angeles: NCHS, 1996); Gary Nash, *All Things Considered,* NPR, September 4, 1995 and April 3, 1996.

38. Arthur M. Schlesinger, Jr., "Extremists Reduce History to Cheerleading," *Cleveland Plain Dealer,* May 20, 1996, B11.

39. Diane Ravitch, "The Controversy over National History Standards," in Elizabeth Fox-Genovese and Elisabeth Lasch-Quinn, eds., *Reconstructing History: The Emergence of a New Historical Society* (New York: Routledge, 1999), 244, 245, 246, 247, 249, 251.

40. Barton J. Bernstein, "The Struggle over History: Defining the Hiroshima Narrative," in Philip Nobile, ed., *Judgment at the Smithsonian: The Uncensored Script of the Smithsonian's 50th Anniversary Exhibit of the Enola Gay* (New York: Marlow, 1995), 127–240; Richard H. Kohn, "History at Risk: The Case of the *Enola Gay,*" in Edward T. Linenthal and Tom Engelhardt, eds., *History Wars:*

The Enola Gay *and Other Battles for the American Past* (New York: Henry Holt, 1996), 140–71.

41. On public historians, See James A. Percoco, "The Wide, Challenging, and Wonderful World of Public History," *OAH Magazine of History* 16 (Winter 2002); Linda Shopes, "Public History, Public Historians, and the American Historical Association," draft report, AHA Task Force on Public History to the AHA's Professional Division, October 4, 2003, 7; the "welcome page" of the National Council of Public Historians' website, www.ncph.org.

42. Martin Harwit, *An Exhibit Denied: Lobbying the History of* Enola Gay (New York: Springer, 1996), 47–48, 52–53, 78, 103, 108, 120, 128, 151, 155–56, 165, 183, 278–79, 285–86, 306, 318–20, 429.

43. Ibid., 345, 392–93 (OAH resolution and Flint letter). I got to know Roy Flint when he taught at the University of Georgia. He was a straight shooter, a West Pointer who became dean at West Point, a decorated combat veteran of the Korean and Vietnam wars, and a first-rate teacher of military history.

44. Tom Crouch and Michael Neufeld (curators of the Air and Space Museum), quoted in *The Columbian,* June 22, 1994, C3.

45. "The Crossroads: The End of World War II, the Atomic Bomb, and the Origins of the Cold War," in Nobile, *Judgment at the Smithsonian,* 3, 11, 14, 17–18, 19, 20, 21, 31, 32, 34, 36, 38, 47, 57–86, 101, 103, 108–111, 117, 121.

46. Paul Schadewald, "Chronology of the *Enola Gay* Controversy," *Journal of American History* 82 (December 1995): 1083–84; I. Michael Heyman, quoted in Kohn, "History at Risk," 166.

47. George Will, "The Real State of the Union," *Washington Post,* January 26, 1995, A25; David Thelen, "History After the *Enola Gay* Controversy: An Introduction," *Journal of American History* 82 (December 1995): 1033. Gingrich, "History Standards Are Bunk."

48. Harwit, *Exhibit Denied,* 313, 314, 315, 316; *Wall Street Journal,* editorial, August 29, 1994, A10; *Washington Post,* editorial, February 11, 1995, A11.

49. "Smithsonian Unveils the Restored *Enola Gay,*" Associated Press, August 19, 2003; Ilse Metchek (of the California Fashion Association), quoted in George White, "Smithsonian Exhibit Plan Wins Backing," *Los Angeles Times,* September 12, 1997.

50. On impeachment, see Peter Charles Hoffer and N. E. H. Hull, *Impeachment in America, 1635–1805* (New Haven: Yale University Press, 1984); Richard A. Posner, *Affair of State: The Investigation, Impeachment, and Trial of President Clinton* (Cambridge, Mass.: Harvard University Press, 1999), 96 n. 5; 98 nn. 9, 11, 12, 13; 100; 104 n. 25; 106 n. 28; 110 n. 39; 117 nn. 47, 49, 51; Robert Byrd, *The Senate, 1789–1989* (Washington D.C.: U.S. Government Printing Office, 1991) 2: 61, 63–66, 70–71, 75; and www.senate.gov/artandhistory/history/common/briefingt/Senate_Impeachment_Role.htm.

51. Tom Baxter, Rebecca Carr, "The President on Trial," *Atlanta Journal and Constitution,* January 16, 1999, A9.

52. "Historians in Defense of the Constitution," *New York Times,* October 30, 1998, A15.

53. "Capitol Hill Hearing with White House Personnel," Federal News Service, December 8, 1998, 9 (quoting Sean Wilentz); Jack Rakove, "High Crimes," *Los Angeles Times,* November 22, 1998, M2; Jack Rakove, "Panel on Impeachment and the Historians," presentation made to the American Historical Association, Chicago, January 8, 2000. I served on the same panel.

54. "Capitol Hill Hearing," 9, 10, 11, 49.

55. On historians as expert witnesses see Brian W. Martin, "Working with Lawyers: A Historian's Perspective," *OAH Newsletter* 30 (May 2002): 4–5; John A. Neuenschwander, "Historians as Expert Witnesses: The View from the Bench," ibid. (August 2002): 1–6; Patricia Cohen, "History for Hire in Industrial Lawsuits," *New York Times,* June 14, 2003, B7–8; Peter Charles Hoffer and N. E. H. Hull, "Historians and the Impeachment Imbroglio: In Search of A Serviceable History," *Rutgers Law Journal* 31 (2000): 473–90. The firm that recruits and trains expert historical witnesses is History Associates Incorporated. A full description of their services is available at www.historyassociates.com.

56. Jonathan D. Martin, "Historians at the Gate: Accommodating Expert Historical Testimony in Federal Courts," *New York University Law Review* 78 (October 2003): 1524.

57. American Historical Association, *Statement on Standards of Professional Conduct* (Washington, D.C.: AHA, 2003), 1. J. Morgan Kousser, "Are Expert Witnesses Whores? Reflections on Objectivity and Scholarship in Expert Witnessing," *Public Historian* 6 (1984): 7, 6; William Stueck, personal communication, December 4, 2003; Laura Maggi, "Bearing Witness for Tobacco," *The American Prospect,* March 27, 2000, available at www.prospect.org/print/V11/10/maggi-l.html. Martin, "Historians at the Gate," 1539.

58. James Mohr went public about the *Webster v. New Lenox School District* brief in "Historically Based Legal Briefs: Observations of a Participant in the *Webster* Process," *Public Historian* 12 (Summer 1990), 19–24. On Foner's case, see Martin, "Historians at the Gate," 1529.

59. On the Sears imbroglio, see Martin, "Historians at the Gate," 1536–38; Thomas Haskell and Sanford Levinson, "Academic Freedom and Expert Witnessing: Historians and the Sears Case," *Texas Law Review* 66 (1988): 1629ff.; Thomas Haskell and Stanford Levinson, "On Academic and Hypothetical Pools: A Reply to Alice Kessler-Harris," ibid., 67 (1989), 1591ff.; Alice Kessler-Harris, "Academic Freedom and Expert Witnessing: A Response to Haskell and Levinson," ibid., 67 (1988): 429ff.

60. Henry Hyde, quoted in Christopher Shea, "The Gap: The Chasm Between Academe and the Rest of America Is Wide—and Getting Wider," *Washington Post,* April 11, 1999, W14; Ann Coulter, quoted on *Rivera Live,* "Judiciary Hearings," CBS, December 8, 1998, available on Lexis, *s.v.* "CNBC News Transcripts"; Robert George and Gerard V. Bradley, "The Scandal Histrionics: Where's the History in the Historians' Argument?" *National Review,* December 7, 1998; Bruce J. Schulman, "History: As American as Hating Intellectuals," *Los Angeles Times,* February 21, 1999, M2; Michael Beschloss,

introduction to *The Impeachment and Trial of President Clinton: The Official Transcripts,* ed. Merrill McLoughlin (New York: Times Books, 1999), xii. I spent an afternoon with Robbie George years before the Clinton affair and came away immensely impressed with his expertise and with the professorial manner in which he expressed his opinions—he seemed to me the very epitome of "the professors," hence my use of the term "ironically."

61. Marc Trachtenberg, quoted in David R. Sands, "Historians Mount Challenge to Postmodern Orthodoxy," *Washington Times,* April 29, 1998; Marc Trachtenberg, "The Past Under Siege," in Fox-Genovese and Lasch-Quinn, *Reconstructing History,* 9–10; Eugene Genovese, quoted in Courtney Leatherman, "Organizers of New Society for Historians Call It an 'Antidote' to Existing Groups," *Chronicle of Higher Education Daily News,* Wednesday, April 29, 1998, and Courtney Leatherman, "Historians Set Up a New Society," *Chronicle of Higher Education,* May 8, 1998, A12; Eugene Genovese, "A New Departure," in Fox-Genovese and Lasch-Quinn, *Reconstructing History,* 6, 7, 8.

62. The battle lines are laid out in a dialogue between David Horowitz, "In Defense of Intellectual Diversity," and Stanley Fish, "Intellectual Diversity: The Trojan Horse of a Dark Design," both in *Chronicle of Higher Education,* February 13, 2004, B12–14.

63. David Brooks, "Lonely Campus Voices," *New York Times,* September 27, 2003, A27. For an outlet for anonymous denunciation of biased professors, see www.NonIndoctrination.org.

64. Shea, "The Gap," W14; "Interchange: The Practice of History," *Journal of American History* 90 (September 2003): 577, 578, 590.

65. Thelen, quoted in David Oshinsky, "The Humpty Dumpty of Scholarship," *New York Times,* August 26, 2000. "Interchange," 592, 593, 594.

Part II

1. For a review essay reviving these charges see Charles L. Glenn, "PC Censorship of Textbooks," *The Journal of the Historical Society* 4 (Winter 2004): 31–41.

2. Bernard Bailyn, "The Challenge of Modern Historiography," presidential address to the American Historical Association, December 27, 1981, in *American Historical Review* 87 (February 1982): 24.

3. Joyce Appleby, "The Power of History," presidential address to the American Historical Association, December 27, 1997, in *American Historical Review* 103 (February 1998): 2, 17.

4. AHA, introduction, on-line version of the *Statement on Standards of Professional Conduct,* www.theaha.org/pub/standard.html#introduction; AHA, *Statement on Standards of Professional Conduct* (Washington D.C.: AHA, 2003), 1.

5. See Carl Guarneri, "Learning from Larceny: The AHA and the Sokolow Case," paper read to the Society of Historians of the Early American

Republic, Berkeley, California, July 13, 2002 (in author's collection); Thomas Mallon, *Stolen Words*, rev. ed. (San Diego: Harcourt Brace, 2001), 189–93; *Statement on Standards of Professional Conduct* (Washington, D.C.: AHA, 2003), 10. The substantive question raised by Oates's techniques are the subject of his and other scholars' articles in *Journal of Information Ethics* 3 (Spring 1994).

6. Sharmin Stein, "Lincoln Author Under Siege," *Chicago Tribune*, December 7, 1990, C1; "Historians Rebut Plagiarism Charge," *New York Times*, May 1, 1991, C16; David Streitfeld, "The Case of the Too-Familiar Lincoln Book," *Washington Post*, May 19, 2002, B1; "Historical Group: Lincoln Biographer Borrowed Material," United Press International, May 21, 1992; Philip J. Hilts, "When Does Duplication of Words Become Theft?" *New York Times*, March 29, 1993, A10; Anthony Flint, "Historian Seeks to Face His Accusers," *Boston Globe*, June 2, 1993, Metro ed., 20; Michael Kenney, "A More Honest Picture of Abe," *Boston Globe*, November 28, 1995, "Living" section, 43; Philip Paludan, personal communication, March 27, 2004.

7. Emily Eakin, History News Network, excerpted, and Stephen B. Oates, "I Stood Accused of Plagiarism," History News Network, at hnn.us/articles/658.html.

8. Arnita A. Jones, "Response to Stephen Oates," History News Network, April 23, 2002, historynewsnetwork.org/articles/article.html?id=693; Robert L. Zangrando, "Response to Stephen Oates," History News Network, April 15, 2002, historynewsnetwork.org/articles/article.html?id=659.

Chapter 5: Falsification: The Case of Michael Bellesiles

1. On Bellesiles's advice to his students, I rely on Michael Gagnon, personal communication, December 1, 2003. Others who wish their remarks to remain confidential but who were Bellesiles's students or colleagues have confirmed what Gagnon told me.

2. Richard Bernstein, personal communication, December 13, 2003; Bellesiles quoted in David Glenn, "Small Press Republishes Controversial Book on America's Gun Culture," *Chronicle of Higher Education*, January 9, 2004.

3. Stanley N. Katz, Hanna H. Gray, and Laurel Thatcher Ulrich, "Report of the Investigative Committee in the Matter of Professor Michael Bellesiles, July 10, 2002," unpublished report (ms. supplied to the author by Stanley N. Katz), 7. The controversy over consumerism on the frontier grew out of studies by Christopher Clark, *The Roots of Rural Capitalism, Western Massachusetts, 1780–1860* (Ithaca, N.Y.: Cornell University Press, 1990), and Winifred Barr Rothenberg, *From Market-Places to a Market Economy: The Transformation of Rural Massachusetts, 1750–1850* (Chicago: University of Chicago Press, 1992), but their theses were known before the books came out.

4. Sanford Levinson, "The Embarrassing Second Amendment," *Yale Law Journal* 99 (December 1989): 637–59. For a survey of the impact of

Levinson's article, see Jack Rakove, "Words, Deeds, and Guns: Arming America and the Second Amendment," *William and Mary Quarterly,* 3rd ser., 59 (January 2002): 206–7; Saul Cornell, "The Current State of Second Amendment Scholarship," speech given at a meeting of the Society for the History of the Early American Republic, July 2001, available www.h-net.msu.edu/~shear/paper/CornellSaulPaper.htm. Cornell notes and Rakove confirms that Bellesiles's work became an important element supporting the collective-right case and against the individual right to bear arms. On Bellesiles's relation to the Emory Violence Studies program, see Bellesiles's posting to H-Law (www.h-law.msu.edu/~law), February 7, 1998.

5. Katz, Gray, and Ulrich, "Report of the Investigative Committee," 7, 19.

6. Ibid., 7–8.

7. Michael Bellesiles, "The Origins of Gun Culture in the United States, 1760–1865," *Journal of American History* 83 (September 1996): 426.

8. Bellesiles, "Origins of Gun Culture," 427–431; Saul Cornell, introduction to *Whose Right to Bear Arms Did the Second Amendment Protect?* (Boston: St. Martin's Press, 2000), 20–21.

9. Jacques Barzun and Henry F. Graff, *The Modern Researcher,* 4th ed. (New York: Harcourt Brace, 1985), 239; For a survey of quantitative methods at the time, see Richard E. Beringer, *Historical Analysis: Contemporary Approaches to Clio's Craft* (New York: John Wiley, 1978), 193–317.

10. Michael Bellesiles, *Arming America* (New York: Knopf, 2000), 262 (cited hereafter as *Arming America* [2000]).

11. Bellesiles, "Origins of Gun Culture," 427; Charles M. Dollar and Richard Jensen, *Historian's Guide to Statistics: Quantitative Analysis and Historical Research* (New York: Henry Holt, 1971), 36; Herbert M. Blalock, Jr., *Social Statistics,* 2nd rev. ed. (New York: McGraw-Hill, 1979), 32–34.

12. Bellesiles, "Origins of Gun Culture," 427; Randolph Roth, "Guns, Gun Culture, and Homicide: The Relationship Between Firearms, the Uses of Firearms, and Interpersonal Violence," *William and Mary Quarterly,* 3rd ser., 59 (January 2002): 228 n. 17; Gloria L. Main, "Many Things Forgotten: The Use of Probate Records in *Arming America*," ibid., 211–16.

13. Bellesiles, "Origins of Gun Culture," 427, 428. Alice Hanson Jones, *American Colonial Wealth: Documents and Methods* (New York: Arno Press, 1978), 3v., and Alice Hanson Jones, *Wealth of a Nation to Be: The American Colonies on the Eve of Independence* (New York: Columbia University Press, 1980); James Lindgren and Justin L. Heather, "Counting Guns in Early America," *William and Mary Law Review* 43 (April 2002): 1777–1842, and Robert H. Churchill, "Gun Ownership in Early America: A Survey of Manuscript Militia Returns" *William and Mary Quarterly,* 3rd ser., 60 (July 2003): 615–42. Both of these essays are models of research technique, explaining where the material was found and giving exact page numbers. For Bellesiles's use of Jones's findings, see Katz, Gray, and Ulrich, "Report of the Investigative Committee," 10.

14. Bellesiles, "Origins of Gun Culture," 427.

15. Bellesiles, "The Establishment of Legal Structures on the Frontier: The Case

of Revolutionary Vermont," *Journal of American History* 73 (March, 1987): 901; 901 nn. 10, 11; 910 n. 32; 911 n. 37.

16. For another table with *N* base clearly noted, see Steven A. Reich, "Soldiers of Democracy: Black Texans and the Fight for Citizenship, 1917–1921," *Journal of American History* 82 (March 1996): 1493 (table 1).

17. Bellesiles, *Arming America* (2000), 582; David Thelen, "A Round Table: Martin Luther King, Jr.," *Journal of American History* 74 (September 1987), 436–37; David Thelen, introduction to *The Constitution and American Life*, special issue, *Journal of American History* 74 (December 1987): 662; David Thelen, "History After the *Enola Gay* Controversy: An Introduction," *Journal of American History* 82 (December 1995): 1035. For examples of Bellesiles's critics' blaming the *JAH*, see John G. Fought, "The Bellesiles' Affair: *Origins* (1996) and Consequences," http://users.adelphia.net/~jgfought; Ralph Luker, "Clio's Malpractice: or, What's a Fallen Girl to Do?" http://hnn.us/articles/1696.html, posted on September 22, 2003; Melissa Sekora, "Disarming America, Part II: Why Won't Michael Bellesiles Seriously Respond to His Critics?" www.nationalreview.com/nr_comment/nr_commentprint 112601.html, posted on November 26, 2001.

18. Don Hickey, H-Law (www.h-law.msu.edu/~law), September 29, 2001; David Paul Nord, "Editor's Annual Report, The *Journal of American History* 1999–2000," www.historycooperative.org/journals/jah/87.2/edreport.htm; Joanne Meyerowitz, "Editor's Annual Report, 2001–2002," www.historycooperative.org/journals/jah/89.2/ed_report.html.

19. Bellesiles, *Arming America* (2000), 582; Joanne Meyerowitz, "History's Ethical Crisis: An Introduction," *Journal of American History* 90 (March 2004): 1326.

20. Bellesiles, *Arming America* (2000), 445 (Table 1). Bellesiles's inability to locate the source of the San Francisco probate figures, after much questioning, was one of the most telling charges against him. Katz, Gray, and Ulrich, "Report of the Investigative Committee," 17.

21. Bellesiles, *Arming America* (2000), 13, 266. I should disclose that I have counted criminal cases of various sorts in a wide variety of colonial court records. I have every tally—it's almost impossible to write anything about court cases or figures without the raw numbers at hand.

22. For a slightly different critique of the sampling design, see Lindgren and Heather, "Counting Guns," 1825–26.

23. Michael Bellesiles, *Arming America*, paperback ed. (New York: Vintage Books, 2001), Table 1, 445, includes new copy, "A total of 11,170 probate records were examined" (cited hereafter as "paperback ed.").

24. The flood was confirmed by Professor John Jurisek, Bellesiles's colleague at Emory, and by Jeff Young, formerly a graduate student there, in personal communications to the author, September 2003.

25. Bellesiles, *Arming America* (2000), 109–10, 485 n. 133; Bellesiles, *Arming America*, paperback ed., 109–10, 485 n. 133.

26. Katz, Gray, and Ulrich, "Report of the Investigative Committee," 9–11. The committee of inquiry sent a researcher to find the sources Bellesiles might

have used when he said that he could not remember precisely where he went or what he saw in the court records (see ibid., 3). The report found strong evidence that he could not have used the manuscript records he recalled examining (see ibid., 22–27). Justin Heather, a researcher working with Lindgren, also tried to find matching documentation for Bellesiles's claims in the archives he might have visited and in the published records he claimed to have used and found massive repeated errors, miscounts, and falsifications (see Lindgren and Heather, "Counting Guns," pp. 1788–89 [guns in Providence], p. 1805 [guns more common in rural than in urban areas], pp. 1820–21 [wills miscounted as inventories and women's inventories included in data supposedly all-male]). Clayton E. Cramer found errors in the anecdotal evidence as a result of Bellesiles's reading the travel journals selectively (Cramer, "Gun Scarcity in the Early Republic," unpublished paper, revised November 19, 2001, available at www.claytoncramer.com, p. 2); James Lindgren collected all these and more errors (see Lindgren, "Fall from Grace: *Arming America* and the Bellesiles Scandal," book review, *Yale Law Journal* 111 [June 2002]: 2195–49).

27. Richard Jensen, H-Net (http://ftp.cac.psu.edu/pub/internexus/HNET. INFO), June 24, 1993; www.h-net.org/about; www.h-net.org/lists.

28. Michael Bellesiles, H-Law, January 8, 1995; Clayton Cramer, personal communication, October 10, 2003.

29. Clayton Cramer, "Letters to the Editor," *Journal of American History* 84 (December 1997): 1188–89.

30. Michael Bellesiles, "Letters to the Editor," ibid.: 1189–90.

31. Clayton Cramer, H-South (www.h-net.org/~south) October 9, 2000; Michael Bellesiles, H-South, October 9, 2000. Cramer strongly believes not only in the right to own and bear handguns, but in their absolute necessity for personal self-defense (Clayton Cramer, personal communication, March 25, 2004).

32. Michael Bellesiles, introduction to *Lethal Imagination: Violence and Brutality in American History* (New York: New York University Press, 1999), 10; Michael Bellesiles, H-Law, February 7, 1998.

33. Richard Bernstein, personal communication, December 12, 2003. David Yassky's friend-of-the-court brief, and a list of signers, is available at the website of the Potomac Institute, www.potomac-inc.org/yass.html, pages 22–23.

34. Bellesiles, H-South, October 9, 2000; ibid., October 16, 2000.

35. Michael Bellesiles, "Disarming the Critics," *OAH Newsletter,* November 2001, available at www.oah.org/pub/nl/2001nov/bellesiles.html; James Lindgren, H-OIEAHC (www.h-net.org/~oieahcweb), September 21, 2001; John G. Fought, "Was Bellesiles Really Threatened?," posted at History News Network, http://hnn.us/articles/888.html, on August 8, 2002.

36. Richard Bernstein, H-Law, April 27, 2001; Richard Bernstein, posting to H-Law editorial Board, May 9, 2001; Peter Hoffer, H-Law, December 7, 2001; Bellesiles interview cited in Danny Postel, "Did the Shootouts over *Arming America* Divert Attention from the Real Issue?" *Chronicle of Higher Education,* February 1, 2002, 12; John Wiener, "Fire at Will," *The Nation,* November 4,

2002, 28; Ronald Hoffman, H-OIEAHC, May 7, 2001; the OAH and AHA resolutions appear in Bellesiles, "Disarming the Critics," and are available at www.theaha.org/perspectives/issues/2001/0109 and www.oah.org/pubs/ nl/2001nov.

37. See, for example, Bellesiles, H-OIEAHC, November 25, 2000, where he states, "I would like to thank those who have joined in the discussion of *Arming America* in a spirit of scholarly inquiry. It is deeply satisfying to have one's research spark discussion and maybe even a reconsideration of some shared assumptions." On the reported hacking of the website, see James Lindgren, H-OIEAHC, September 15, 2001.

38. Robert A. Paul, Emory University, Office of Media Relations, press release, October 25, 2002; Jack Rakove, H-Law, April 18, 2001; Michael Johnson, personal communication, December 29, 2003; Paul Finkelman, "A Well Regulated Militia: The Second Amendment in Historical Perspective," *Chicago-Kent Law Review* 76 (2000): 234–35; Paul Finkelman, H-Law, April 18, 2001.

39. Sanford Levinson, H-Law, October 5, 2001; comments by Greg Nobles, Peter Onuf, Alfred Young, Robert Richie, Michael Kammen, Michael Zuckerman, all university professors of history, inside the paper covers of *Arming America*, paperback ed. On Heston: See Bellesiles, "Disarming the Critics."

40. Edmund Morgan, review of *Arming America*, by Michael Bellesiles, *New York Review of Books*, October 19, 2000, 30–32; Garry Wills, review of *Arming America*, by Michael Bellesiles, *The New York Times Book Review*, September 10, 2000, 5–6.

41. Roger Lane, review of *Arming America*, by Michael Bellesiles, *Journal of American History* 88 (September 2001): 614, 615.

42. Clayton Cramer, *National Review*, October 9, 2000, 54–55; Robert H. Churchill, *Reviews in American History*, 29 (2001): 329–37; Joyce Lee Malcolm, *Texas Law Review* 79 (May 2001): 1657–76.

43. Justin Herman, "Gun Battles," review of *Arming America*, by Michael Bellesiles, posted at H-Pol (H-Pol@h-net.msu.edu), May 2001; see also Katz, Gray, and Ulrich, "Report of the Investigative Committee," 15.

44. Richard Bernstein, H-Law, January 29, 2002.

45. Gloria Main, "Many Things Forgotten," *William and Mary Quarterly*, 3rd ser., 59 (January 2002): 215; Ira D. Gruber, "Of Arms and Men: *Arming America* and Military History," ibid.: 219; Randolph Roth, "Guns, Gun Culture, and Homicide: The Relationship between Firearms, the Uses of Firearms, and Interpersonal Violence," ibid.: 224, 227.

46. Michael Bellesiles, "Exploring America's Gun Culture," *William and Mary Quarterly*, 3rd ser., 59 (January 2002): 247, 244; Bellesiles, *Weighed in an Even Balance* (Brooklyn, N.Y.: Soft Skull Press, 2003), 5.

47. Michael Bellesiles, H-OIEAHC, December 21, 2000; Bellesiles, *Arming America* (2000), 109. For other examples of Bellesiles's claims concerning the probate records confirming his central arguments, see ibid., 74, 148–49, 262, 266, 386.

48. Bellesiles, *Weighed in an Even Balance*, 5, 6.

49. Prior to that, Emory had asked the Professional Division if we would examine

the evidence and offer our judgment, but Emory would not make the formal complaint required by our internal rules and dropped its request. No record was kept of the Emory request to the Professional Division, but the matter was mentioned at a meeting of the Professional Division in April 2002. When I asked why the request was not included in the log of all other requests appended to our briefing book, I was told that a clerical error had been made and would be remedied. On the formal basis for the Emory inquiry, see Katz, Gray, and Ulrich, "Report of the Investigative Committee," 1.

50. Roth, *Morning Edition,* NPR, March 4, 2002; Hoffman quoted in Florence Olson, "Historian Resigns After Report Questions His Gun Research," *Chronicle of Higher Education,* November 8, 2002, 17; Jen Sansbury, "Fiery Author, Teacher Has Unsure Future with Emory," *Atlanta Journal-Constitution,* April 20, 2002, H4; Jen Sansbury, "Emory Widens Probe of Book," ibid., April 26, 2002, D1; Jacqueline Trescott, "Book Flap Prompts NEH to Pull Name from Fellowship," *Washington Post,* May 22, 2002, C3; Jen Sansbury, "Emory Author Won't Be in Class," *Atlanta Journal-Constitution,* August 23, 2002, D9.

51. Katz, Gray, and Ulrich, "Report of the Investigative Committee," 19; Karen Hill, "Scolded Author Quits Emory," *Atlanta Journal-Constitution,* October 26, 2002, E1; Robert A. Paul, Emory University, Office of Media Relations, press release, October 25, 2002; Andrew Ackerman, "Bellesiles Resigns University Position," *Emory Wheel,* October 29, 2002.

52. David Skinner, "The Cowards of Academe," *The Weekly Standard,* June 10, 2002, 21; Melissa Sekora, "Prized, No Longer," National Review Online, December 17, 2002; Jane Garrett, quoted in Publisher's Lunch (on-line magazine), January 9, 2003, www.publishersmarketplace.com/lunch/archives/2003_01_08.html; Larry Pratt, "Michael Bellesiles," March 2001, reports conversations with Gabrielle Brooks, promotion director, "Janet," an assistant to the publisher Sonny Mehta, production editor Kathy Hourigan, and Alexis Gargalino, Jane Garrett's assistant; www.gunowners.org/op agnyo1pt7.htm; Joyce Seltzer, "Honest History," *Journal of American History* 90 (March 2004): 1347. Full disclosure: I edit a series of books on American legal history for the University Press of Kansas. The series format does not allow any reference notes at all. I have to trust my authors' honesty explicitly.

53. William Grimes, "Jane Garrett: A Woman of Words That Win Pulitzers," *New York Times,* June 4, 1996; University of Delaware, Office of Public Relations, "Molding Two Lifelong Passions into One Career," *Messenger* 6 (1996), www.udel.edu/PR/Messenger/97/1/17.html; Edward Shanahan, "Jane Garrett of Knopf," July 2, 2003, www.downstreet.net/archives/JaneGarrett. htm; Lizabeth Cohen, "The Cover Story for *A Consumer's Republic,*" July 2, 2003, www.randomhouse.com/knopf/authors/lizcohen/behind.html.

54. Michael Bellesiles, *Arming America,* rev. ed. (Brooklyn, N.Y.: Soft Skull Press, 2003), 445.

55. Pauline Maier, personal communication, January 27, 2004; Elliott J. Gorn, "The Historian's Dilemma," *Journal of American History* 90 (March 2004): 1330.

56. "Citizens Committee for the Right to Keep and Bear Arms Calls Upon

Libraries to Remove Discredited Bellesiles Book from Shelves," U.S. Newswire, January 8, 2003; Jason Hoppin, "Ninth Circuit: Gun Ownership Is Not an Individual Right," *Legal Intelligencer,* December 9, 2002, 4; Jack Rakove, quoted in Don Williams, H-OIEAHC, January 23, 2003; Roger Lane, quoted in Joyce Lee Malcolm, "Disarming History," *Reason,* March 1, 2003, 22. Circling the wagons: see Jack Rakove, H-OIEAHC, May 23, 2002; Peter Hoffer, H-OIEAHC, May 23, 2002.

Chapter 6: Plagiarism: The Cases of Stephen Ambrose and Doris Kearns Goodwin

1. Laura Miller, "I Couldn't Have Put It Better Myself," *New York Times Sunday Book Review,* July 23, 2003, 31; Scott McLemee, "Seeing Red," *Chronicle of Higher Education,* June 27, 2003, A11 (covering the Foner story); Jacques Steinberg, "New Book Includes Passages from Others," *New York Times,* May 31, 2003, G9 (announcing the VanDeMark case). The Jayson Blair affair burst on us in May 2003. See Howard Kurtz, "N.Y. Times Uncovers Dozens of Faked Stories by Reporter," *Washington Post,* May 11, 2003, A1, and *Los Angeles Times,* September 11, 2003, Business section, part 2, 3.

2. David Thelen, "Becoming Martin Luther King, Jr.: An Introduction," introduction to a roundtable on King's plagiarism, *Journal of American History* 78 (June 1991): 11–22, and the articles that followed; James Cox, "A Plague of Plagiarism," *USA Today,* July 25, 1991, B1.

3. American Historical Society, *Statement on Standards of Professional Conduct* (Washington, D.C.: AHA, 2003), 10; Peter Charles Hoffer, "Reflections on Plagiarism, Part I–A Guide to the Perplexed," *Perspectives of the American Historical Association* 42 (February 2004): 17; see also Peter Charles Hoffer, "Reflections on Plagiarism, Part II–The Object of Trials," ibid. (March 2004): 21–26.

4. Richard Posner, "The Abuses and Uses of Plagiarism," *Bergen County (New Jersey) Record,* May 27, 2003, L7; "all deliberate speed": see Alwin Thaler, "With All Deliberate Speed," *Tennessee Law Review* 27 (1960): 510. Judges and lawyers are not the only ones who claim exemption from the rules of plagiarism. Poets call plagiarism "imitation" and it is often regarded as a form of compliment. Historical novelists borrow shamelessly from historical scholarship and do not credit the sources, much less quote them. Even within historical writing, there are some exceptions that are conventionally exempted from the strict rules against plagiarism. For example, those who prepare documents as precis or summaries of existing scholarship in government offices, travel guidebooks, captions at museum exhibitions, pamphlets distributed at historical sites, talks or performances by reenactors or historical interpreters, lectures by history teachers to their classes and speeches at public meetings, and textbooks are not expected to quote or cite precisely each secondary source they have used.

5. Hoffer, "Reflections on Plagiarism–Part I," 17; Bryan Garner, ed., *Black's Law Dictionary*, 7th ed., s.v. "Plagiarism," 1170 (quoting Paul Goldstein); AHA, *Statement on Standards*, 10; Joseph Gibaldi, *MLA Handbook for Writers of Research Papers*, 6th ed. (New York: Modern Language Association, 2003), 66.

6. Eugene Volokh, *Academic Legal Writing* (New York: Foundation Press, 2003), 156.

7. Hoffer, "Reflections on Plagiarism–Part I," 20.

8. Stephen E. Ambrose, *To America: Personal Reflections of an Historian* (New York: Simon & Schuster, 2002), 196; Stephen Ambrose, "Ambrose on Ambrose," available on his website, www.stephenambrose.com/bio.html. Richard Goldstein, "Stephen Ambrose," *New York Times*, October 14, 2002, B7; David D. Kirkpatrick, "As Historian's Fame Grows, So Do Questions on Methods," *New York Times*, January 11, 2002, A5.

9. Stephen Ambrose, "Old Soldiers Never Lie," www.forbes.com/asap/2000/1002/110.html; Ambrose, "To America," 159; Ambrose on Ambrose, www.stephenambrose.com/bio.html.

10. Fred Barnes, "Stephen Ambrose, Copycat," *Weekly Standard*, January 4, 2002; "Ambrose Issues Apology for Plagiarizing Book," *Los Angeles Times*, January 7, 2002, A14. A summary of the charges with accompanying text appears in Mark Lewis's series of articles for Forbes.com: "Ambrose Problems Date Back to Ph.D. Thesis"; "Did Ambrose Write *Wild Blue* or Just Edit It"; "Dueling D-Day Authors: Ryan Versus Ambrose"; "Nothing Like It in the World? Hardly"; "More Controversy for Stephen Ambrose," at, respectively, www.forbes.com/2002/05/10/0510ambrose.html; 02/27/0227/ambrose.html; 01/17/0117ambrose.html; 01/09/0109/ambrose.html; 01/07/0107/ambrose.html.

11. Randall Pinkston, "Stephen Ambrose Dies at the Age of 66," *CBS News*, October 14, 2002 (CBS News transcript); Stephen Ambrose, "Historian Defends Himself Against Plagiarism Charges," Newhouse News Service, "Commentary," May 2, 2002; Richard Goldstein, "Stephen Ambrose," *New York Times*, October 14, 2002, B7 (includes quotation from *Los Angeles Times*); Susan Larson, "Historian Ambrose Dies at 66 of Cancer," *New Orleans Times-Picayune*, October 14, 2002, A1.

12. J. Anthony Lukas, *Big Trouble* (New York: Simon & Schuster, 1997), 831; that Mayhew is worth listening to, Martin Arnold, *New York Times*, "Making Books," September 17, 1998, E3; Sam Whiting, "Working on the Railroad, Historian Stephen Ambrose Rides the Rails to the Top of the Best Seller List," *San Francisco Chronicle*, September 18, 2000, F1; that Mayhew is tough: Keith Kelly, "Mouse Droppings—Disney Expose Killed by Publisher," *New York Post*, May 27, 1999, 40; Gayle Feldman, "What Becomes an Editor Most," *Publisher's Weekly*, June 30, 2003, 47; that Mayhew is "legendary": Lawrence O'Donnell, on *Hardball with Chris Matthews*, *CBS News*, August 25, 1999 (CNBC News transcript); Matthew Flamm and Clarissa Cruz, "Books/Between the Lines" *Entertainment Weekly*, June 2, 2000, 73; on Mayhew's loyalty to her

authors: Rob Hiaasen, "History Lessons," *Baltimore Sun,* January 18, 1998, J1; Blaine Harden, "Troubled Ground," *Washington Post,* July 20, 1997, W16.

13. Doris Kearns Goodwin, interview, June 28, 1996, The Hall of Arts, www. achievement.org/autodoc/page/goo)int–1, accessed October 28, 2003.

14. Goodwin, June 28, 1996, interview; Allan Nevins, *Gateway to History* (New York, Doubleday, 1962), 355, 348; Alan Shelstron, *Biography* (London, Methuen, 1977), 3.

15. Goodwin, June 28, 1996, interview.

16. Phil Kloer, "Doris Kearns Goodwin Says She'll Confront Controversy in Atlanta Lecture Monday," *Atlanta Journal-Constitution,* March 24, 2002, F1; "How the Goodwin Story Developed," History News Network, October 27, 2003, http: //hnn.us/articles/590.htm.

17. Ambrose, "Historian Defends Himself," May 2, 2002.

18. "Douglas Brinkley Discusses Stephen Ambrose," *CNN News,* October 13, 2002 (CNN transcript #101302C.Voo); "Life of Stephen Ambrose," *CNBC News,* October 18, 2002 (CNBC News transcript).

19. Apparently he did this once or twice too. For example, he took two letters from Cornelius Ryan's *The Longest Day* and credited the source in one book, but failed to properly credit Ryan when he used the letters again in a second book (see Lewis, "Dueling D-Day Authors: Ryan Versus Ambrose").

20. Stephen Ambrose, *The Wild Blue: The Men and Boys Who Flew the B–24s Over Germany* (New York: Simon & Schuster, 2001), 18.

21. Ambrose, *Wild Blue,* 65; Thomas Childers, *Wings of Morning: The Story of the Last American Bomber Shot Down over Germany in World War II* (Reading, Mass.: Addison-Wesley, 1995), 13.

22. Ambrose, "Historian Defends Himself"; Ambrose, *Wild Blue,* 64, 165; Childers, *Wings of Morning,* 11, 86.

23. Ambrose, *Wild Blue,* 94, 164, 165; Childers, *Wings of Morning,* 17, 83, 88.

24. Rosenthal and Foner quoted in David D. Kirkpatrick, "As Historian's Fame Grows, So Do Questions on Methods," *New York Times,* January 11, 2002, A5.

25. Thomas Mallon, "Thomas Mallon Discusses Plagiarism," *All Things Considered,* NPR, January 10, 2002; the quotation was reproduced in Jonathan Pitts, "A Twice Told Tale," *Baltimore Sun,* March 10, 2002, E7.

26. Kirkpatrick, "As Historian's Fame Grows," *New York Times,* January 11, 2002, A5; Jeff Guinn, "In Defense of Stephen Ambrose," *Fort Worth Star-Telegram,* January 24, 2002.

27. Eric Foner, *The News Hour with Jim Lehrer,* "Writing History," segment, January 28, 2002, transcript 7254.

28. Childers quoted in Karen Heller, "Plagiarized Prof Speaks Out on Ambrose," *Philadelphia Inquirer,* January 2002, acc. no. K2868.

29. Ambrose, *Wild Blue,* 110 (quoting from Wesley Frank Craven and James Lea Crate, eds. *Army Air Forces in World War II* [1948]); Stephen Ambrose, *Upton and the Army* (Baton Rouge: Louisiana State University Press, 1964), the published version of his dissertation at Wisconsin cited primary and secondary sources; but even then he was sloppy. See pp. 190–194 above.

30. Ambrose quoted in Tim Rutten, "Ambrose Told the Stories from History that We Needed to Hear," *Los Angeles Times*, October 16, 2002, 5.

31. James Patterson quoted in Jonathan Noble, "Profs Say Charges of Plagiarism against Ambrose Are Serious Affair," *Brown Daily Herald*, January 30, 2002.

32. Stephen Ambrose, *Halleck: Lincoln's Chief of Staff* (Baton Rouge: Louisiana State University Press, 1962).

33. Ambrose, *Upton and the Army*, 110, 130, 170 n. 31; Russell Weigley, *Towards an American Army: Military Thought from Washington to Marshall* (New York: Columbia University Press, 1962), 100–127, 180.

34. Ambrose's dissertation, "Upton and the Army," University of Wisconsin, 1963, can be obtained from ProQuest Digital dissertations, www.lib.umi.com/dissertations/fullcit/6307573; Mark Lewis's series of articles for Forbes.com: "Sources Echoed in Ambrose's Doctoral Thesis," "Problems Date Back to Ph.D. Thesis," www.forbes.com/2002/05/10/0510ambrose_2.html. All that I can say about Lewis's fine detective work is that "he missed some," but he certainly found enough evidence to support his point.

35. Ambrose, *Upton and the Army*, 154; Walter Millis, *The Martial Spirit* (New York: Literary Guild, 1931), 152.

36. Ambrose, *Upton and the Army*, 158, 175 n. 16; Weigley, *Towards an American Army*, 218.

37. Ambrose, *Upton and the Army*, 156, 157, 174 n. 11, 175 n. 14.

38. Stephen Ambrose, *Custer and Crazy Horse: The Parallel Lives of Two American Warriors* (Garden City, N.Y.: Doubleday, 1975), preface, 156.

39. Ambrose, *Custer and Crazy Horse*, 96, 97; Jay Monaghan, *Custer: The Life of General George Armstrong Custer* (Boston: Little, Brown, 1959), 19, 33.

40. Benjamin Thomas's 1952 *Abraham Lincoln: A Biography* was similarly in the old consensus vein, making it potentially an easy target for a plagiarist.

41. Stephen Ambrose, *Undaunted Courage: Meriwether Lewis, Thomas Jefferson, and the Opening of the American West* (New York, Simon & Schuster, 1996), 68, 488; Donald Jackson, *Jefferson and the Stony Mountains: Exploring the West from Monticello* (Urbana: University of Illinois Press, 1981), 8.

42. Ambrose, *Undaunted Courage*, 74, 489; Jackson, *Jefferson and the Stony Mountains*, 94; Susan Thompson, "Student Found Ambrose's Work Similar to Others'," *St. Louis Post-Dispatch*, February 4, 2002.

43. Balkowski quoted in Pitts, "Twice Told Tale," 7; E; G. J. "Chris" Graves, Edson T. Strobridge, and Charles N. Sweet, "The Sins of Stephen E. Ambrose," review of *Nothing Like It in the World: The Men Who Built the Transcontinental Railroad, 1863–1869*, by Stephen Ambrose, http://utahrails.net/utahrails/ambrose.htm, accessed May 1, 2003; and see Mark Lewis's reporting for Forbes.com.

44. Bo Crader, "A Historian and Her Sources," *Weekly Standard*, January 18, 2002; Lynne McTaggart, *Kathleen Kennedy: Her Life and Times* (Garden City: Dial, 1983); Doris Kearns Goodwin, *The Fitzgeralds and the Kennedys* (New York: Simon & Schuster, 1987); HNN, "How the Goodwin Story Developed."

45. Stacey Stowe, "University President Accused of Plagiarism," *New York Times*, March 12, 2004, C14; Maurice Isserman, "Plagiarism: A Lie of the Mind,"

The Chronicle Review: Chronicle of Higher Education, May 2, 2003, B12–13.

46. John Podhoretz, "Historians and Thieves," *New York Post,* February 26, 2002, 23; Lynne McTaggart, "Fame Can't Excuse a Plagiarist," *New York Times,* March 16, 2002, A15; David Mehegan, "When Words Collide," *Boston Globe,* March 24, 2002, E1; McTaggart quoted in Fred Bruning, "Difficult Days," *Newsday,* April 8, 2002, II B6.

47. Samar Farah, "Taking a Page Out of Another's Book," *Christian Science Monitor,* January 31, 2002, 11; Goodwin quoted in Peter H. King, "As History Repeats Itself, the Scholar Becomes the Story," *Los Angeles Times,* August 4, 2002, 1.

48. Doris Kearns Goodwin, *No Ordinary Time: Franklin and Eleanor Roosevelt—The Home Front in World War II* (New York: Simon & Schuster, 1994); Goodwin quoted in Thomas C. Palmer, Jr., "Goodwin Discloses Settlement Over Credits," *Boston Globe,* January 22, 2002, A1; Goodwin quoted in King, "As History Repeats Itself."

49. Goodwin, *No Ordinary Time,* 99; Joseph P. Lash, *Eleanor and Franklin: The Story of Their Relationship* (New York: Norton, 1971), 635.

50. John J. Duncan, "Liberal Bias in America's Colleges and Universities," *Congressional Record,* March 6, 2002, House of Representatives, H718; David Horowitz, "Study of Bias in the Selection of Commencement Speakers at 32 Elite Colleges and Universities," http://studentsforacademicfreedom.org/reports/liberalbias.html; L. Brent Bozell, "Historians Hoist the Whitewash for Clinton, February 19, 1999, www.mediaresearch.org/bozellcolumns/newscolumn/1999/col19990219.asp.

51. On Goodwin and the Clintons, see Goodwin, June 28, 1996, interview. The text of the letter with the additional signers was posted at the History News Network website, http://hnn.us/articles/1195.html, and the letter to the editor appeared in the *New York Times* on October 25, 2003.

52. Mark Lewis, "Doris Kearns Goodwin and the Credibility Gap," Forbes.com, February 27, 2002, www.forbes.com/2002/02/07/0227goodwin.html; Goodwin quoted in King, "As History Repeats Itself."

53. Ulrich and Rakove quoted in David Mehegan, "When Words Collide," *Boston Globe,* March 24, 2002, E1.

54. Thomas Mallon, *Stolen Words,* rev ed. (San Diego: Harcourt Brace, 2001), 117–18.

55. Greta Sharma Jensen, "Word Problems: How Bad Is It When Historians Plagiarize?" *Milwaukee Journal Sentinel,* March 17, 2002, L1.

56. Elliott J. Gorn, "History for Sale," *The Chronicle of Higher Education,* March 1, 2002, "Chronicle Review," 10.

57. I know that some authors submit "reader reviews" to Amazon.com under assumed names and give their books five stars, but I do not think these ringers alter or undermine my results. See Amy Harmon, "Amazon Glitch Unmasks War of Reviewers," *New York Times,* February 14, 2004, A1, A16. My Amazon.com methodology involved beginning with the Pulitzer Prize winners in history, biography, and general nonfiction, then looking at the

"Customers who bought this book also bought" column and working through those books. Books whose reader reviews I examined included Diane McWhorter, *Carry Me Home* (2001), Robert A. Caro, *Master of the Senate* (2002), David McCullough, *John Adams* (2001), Joseph J. Ellis, *Founding Brothers* (2000), and H. W. Brands, *The First American* (2000), in that order, with a total of 1,038 reviews as of February 19, 2004.

58. Timothy Noah, "How to Curb the Plagiarism Epidemic," *Slate* magazine, January 28, 2002.

Chapter 7: Fabrication: The Case of Joseph Ellis

1. See, for example, Jacques Steinberg, "A Question of Credibility," *New York Times,* January 19, 2004, C1, C9. On the "weasonable" non-lie, see Scott Adams, *Dilbert and the Way of the Weasel* (New York: HarperBusiness, 2002), 5; on lying as a way of life, see Al Franken, *Lies (And the Lying Liars Who Tell Them): A Fair and Balanced Look At the Right* (New York: Dutton, 2003), 352.

2. See, for example, David Callahan, *The Cheating Culture: Why More Americans Are Doing Wrong to Get Ahead* (Orlando, Fla.: Harcourt Brace, 2003), 220–23; Jana Ritter, "The Lying Game: A Matter of Fact Approach to Résumé Fraud," The Galt Global Review, November 13, 2002, www.galtglobalreview.com/career/lying_game.html; Marl Wrolstad, "Lying on Résumés," *Dallas Morning News,* December 22, 2001, A1; American Historical Association, *Statement on Standards of Professional Conduct* (Washington, D.C.: AHA, 2003), 5.

3. Arthur Schlesinger Jr., statement, House Judiciary Committee Constitutional Subcommittee, November 9, 1998, 4 (from Federal News Service).

4. James H. Merrell, *Into the American Woods: Negotiators on the Pennsylvania Frontier* (New York: Norton, 1999), 40–41; Christine Leigh Heyrman, *Southern Cross: The Beginnings of the Bible Belt* (New York: Knopf, 1997), 234; Edmund Morris, "Just Our Imaginations, Running Away," *New York Times,* June 22, 2001, A21.

5. Simon Schama, *Dead Certainties (Unwarranted Speculations)* (New York: Oxford University Press, 1991), 322; John Demos, *The Unredeemed Captive: A Family Story from Early America* (New York: Knopf, 1994), 190–91; John Demos, "In Search of Reasons for Historians to Read Novels," *American Historical Review* 103 (1998): 1526–29; Thomas A. Sebeok, *A Sign Is Just a Sign* (Bloomington: Indiana University Press, 1991), 12–13.

6. Student quotations in Walter V. Robinson, "Professor's Past in Doubt," *Boston Globe,* June 18, 2001, A1; Walter V. Robinson, "College Notes Regrets on Falsities by Professor," *Boston Globe,* June 20, 2001, B1.

7. Mark Feeney, "In the Name of the Fathers," *Boston Globe,* November 1, 2000, C1; Joseph Ellis, "Putting History in Perspective," *Vista* 4 (Spring 2000); Joseph Ellis, "A Look at the Science of History," *Washington Post,* February 7, 1999, B3. My thanks to Peter Onuf for information on Ellis's comments in private sessions.

8. Ellis, "A Look at the Science of History"; Joseph Ellis, "A Contrarian's View of the Lessons of Vietnam," *Chicago Tribune,* October 10, 1999, C1; Erich Carey, quoted in *The Early Show: CBS News,* June 30, 2001; Pamela Ferdinand, "A Historian's Embellished Life," *Washington Post,* June 23, 2001, C1.

9. Jack Thomas, "The Road to the Ellis Story," *Boston Globe,* July 2, 2001, A11; Robinson, "Professor's Past in Doubt."

10. Robinson, "Professor Apologizes for Fabrications," *Boston Globe,* June 19, 2001, A1; Robinson, "College Notes Regrets."

11. Organization of American Historians, "Professional Integrity and the OAH," *OAH newsletter,* May 2003, available at www.oah.org/pubs/nl/2003may/integrity.html; Mount Holyoke statement: www.mtholyoke.edu/cic/about/introduction.shtml.

12. Robinson, "Professor Faces Investigation at Mount Holyoke," *Boston Globe,* June 21, B3.

13. James M. Banner, "Historical, Personal Truths," *Tulsa World,* July 15, 2001; David Oshinsky, "The Way We Live Now: You Had to Be There Then," *New York Times,* July 1, 2001, A6, 21; David Hackworth, "Poseurs of Heroic Dimensions," *Washington Times,* June 30, 2001, A12; Garrow quoted in Robinson, "Professor Faces Investigation."

14. Walter Robinson, quoted in *Talk of the Nation,* NPR, June 25, 2001; Joseph J. Ellis, *Passionate Sage: The Character and Legacy of John Adams* (New York: Norton, 1993), 87.

15. David Abel, "College Suspends History Professor," *Boston Globe,* August 18, 2001, A1; Ann Coulter, "Creative History," *The American Enterprise,* September 1, 2001, 12; Patrick Healy, "Ellis Returns to Classroom Following a Year's Suspension," *Boston Globe,* September 10, 2002, B1.

16. Joseph J. Ellis, *American Sphinx: The Character of Thomas Jefferson,* rev. ed. (New York: Vintage Books, 2001), 15; Ellis, *Passionate Sage,* 13.

17. Joseph J. Ellis, *Founding Brothers: The Revolutionary Generation* (New York: Knopf, 2000), 43, 51.

18. Ibid., 130.

19. Ibid., 20, 49–50, 129, 164.

20. Ibid., 224, 225.

21. Ellis, *American Sphinx,* 203, 6, 7.

22. Ibid., 15.

23. Ibid., 27, 37, 38, 39–40, 44.

24. Ellis, *Passionate Sage,* 14, 15; *American Sphinx,* xix, *Founding Brothers,* x.

25. Ellis, *American Sphinx,* 370, 371.

26. Ibid., 58, 92.

27. Ibid., 171; Ellis, *Passionate Sage,* 24, 39.

28. Joseph Ellis, *After the Revolution: Profiles of Early American Culture* (New York: Norton, 1979), xiii, xiv, xv.

29. Ibid., 21, 36, 37, 187–188, 70, 110, 41, 154.

30. Ellis, *Passionate Sage,* 27, 12; *American Sphinx,* 5; *Founding Brothers,* ix.

31. Ellis, *American Sphinx,* 19, 371 n. 16. Paul Finkelman, personal communica-

tion, November 14, 2003; Peter Onuf, personal communication, December 1, 2003.

32. Ellis, *Passionate Sage,* 78, 79; *American Sphinx,* 260, 176.

33. Ellis, *Passionate Sage,* 83; Bruce J. Schulman, "'I' and History Make for Strange Bedfellows," *Los Angeles Times,* July 8, 2001, M6; Michael Eric Dyson, "A Macho-Obsessed Culture," *Chicago Sun Times,* June 26, 2001, 27.

34. History News Network, "Poll: Readers Sound Off about Joe Ellis's Suspension," http://hnn.us/articles/205.html.

Chapter Eight: History as "Fair Game"

1. Scott Smallwood, "The Fallout," *Chronicle of Higher Education,* December 17, 2004, A12; Sara Rimer, "When Plagiarism's Shadow Falls on Admired Scholars," *New York Times,* November 24, 2004, B9.

2. Marcella Bombardieri "Tribe Admits Not Crediting Author," *Boston Globe,* September 28, 2004, B1; Joseph Bottum, "The Big Mahatma," *The Weekly Standard,* October 4, 2004; Tribe e-mail to author, February 1, 2005.

3. Lauren A. E. Schuker, "Harvard Professor Accused of Plagiarism," *Harvard Crimson,* September 29, 2003; Alexander Cockburn, "Beat the Devil," *The Nation,* October 13, 2003, 9; Alan Dershowitz, with a reply by Cockburn, "Plagiarized! Total Nonsense; Exchange," *The Nation,* October 27, 2003, 2; Marcella Bombardieri, "Academic Fight Heads to Print," *Boston Globe,* July 9, 2005, B1; Jennifer Howard, "Calif. Press Will Publish Controversial Book on Israel," *Chronicle of Higher Education,* July 22, 2005, A1; Mandy Garner, "The Good Jewish Boys Go Into Battle," *The Times (London) Higher Education Supplement,* December 16, 2005, 16.

4. David Hackett Fischer and William Cronon quoted in David Mehegan, "Is the Author Really the Author," *Boston Globe,* September 11, 2004, C1.

5. Alan Brinkley quoted in Mehegan, "Is the Author Really the Author."

6. On platforms: "Platform. These days it's the magic word in publishing. When a publisher wants to buy, they're not just buying your book or your idea, they're buying you and the many ways you reach people." Sophfronia Scott, "How to Build Your Author's Platform From Scratch," www.ezinearticles.com/?How-to-Build-Your-Authors-Platform-From-Scratch&id=163517; On mentoring: Rochelle Cooper Dreyfuss, "Collaborative Research: Conflicts on Authorship, Ownership, and Accountability," *Vanderbilt Law Review* 53, May 2000, 1230.

7. My source is Thomas Whigham.

8. www.valley.vcdh.virginia.edu/usingvalley/valleystory2.html; Edward L. Ayers, *In the Presence of Mine Enemies: The Civil War in the Heart of America, 1859–1863* (New York: Norton, 2003), 455–58.

9. Goodwin, *No Ordinary Time,* 727; Goodwin, *Team of Rivals: The Political Genius of Abraham Lincoln* (New York: Simon and Schuster, 2004), front matter; Cokie Roberts, *Founding Mothers: The Women Who Raised Our Nation* (New

York, Morrow, 2004), xi, xiii; Esther Forbes, *Paul Revere and the World He Lived In* (Boston: Houghton Mifflin, 1942), front matter.

10. Laurence Tribe, *Abortion: The Clash of Absolutes* (New York: Norton, 1990), xv–xvi.

11. Lawrence W. Levine, *The Opening of the American Mind* (New York: Oxford, 2001), frontmatter.

12. Edward Tenner, "The Pitfalls of Academic Mentorship," *Chronicle of Higher Education*, August 13, 2004, B17.

13. Allen Nevins, *John D. Rockefeller, the Heroic Age of American Enterprise*, 2v. (New York: Scribners, 1940), 2:725; Gerald L. Fetner, *Immersed in Great Affairs: Allen Nevins and the Heroic Age of American History* (Albany: SUNY Press, 2004), 119, 121, 129.

14. I protested against the language when I was sent the contract, changed and initialed the change, and the *Review* editor accepted my comments. The language no longer appears, but the *Review* has taken steps to work with reviewers to lessen the chance of a lawsuit.

15. Susan J. Douglas, "Plagiarists: Catch Your Own Clue," September 1, 2006, In These Times; /www.inthesetimes.com/site/main/article/2782/. On the reuse of ideas—the leading cases involve scriptwriters who submit scripts to producers and discover, after they have been told that their work will not be used, that the basic ideas, plot lines, and characters in the script have been adapted by a producer for a movie project. Lawyers for the authors argued that the use of the author's ideas created an "implied contract," and that the producer who ultimately based a movie on the script owed something to the author. Judges have not bought this argument, relying instead on traditional copyright law. Thus the original svriptwriters have not been able to win their suits, even though they registered the copyright and it was clear to the producers whence the ideas had come. "Court Case Prompts Hollywood Plagiarism Debate," NPR "Weekend Edition," September 16, 2006.

16. On historical "facts": Carl Becker, "What Are Historical Facts?" in Becker, *Detachment and the Writing of History: Essays and Letters of Carl L. Becker*, ed. Phil L. Snyder (Ithaca, N.Y.: Cornell University Press, 1958), 47.

17. Pam McCarthy to Valerie Lawson, December 20, 2005, in "The Secret Life of a Letter to the Editor," *Columbia Journalism Review*, January/February 2006; /www.cjr.org/issues/2006/1/lettertoeditor.asp.

18. "The Secret Life of a Letter to the Editor" *Columbia Journalism Review* January/February 2006; /www.cjr.org/issues/2006/1/lettertoeditor.asp; Tim Wu, "Culturebox: Holy Grail Wars," *Slate*, March 13, 2006.

19. Ben Sisario, "Reworking, but no Theft," *New York Times*, March 16, 2006, E2.

20. On the decline and fall of historical fiction, Christopher Caldwell, "A Da Vinci tangle of copyright code," *Financial Times* (London), March 4, 2006.

21. Dan Brown, "Witness Statement," *London Times* Law News, March 14, 2006; Neutral Citation Number: [2006] EWHC 719 (Ch); Case No: HC04C03092; High Court of Justice, Chancery Division, Summary of Judgment, April 7, 2006.

22. www.copyright.gov/circs/circ21.pdf#search=%22copyright%20office%
    20circular%2021%22.
23. Charles Matthews, "The Devil's in the Details," *Houston Chronicle,* January 19,
    2007; Tom Connor, "The Age of Embellishment," *Writer's Digest,* October
    2006, 29. For example, Timothy Noah, "How to Curb the Plagiarism
    Epidemic (Or How Alice Mayhew Got Her Groove Back)," Slate.com,
    January 28, 2002, www.slate.com/?id=2061281.
24. Mark Lewis, "Accusations Won't Hurt Ambrose Book Sales," Forbes.com,
    November 11, 2002, www.forbes.com/2002/01/11/0111ambrose.html.
25. Andrew Sean Greer, "Almost Sane," *New York Times Book Review,* October 15,
    2006, 30.
26. John J. Seydow, "Chatty, Academic Tones Clash in Tale of Pocahontas and
    Smith, Review of David A. Price, *Love and Hate in Jamestown,*" *Philadelphia
    Inquirer,* January 15, 2004, E2; Zoe Heller, "The Book You Have to Read," on
    Melvin Konner's *Unsettled* (2004), in *Entertainment Weekly,* February 6, 2004,
    155; Scott McLemee, "The Third Reich–Solidarity Prevails," *Baltimore Sun,*
    March 14, 2004, F13.
27. See, e.g., Stephen Ambrose, "Victory in Europe: May 1945," http://
    smithsonianassociates.org/programs/Ambrose/ambrose.asp; Michael
    Bellesiles, "The Limits of Shock and Awe," History News Service, www.h-net.org/
    ~hns/articles/2003/111103a.html (posted November 13, 2003, accessed
    November 16, 2003), Bellesiles to H-Law, December 7, 2003 (commenting on
    Justice Antonin Scalia's use of history); Joseph J. Ellis, "The Right Men, But
    Not the Real Story," Los Angeles Times Book Review, November 16, 2003, 3;
    Ellis, "Sit Down You're Rocking the Boat," New York Times Book Review,
    February 14, 2004, 13; Ellis, "A New Topic for an Old Argument," New York
    Times, February 29, 2004, WK13; Doris Kearns Goodwin, talk to the Abraham
    Lincoln Fifth Annual Symposium, March 16, 2002, www.loc.gov/loc/lincoln.
28. Michael D. Schaffer, "Lessons of War," *Philadelphia Inquirer,* April 7, 2004, F1;
    Gerri Miller, "Wild Times," *Satellite Direct,* March 2004, 20–21.
29. David Eldridge, *Hollywood's History Films* (London: Tauris, 2006), 127–51.
30. Timothy J. Gilfoyle, "Scorsese's *Gangs of New York:* Why Myth Matters," *Journal
    of Urban History* 29 (July 2003), 626.
31. Toplin, *Reel History: In Defense of Hollywood* (Lawrence: University Press of Kansas,
    2002), 92, 94–95; James M. McPherson, "Glory" in Mark C. Carnes, et al., eds.,
    Past Imperfect: History According to the Movies (New York, Holt, 1995), 128.
32. My account is largely derived from Earl J. Hess, *The Union Soldier in Battle:
    Enduring the Ordeal of Combat* (Lawrence, Kans., 1997),15–19.
33. Daniel B. Wood and Gloria Goodale, "History by Miniseries: Too Fast and
    Too Loose," *Christian Science Monitor,* September 13, 2006, 1; Ruth Marcus,
    "Undocumented Drama," *Washington Post,* September 13, 2006, A17;
    Edward Wyatt, "More Questions of Accuracy Raised About ABC Mini-Series
    on Prelude to 9/11," *New York Times,* September 12, 2006, E1.
34. See, e.g., Mark C. Carnes, general editor, *Past Imperfect: History According to the
    Movies* (New York: Holt, 1995); Robert Brent Toplin, *History by Hollywood: The*

Use and Abuse of the American Past (Urbana: University of Illinois Press, 1996); Toplin, *Reel History*; William Guynn, *Writing History in Film* (New York: Routledge, 2006); Philip Rosen, *Change Mummified: Cinema, Historicity, Theory* (Minneapolis: University of Minnesota Press, 2001).

35. Based on conversations with my colleagues who have appeared on these documentaries: Karl Friday, Lester Langley, Edward Larson, John Morrow, William Stueck, and Thom Whigham.

36. Douglas, "Plagiarists: Catch Your Own Clue."

37. Ulrich quoted in Matthew Price, "Hollow History" *Boston Globe*, October 24, 2004, E1.

Conclusion: The Future of the Past

1. OAH "Professional Integrity and the OAH," OAH Newsletter, www.oah.org/pubs/nl/2003may/integrity.html; AHA, "AHA Announces Changes in Efforts Relating to Professional Misconduct" Press release, May 5, 2003; www.historians.org/Press/PR_Adjudication.htm. For example, in the investigation of the alleged misconduct of Professor Ward Churchill by a special University of Colorado faculty committee, the final report on May 9, 2006, used the "Statement on Standards" as an authority on the definition of plagiarism.

2. Sara Hebel, "Patrolling Professors' Politics" *Chronicle of Higher Education*, February 13, 2004, 18; Saree Mikdisi, "Witchhunt at UCLA," *Los Angeles Times*, January 22, 2006, M1; Jennifer Jacobsen, "A Liberal Professor Fights A Label" *Chronicle of Higher Education*, November 26, 2004, 8; but see John Leo, "A Kick Where It's Needed," *U.S. News and World Report*, February 23, 2004, 20; "From the Desk of David Horowitz" Frontpagemag.com, at http://www.frontpagemag.com/Content/read.asp?ID=50.

3. J. L. Bell, "History 101 Florida's Flawed Plan," HNN, July 17, 2006, http://hnn.us/articles/28095.html.

4. See, e.g., William Kelleher Storey, *Writing History A Guide for Students* second edition (New York: Oxford, 2004), 35, and compare it with the 1996 edition. Mary Lynn Rampolla, *A Pocket Guide to Writing in History* 5th ed. (Boston: Bedford, 2007), 88–95, devotes an entire chapter to the subject of plagiarism. Compare these with older works, like Anthony Brundage, *Going to the Sources: A Guide to Historical Research and Writing* (Wheeling, Ill.: Harlan Davidson, 2002).

5. Thomas Bartlett, "Missouri Dean Appears to Have Plagiarized Commencement Speech by Cornel West," *Chronicle of Higher Education*, June 13, 2005, chronicle.com/prm/daily/2005/06/2005061304n.htm; www.humanity.org/voices/commencements.

6. Alan Taylor quoted in Matthew Price, "Hollow History," *Boston Globe*, October 24, 2004; www.boston.com/news/globe/ideas/articles/2004/10/24/hollow_history?pg=full.

INDEX

310

Index

Organization of American Historians
(*cont.*)
and lying by teachers, 215
and violation of professional
standards, 256
"Origins of Gun Culture in the
United States 1760–1865, The"
(Bellesiles), 145–151, 155
Oshinsky, David, 215–216

Painter, Nell Irvin, 76, 129, 139
Palmer, Frederick, 193
Palmer, Thomas, 200
Parallel text comparisons, 181–182
Paraphrasing. *See* Ambrose, Stephen,
use of paraphrasing; Goodwin,
Doris Kearns, use of paraphrasing;
under Plagiarism
Parkman, Francis, 21, 25–28, 41, 49,
59, 188
Boorstin on, 52
Partisan amateurism, 156, 158
Passionate Sage (Ellis), 219, 226
Path to 9/11, The (television
miniseries), 251, 252
Patterson, James, 190, 204
Paul, Robert, 160
*Peacemakers, The: The Great Powers and
American Independence* (Morris), 92
Peale, Charles Willson, 223, 224
Pelzer Prize, 149
Pennsylvania, University of, 88, 128
People and a Nation, A (Norton et al.),
82–83, 84
People of color, 3, 13, 24, 80. *See also*
Blacks; Minorities
Perspectives in History (Bailyn), 168
Peterson, Merrill, 91
Phillips, Wendell, 69
Phrenology, 27
Piggybacking an author's books, 181,
219
Piracy of findings, work, 238, 239, 241
and ethics of acknoweldging
source, 241
Pitcher, Molly, 108

Plagiarism, 13, 14, 15, 30, 33, 34, 135,
173, 203–207. *See also* under
Popular history
and accuracy/inaccuracy, 174
definitions, 137, 173, 174, 180, 202,
203
and early use of facts, 20
and Francis Parkman, 25–26
mosaic, 175, 193
and paraphrasing, 175, 180. *See also*
Goodwin, Doris Kearns, use of
paraphrasing; Ambrose,
Stephen, use of paraphrasing;
Goodwin, Doris Kearns, use of
paraphrasing
and piggybacking author's books,
181
reader as victim of, 199
and research assistants' errors, 231,
232–233
serial, 175
and Stephen B. Oates, 136–138
students made party to, 231
and textbooks, 45, 85
and use of nonauthorial
collaborators, 236–237
Planned Parenthood, 253
Pocket History of the United States
(Nevins and Commager), 44
Podhoretz, Norman, 4–5
Poe, Edgar Allen, 26
Political correctness, 108, 109–110,
112, 128
Political parties, 18, 23, 55
Politicization, 16, 109–110, 117, 124,
128, 156, 170, 171
Popular history, 8, 16, 33, 43, 45, 53,
61, 172, 178, 196
and consensus history, 93
and immunity from professional
scrutiny, 143
marketing of, 8
and plagiarism, 137–138, 139, 187,
188, 205
and professional history, 16, 83, 94,
206–207, 208

PETER CHARLES HOFFER is distinguished research professor of history at the University of Georgia. He is the author of many books of academic history, including *Seven Fires: The Urban Infernos that Reshaped America*. He lives in Athens, Georgia, and Cherry Hill, New Jersey.

PublicAffairs is a publishing house founded in 1997. It is a tribute to the standards, values, and flair of three persons who have served as mentors to countless reporters, writers, editors, and book people of all kinds, including me.

I.F. STONE, proprietor of *I. F. Stone's Weekly*, combined a commitment to the First Amendment with entrepreneurial zeal and reporting skill and became one of the great independent journalists in American history. At the age of eighty, Izzy published *The Trial of Socrates*, which was a national bestseller. He wrote the book after he taught himself ancient Greek.

BENJAMIN C. BRADLEE was for nearly thirty years the charismatic editorial leader of *The Washington Post*. It was Ben who gave the *Post* the range and courage to pursue such historic issues as Watergate. He supported his reporters with a tenacity that made them fearless and it is no accident that so many became authors of influential, best-selling books.

ROBERT L. BERNSTEIN, the chief executive of Random House for more than a quarter century, guided one of the nation's premier publishing houses. Bob was personally responsible for many books of political dissent and argument that challenged tyranny around the globe. He is also the founder and longtime chair of Human Rights Watch, one of the most respected human rights organizations in the world.

·   ·   ·

For fifty years, the banner of PublicAffairs Press was carried by its owner Morris B. Schnapper, who published Gandhi, Nasser, Toynbee, Truman, and about 1,500 other authors. In 1983, Schnapper was described by *The Washington Post* as "a redoubtable gadfly." His legacy will endure in the books to come.

Peter Osnos, *Founder and Editor-at-Large*

CPSIA information can be obtained at www.ICGtesting.com
Printed in the USA
LVOW07s1001110814

398554LV00001B/7/P